Globalizing Seoul:
The City's Cultural and Urban Change

In the decades following the 1997 Asian economic crisis, South Korea sought *segyehwa* (globalization). Evidence of this is no more evident than in the country's capital, Seoul, where urban development has been central to making the city a global hub and not just the centre of the national economy.

However, recent development projects differ from those of the past in that they no longer focus solely on economic efficiency, but on the deployment of a new urban aesthetics. As Jieheerah Yun reveals in *Globalizing Seoul: The City's Cultural and Urban Change*, the pursuit of globalization and the rebranding of Seoul's image from hard industrial city to soft cultural city have shaped the urban development of the city.

Following a brief urban history of Seoul, she focuses on two key themes. In the first, how globalization has contributed to refashioning Korean traditions, she analyzes the policies and actions to preserve Korean folk houses and pre-industrial street layouts, looking in detail at the Bukchon and Insadong areas of the city.

Her second theme is an examination of migration and the generation of new minority neighbourhoods amidst the *segyehwa* policies and the state's efforts to build a multicultural society. In detailed case studies of the redevelopment of Dongdaemun Market as part of rebranding Seoul as the 'world design capital' and of the Itaewon area as both a Special Tourist Zone and a Global Cultural Zone, she shows how multi-ethnic neighbourhoods are threatened by lack of consideration for economic justice and housing provision.

Jieheerah Yun is an Assistant Professor in the College of Architecture, Hongik University, Seoul, South Korea.

Planning, History and Environment Series

Selection of published titles

Globalizing Seoul: The City's Cultural and Urban Change

Jieheerah Yun

Routledge
Taylor & Francis Group

LONDON AND NEW YORK

First published 2017
by Routledge
2 Park Square, Milton Park, Abingdon, Oxfordshire OX14 4RN

and by Routledge
711 Third Avenue, New York, NY 10017

Routledge is an imprint of the Taylor & Francis Group, an informa business

This book was commissioned and edited by Alexandrine Press, Marcham, Oxfordshire

British Library Cataloguing in Publication Data
A catalogue record of this book is available from the British Library

Library of Congress Cataloging in Publication Data
A catalog record for this book has been requested

ISBN: 978–1–138–77773–6 (hbk)
ISBN: 978–1–315–20572–4 (ebk)

Typeset in Aldine and Swiss by PNR Design, Didcot

Contents

Acknowledgements

I would like to thank the following teachers, mentors, colleagues, and friends who have guided me throughout my education, research, and career. Without their inspiration and support, this work would not have been possible.

First and foremost, I thank my dissertation advisor, Professor Nezar AlSayyad. For me he has always been a role model of what a great teacher and scholar should be. He has always been helpful whenever I needed advice regarding academic and career-related problems. His seminars which I took as a graduate student were tremendously influential in shaping my academic interests. Most significantly, his seminal work on traditions in built environments have profoundly influenced the ultimate direction of my research. Second, I thank Professor Greig Crysler, who not only provided insight into globalization theories but taught me a lot about spatial politics and critical theory of architecture. He has provided me with judicious advice and insightful counsel. I also thank Professor You-tien Hsing who taught me a lot about East Asian perspectives on globalization. I am indebted also to Professor Paul Groth and Professor Ananya Roy for serving on my dissertation committee.

This book is a result of several years of research and collaboration with various people in United States and South Korea. I am indebted to Young-guk Kim and Gyung-ae Kim, the librarians at Korean National Assembly Library, who helped me enormously with finding archival data. I also want to thank others in South Korea, including members of FF Group, who did not hesitate in sharing their opinions and experiences with me. Many thanks to my colleagues at Hongik University for their advice. I also thank Ahmed El Antably, Gabriel Arboleda, Tiago Castella, Eunah Cha, Susanne Cowan, Seungwan Hong, Hueyying Hsu, Varun Shiv Kapur, Gokce Kinayoglu, Jing-in Kim, Mpho Matsipa, Clare Robinson, Carmen Tsui for their generous help and intellectual companionship.

I thank following mentors and colleagues for reading and commenting on various parts and stages of this manuscript: Professor Bong-hee Jeon at Seoul National University, Yael Allweil, Yishi Liu, Jennifer Choo, Cecilia Chu, Shih-Yang Kao, Seung-Youn Oh, Aileen Cruz, Orna Shaughnessy, Youjeong Oh. Thanks to Vitalee Giammalvo for editing part of the book and making valuable suggestions. In particular, I would like to thank William Heidbreder for the considerable effort and great skill he applied to editing the manuscript. I also thank staff at University of California, Berkeley and Hongik University Architecture Department for their support.

This research would not have been possible without the financial support of many institutions. The work was supported by the Ministry of Education of the Republic of Korea and the National Research Foundation of Korea (NRF-2013S1A5A8020542). The writing of this book was also supported by the Chancellor's Fellowship for Dissertation Research, University of California, Berkeley, and Haas Junior Scholars Program Grant at the Institute of East Asian Studies. I am grateful for the continuous support of the PhD Committee of the Department of Architecture at Berkeley. Part of Chapter 2 was published in 2012 as 'The remodeling of the vernacular in Bukchon *hanoks*', in *Open House International* (Volume 37, no. 1, pp. 40–47). I am grateful to the publisher and editor for their permission to include this text here.

Last but not least, my deepest appreciation goes to my mother, who patiently mailed me all the books and articles I needed. I also would like to thank my father and my brother for continuous support. I am deeply indebted to my husband, Kwanpyo, who has constantly provided emotional support and encouragement.

Jieheerah Yun
December 2016

List of Illustrations

Figure I.1. Global Zones of Seoul. (*Source*: National Geographic Information Institute, 2007)

Figure 1.1. Old map of Seoul showing waterway and main gates (indicated by crosses. (*Source*: Courtesy of Yeungnam University Museum)

Figure 1.2. Old map of Seoul showing the Gyeongbok and Changdeok Palace complexes. (*Source*: Royal Asiatic Society Korean Branch)

Figure 1.3. Comparison between Sungkyunkwan (*left*) and residences of elite literati named Yun Jeung (*right*). (*Source*: Cultural Heritage Administration)

Figure 1.4. Boundary of Hansong in the late eighteenth century. (*Source*: Courtesy of Kyujanggak Institute for Korean Studies)

Figure 1.5. The Russian Legation Building (*above*) and Myungdong Cathedral (*below*). (*Source*: Seoul Tukbyol Sisawiwonhoe)

Figure 1.6. The photo of the major thoroughfare in front of Gyeongbok Palace Complex. (*Source*: Seoul Tukbyol Sisawiwonhoe)

Figure 1.7. The Japanese Government-General Building. (*Source*: Seoul Tukbyol Sisawiwonhoe)

Figure 1.8. The photo of the Namdaemun area in the 1930s. (*Source*: City History Compilation Committee of Seoul)

Figure 1.9. The boundary of Seoul. (*Source*: Seoul Tukbyol Sisawiwonhoe)

Figure 1.10. Shanty houses. (*Source*: Seoul Tukbyol Sisawiwonhoe)

Figure 1. 11. Saewun Arcade in the 1970s. (*Source*: City History Compilation Committee of Seoul)

Figure 2.1. The old map of Seoul showing Bukchon. (*Source*: Royal Asiatic Society Korean Branch)

Figure 2.2. Remodelled urban *hanoks*. (*Source*: Photographs by Jieheerah Yun)

Figure 2.3. The 1970 advertisement of 'demonstration' apartment houses. (*Source*: Maeil Business News Korea, 20 August 1970)

Figure 2.4. Remodelled *hanok* in Bukchon. (*Source*: Photograph by Jiehcerah Yun)

Introduction: The Production of Korean Global Space

Caught between the restraints of the developed countries and the chase of the late starters, South Korea is currently facing the difficulty of finding a new path. The rapidly aging population and the low birth rate resulting in a declining growth rate are some of the factors threatening our economy… There are many difficulties inside and outside the country. However, there is enough possibility for our economy to achieve a rapid yet sustainable growth. Neighbouring Chinese and Indian markets are on the track of rapid growth, and the Asian economy is undergoing such a dynamic development that it has become a new growth axis of the world. Segyehwa (globalization) presents threats of fierce competition but it can also be an opportunity for our economy to dynamically expand.

Lee Myung Bak, in a speech on 18 October 2007 during his presidential campaign

These words from a campaign speech by then presidential candidate Lee Myung Bak, emphasizing the importance of continued economic growth, illustrate the dilemma faced by South Koreans almost a decade after the 1997 Asian financial crisis. At a time when the Asian economic model and the 'miracle on the Han River' no longer seemed valid, Lee reasserted the possibility of continued prosperity by citing the examples of China and India. The discussion of 'a new growth axis' in Asian countries suggests that there still exists room to incorporate economic developments within the South Korean economic system if Koreans can take full advantages of *segyehwa* and find ways to tap into expanding markets in the larger Asian region. Characterized by economic stagnation and a high unemployment rate, the arrival of the new millennium in South Korea did not seem to quicken the pace of economic recovery. In the context of worsening economic signs, electing Lee, who had a business background and emphasized economic recovery, seemed a logical choice for many South Koreans.

Quite distinct from the controversial term globalization, *segyehwa* has served as a parallel South Korean term that became more widely known as a political slogan in the early 1990s in conjunction with the Kim Young Sam administration. Although the *segyehwa* campaign reflected a continuation of certain aspects of the modernization project, it was also an important break from the previous national campaign to 'catch up with the West'. From the economic perspective, it marked a break from the old model of the developmental state interfering with market forces through protective measures. The government's project of *segyehwa* sought to differentiate itself from the previous regime by addressing the ills of its developmentalist approach, especially its disregard for the natural environment and social justice. The reformist policies reflected the wider processes of the economic restructuring of East Asia and the formation of new institutional bodies such as ASEAN Plus 3 and the East Asia Summit. Yet they contained specificities, as the political economies of East Asian countries differed substantially.

From a cultural perspective, it signified the need for South Koreans to throw out an outdated mode of ethnocentrism and undertake the cosmopolitan tolerance of different cultures. Lee's speech reveals important divergences as well as continuities within the Korean perception of *segyehwa*. Although the Korean term had already been used as a political catchphrase in Kim's administrations, Lee's approach differs in that it acknowledges the dangers and challenges associated with the attempt to nationalize and give regional specificity to the abstract concept of globalization.

In this socioeconomic milieu, efforts to propel the status of Seoul from the centre of the national economy to a global hub have materialized in the initiation of several redevelopment projects. Urban setting and architectural environments have become the central arena in which such efforts have become manifest. The contemporary urban projects differ from development projects of the past in that they renounce top-down and uncommunicative approaches focused solely on economic efficiency. Instead, the mission of many urban projects is to emphasize historical preservation and protection of the natural environment while encouraging balanced growth.[1] In the early 2000s, the city of Seoul embarked on the project of designating 'cultural districts' and 'historical and cultural inquiry streets' in order to improve the urban environments damaged by reckless development. Taking on the notion of 'cultural city' defined at a meeting of the Council of the European Union in June 1985, the city of Seoul sought to renew its image from an industrial *nouveau riche* of the Third World to a sophisticated cosmopolitan cultural axis (SDI, 2002*a*). The effort to preserve cultural traditions resulted not only in a more careful maintenance of national heritage sites but also in the reconstruction and rediscovery of traditional Korean-style houses. At the same time, following the spirit of broadening one's cultural perspective, places promoted as cultural spaces were diversified to include various urban sites previously considered too hectic or heterogeneous. Although the state had paid little attention to exotic cuisines in urban areas such as Itaewon, it now regards the presence of various ethnic restaurants as a source of cultural tourism (Culture and Tourism Department, 1999). In a word, consumption patterns in South Korea have diversified to a significant degree as the result of faster information exchange rates.

This book examines the processes whereby the rhetoric of *segyehwa* has contributed to shaping Seoul's urban environment and how different responses from the social actors including local government, residents, and NGOs are expressed. Rather than engaging in lengthy theoretical discussions of the term 'globalization', I focus on the specific national appropriation of the term and the process by which the abstract qualities associated with globalization in current scholarship become transformed into a new type of urban discourse. The term *segyehwa* – and the more contemporary Korean term *global-hwa* – have been used in describing many high-flown development projects sponsored by both central and local governments. Many local residents, journalists, investors, NGOs, entrepreneurs, and pubic officials have joined the government's ambitious promotion of Seoul as a global city, and used the term 'global' in the pursuit of their interests. Yet amidst the flood of projects and institutions professing to embody the global entrepreneurial spirit, others have questioned the ways the spectre of the 'global' has been used. I analyze how the different local aspirations and aversions to the state-led *segyehwa* project have been expressed through spatial practices in the urban sites targeted for redevelopment.

The Rise of the 'Cultural City' Discourse

Beginning in the early 2000s, the city government of Seoul started to engage in the development of an urban discourse which I shall call the 'cultural city discourse'. In 2002, a study conducted by the Seoul Development Institute (SDI) concluded that there was a need to cultivate 'cultural spaces' in Seoul in order to follow the global transformation from the industrial age to the post-industrial information age. The report introduced a survey conducted in 2001 among public officials and cultural/art department personnel which indicated that the biggest problem in Seoul was that

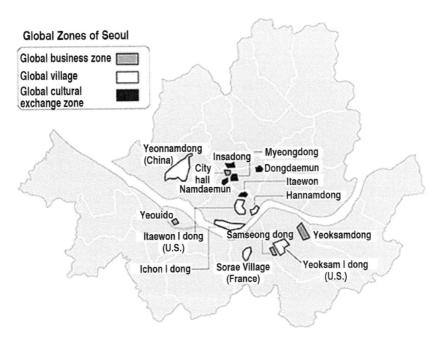

Figure I.1. The global zones of Seoul.

'urban spaces in general are not conducive to the cultivation of cultures' (SDI, 2002*b*). In another study, SDI noted that 'it is possible to generate global investments if Seoul shifts its focus from manufacturing industries to cultural industries and to promoting a higher quality of life, acquiring the image of a "culture city"'(SDI, 2002*a*). Following the definition given in the European Capital of Culture programme which first started in 1985, the study defined the 'cultural city' as 'a new city with prerequisites for growth based on culture – such as environments conducive to cultural activities' (SDI, 2002*a*, p. 21) Similar to the 'culture city', organizations such as Seoul Design Foundation have focused on transforming the image of Seoul from that of a 'hard city' to a 'soft city'. Whereas Seoul represented an industrial 'hard city' emphasizing speed and efficiency, the concept of a soft city emphasizes 'soft' aspects of a city such as appreciation of 'traditional cultures'. The cultural city discourse proposed a new set of urban renaissance projects in order to recover from the ills of modernization and restore the balance between material growth and appreciation of the non-economic aspects of life.

Although the cultural city discourse did not address questions of defining urban culture, it appealed to policy-makers and urban planners enough to influence many urban projects as too much emphasis has previously been placed on economic growth. For instance, several Culture History Routes within the historic part of Seoul were designated as places to preserve the national heritage and foster cultural exchange. In a similar vein, in 2007 the city government of Seoul designated fifteen areas within Seoul as Global Zones (figure I.1) – four business zones, five cultural exchange zones, and six villages – in order to 'strengthen [its] internal stability as a global city' (National Geographic Information Institute, 2007, p. 57). The designation of Global Cultural Zones came with the city government's emphasis on the preservation of traditional Korean customs as well as fostering cultural exchange between Koreans and foreign nationals. For instance, Insadong was promoted as the repository of traditional Korean culture while Dongdaemun and Itaewon were designated as exchange zones due to their diverse cultural forms and shopping opportunities. Undertaken as part of an effort to 're-design' Seoul, this series of new urban projects and the development of Global Cultural Zones (GCZ) represent important assumptions about urban culture which this book will discuss in greater detail.

The process of positioning Seoul as a global city through the deployment of new urban aesthetics, or what I call the 'cultural turn' in development, demonstrates an important break from the previous developmentalism in the sense that the goal of economic efficiency is mediated by the need to acknowledge emotional and social values. After the democratic transition in the mid-1980s, the South Korean state has striven to differentiate itself from the developmentalist authoritarian regime, and the invocation of the 'global' in the early 1990s was one of the important strategies to achieve such a distinction. For instance, emphasis on the appreciation of immaterial things has become an important aspect of the *segyehwa* campaign. As a part of the distancing mechanism, the invocation of *segyehwa* contained a strong reformist overtone that appealed to many South Koreans as both an economic and a political strategy. Thus, I examine the cultural work of *segyehwa* and *global-hwa* in the urban renaissance projects that deploy the discourse of 'culture' and 'tradition'.

In a broader sense, this book analyzes the shifting notions of cultural modernity defined through the promotion of 'tradition' and 'multicultural society' in urban sites of the democratized South Korean society. Although the reformist tendencies in the *segyehwa* drive have resulted in the re-examination of overtly developmentalist approaches, the state's faith in continuous material growth has not been abandoned. In this context, its simultaneous pursuit of cultural modernity and economic efficiency has become a difficult feat requiring a careful balance of power and deliberate planning. The preservation of 'Korean tradition' and the promotion of a 'multicultural society' in South Korea have become new state-led cultural planning strategies that lie behind many redevelopment projects in order to harmonize cultural modernity and economic efficiency. More specifically, I analyze the series of projects to create Global Zones in Seoul beginning in the early 2000s, and the city government's effort to transform the image of Seoul from an industrial to a post-industrial city. By comparing how these specialized districts construct Korean identities and those of the imagined 'others', this study illustrates the processes by which the distinction between them is both exaggerated and understated, and how these terms are contingent on different versions of Korea's past and its future. Contrary to policy-makers' and planners' belief, I argue that the challenges to the transformation of Seoul rise from the narrow ways spaces are imagined rather than the physical inadequacy of built environments. More specifically, the narrow definition of 'the global' and its application in the urban space have become a barrier to the production of Korean global space.

Despite the state's effort to generate an aura of difference or freshness by invoking the spectre of the global, the cultural turn of the developmental impulses contains inherent paradoxes that help to undermine the validity of its projects. The movement against *segyehwa* has started to question the superficial notion of multiculturalism and nostalgic reconstructions of Korean tradition. The movement includes urban residents, NGOs, street vendors, and artists who question the governmental use of the word 'global' in urban redevelopment projects. While the proponents of *segyehwa*-inspired urban redevelopment focus on the promise of a bright future, those who participate in the production of the counter-narrative emphasize the present conditions of structural and representational. This book examines the processes by which the construction of 'tradition' as a state project is mediated by the presence of de-developmentalist approaches. By highlighting the unanticipated consequences of *segyehwa* policies, this study shows that globalization is a multidirectional process that involves constantly shifting and negotiated local articulations rather than a simple top-down process.

Notwithstanding the difficulty of pinpointing the exact historical moment at which a given society becomes 'democratic', this study regards the year 1987 as the pivotal point since that was when democratic transitions through electoral reform began to take place, and when what scholars called the 'crisis of political and economic success' began (Diamond and Kim, 2000). Economically, the rapid rate at which South Korea escaped the poverty associated with the Korean War and propelled itself into the international trade arena has led many scholars to remark on the 'miracle on the Han River'. Politically, democratic movements that gained momentum and middle class support culminated in a peaceful regime change. Ironically, perceptions of successes shared by South Koreans contributed to institutional instability as well as making 'the ideological cleavage' between democracy and developmentalism appear irrelevant (*Ibid.*, p. 69).

Although many South Koreans started to recognize the economic threat of globalization after the experience of financial crisis in 1997, this realization alone could not overturn the tendency of South Korean society to associate economic liberalization with political freedom. Unlike Western Europe and the United States, which gradually transitioned from a liberal economy in the late nineteenth century to a Keynesian economic model, South Korea did not go through a stage of unrestrained capitalist market and unrestrained monopolies. Instead, the combination of Japanese colonial rule and the military dictatorship that followed held capitalism at bay. Korea remained an underdeveloped agrarian society with an extreme minority of wealthy individuals willing to cooperate with the military dictatorship regimes. As Bruce Cumings (2005, p. 205) has noted, capitalism in South Korean society 'did not fit a textbook description of capitalism' due to the colonial legacy of the Japanese developmental regime and state-led industrialization thereafter.

Thus, although much seemed to change after the first successful democratic movement in 1987, some of the older lines of conflict remained. If democratic movements were an organizing principle designed to unite different generations, the following economic liberalization became a source of division even among those who marched together in the streets in the 1980s to support democratization. While the South Korean government began to loosen up its autocratic control in many spheres, the business tycoons gained more independence and power since there was no political authority figure that they had to try to please. Economic liberalization and restructuring resulted not only in a tremendous level of job insecurity and shifts (a decline for some and an increase for others) in economic opportunities but also a realignment of political camps. On the one hand, previous participants in the democratic movement joined hands with the old political camp to promote neoliberal economic policies. On the other hand, labour leaders started to utilize grass-roots democratic organization and formal government channels to oppose further economic liberalization.

The aim of this book is to illustrate how the project of globalization and the efforts to rebrand the image of Seoul from hard industrial city to soft cultural city have shaped urban redevelopment projects. Before delving into the discussion of research sites, this chapter discusses the historical background of South Korea's experience of globalization as well as theoretical issues concerning this book. I first examine the historical development of Seoul and the rise of a new urban discourse following the Asian financial crisis. I then discuss the conceptual frameworks regarding culture and tradition, and how such concepts are being deployed in the South Korean context.

Segyehwa, or the Spectre of the Global

The most controversial, and most discussed, concept used in this book is the term 'globalization'. Some scholars question the ontological status of the term 'globalization' by using the term 'globalony' to describe the contemporary obsession for faster rates of exchange (Veseth, 2005). Similarly, Partha Chatterjee (2004) has pointed out that European countries such as Britain and France in the nineteenth century witnessed a greater rate of flow of international capital in relation to total national income than in the twentieth century. Considering claims that globalization is a problematic term with room for misuse, the question whether the term 'globalization' is useful in examining the built environment has haunted the coterie of scholars interested in current socio-economic changes. Other scholars accept that the contemporary exchange of information, capital, and people entails important differences from previous patterns of exchange. Manuel Castells (2000) has provided an encompassing notion of the information technology revolution not just as an aggregate of new technologies, but also as a process including qualitatively different organization principles arising from previous technological innovations. Hence, despite the ambiguities, it is necessary to acknowledge the existence of a different pattern of exchange in the contemporary period, albeit with different interpretations and qualifications concerning the appropriateness of the term 'globalization'.

In urban studies, the term globalization has induced various academic interpretations and debates. The theory of the global city postulates that the processes of globalization result in the concentration of functions in big cities despite the technological revolution which makes the dispersal of economic functions possible. For instance, Saskia Sassen (1991) has argued that 'global cities' such as New York, London, and Tokyo have become ever more important financial centres due to the networking of specialized firms already located in such big cities. The global city theory, despite its critical analysis of political economies associated with globalization, has generated criticism from post-structuralist and post-colonialist scholars. Scholars such as Aihwa Ong (1999, p. 3) have criticized David Harvey's articulation of globalization and the role of capitalism as reductive in the sense that his account misses 'human agency and its production and negotiation of cultural meanings within the normative milieus of late capitalism'. On the other hand, the post-colonialist critique of global city discourse, unlike the post-structuralist approach, questions the understanding of globalization and modernity in the developmental framework. Jennifer Robinson (2006, p. 96) criticizes Sassen's notion of a global city as 'emphasizing [a] relatively small range of economic processes with a certain "global" reach' while it 'excludes many cities from its consideration'.

In the case of South Korea, the term *segyehwa* signifies something quite different from the meta-term 'globalization'. It cannot be considered separately from the larger political economy within which South Korea is situated. The rhetoric of *segyehwa* was first invoked during the culmination of democratic movement and the growing public awareness of the ills of past military regimes and reckless developmentalist projects. Scholars increasingly pointed out that development projects in the so-called 'four Asian tigers' often ignored the non-economic costs of these projects, such as the environmental and social costs, due to the limited time they had to 'catch up' with other developed nations (McMichael, 1996, p. 36). The fast rate of environmental degradation in urban areas and the depletion of the population in rural areas were understood as the consequence of reckless developments. At the same time, the close ties between *chaebol* (conglomerates) and the central government became a hotly debated issue since cases of corruption and political favouritism often decorated the front pages of South Korean newspapers. Within the urban context, the term 'development dictatorship' was coined to describe the many large construction projects decided without any kind of democratic oversight. Despite being praised for the country's material growth, South Koreans yearned for political participation, social transparency, and environmental justice.

It was during this period of relative economic prosperity and political instability that the Kim Young Sam administration introduced globalization as a political slogan. Confident of recent political achievements such as the peaceful regime change and the successful hosting of the Olympic Games, Kim called for South Korean nationals to throw away 'Korean diseases' (such as close state-conglomerate alliances, the presence of military secret societies, and the lack of financial transparency) associated with the previous developmentalist dictatorship. The new policy initiatives designed to reform the Korean economic system included measures such as the Real Name Financial Transaction System.[2] Instead of resorting to an authoritarian emphasis on ethnocentrism, Kim's political speeches emphasized that Koreans need to adopt broader perspectives and take a proactive role by learning from the rest of the world.

At the same time that the project of *segyehwa* sought to change the political culture of South Korea, it also introduced major policy changes contributing to economic liberalization. It is noteworthy that the project was part of the national development strategy that emphasized sharpening competitive edges 'to become like the rest of the world' (Chang et al., 2009, p. 144). Many public programmes to help the poor were also similar to neoliberal governments' call for greater self-help rather than involving structural welfare reforms (Hoogvelt, 1997). Although Kim's political rhetoric often associated further economic growth with the phrase 'globalization', it mainly served as a political slogan since it lacked practical considerations. Despite the rapid speed at which some South Koreans improved their economic and political conditions, democracy in South Korea was still in its infancy and lacked many institutional and policy reforms. While Kim's regime attempted to address these shortcomings, it was not prepared to handle appropriately the potential backlash from a conservative middle class with vested interests. Consequently, Kim's administration changed its rapid pace of reform and began to restore a business-friendly environment. While labour and financial markets were liberalized, the power of conglomerates remained relatively intact. Gills and Gills (2000, p. 39) argue that an abrupt reversal of the policy from decentralization to a growth-first strategy in the early 1990s left 'Korean workers badly exposed when the subsequent economic crisis in 1997–8 brought high unemployment'.

Yet the mismatch between the ambition and reality associated with *segyehwa*, which clearly manifested itself in the Asian financial crisis, has not resulted in the abandonment of the term. Rather, the phantasm of the global reappeared in a new form and new names such as *global-hwa*. As if using a new term can dispel the negative image of the IMF crisis associated with *segyehwa*, the term 'global' – and related terms such as 'global network', 'global standard', and 'global leaders' – have come back with a vengeance.[3] The targets of reform have widened and diversified as well. The images of 'global' apply not only to business and marketing, but also to other, subtler, areas such as cultivating a sense of humour and appropriate manners for social activities. With respect to state's nation building strategy, the spectre of the global signalled an important transition. For instance, the political power of the ideology of *hanminjok*, or a single Korean ethnicity, started to weaken in the 1990s as the rhetoric of *segyehwa* criticized the ethnocentric tendencies of the previous regime such as blaming undesirable social phenomena on 'foreign' forms of vice (Tipton, 1998, p. 427). While the criticism in the early 1990s was confined to xenophobic reactions to admittedly foreign customs and people, political discussions in the new millennium have increasingly begun to challenge the very idea of a single Korean identity. Although scholars have argued that the ideology of a single Korean identity is largely a myth, it nevertheless played an important part in the nation-building process by generating defensive national sentiments against external powers (Cohen, 1978). However, the concept of *hanminjok* has increasingly been at odds with state policies such as encouraging transnational marriages and migrant labour, designed to ease the labour shortage and compensate for the falling fertility rates in rural regions. In the mid-2000s, increasing numbers of migrant workers in South Korea and transnational marriages prompted the state to engage in 'multicultural campaigns' to embrace various racial and ethnic populations within South Korean society.

In the context of urban development, attempts to deal with the 'crises of successes' and the need to reform have contributed to the rise of a new urban discourse which emphasized the experiential and emotional aspects of urban projects rather than their functional aspects. The perception of the ills of modernist design was even stronger in South Korea, where the functionalist modernist aesthetic was strongly associated with dictatorship, than elsewhere. Instead, exploring the connection to one's past as well as incorporating room for the user's participation became more important. The concept of a 'soft city' promoted in the Design Seoul project emphasized the appreciation of invisible things, such as cultural traditions and emotional wellbeing (Kwon, 2010). In order to achieve the goal, what is imperative is not to provide a comfortable environment but to generate a distinctive image of the place, attractive and unique in its own way. This aesthetic need to differentiate the city of Seoul from other industrial cities was particularly strong because of the contrast between Seoul's long history as a capital and its short history of industrialization.

Tradition as a 'Project': Tradition, Modernity, and In-between

Throughout this book, I engage in discussions of abstract concepts whose meanings need to be explored due to the complex nature of the terms. In particular, this study examines the dual processes of rediscovering Korean 'tradition' and building a 'multicultural society' in the construction of Cultural Zones. Similar to the term 'globalization', 'tradition' and 'modernity' are another set of terms that often become used in very different contexts without close examination.

A group of scholars have remarked on the impossibility of separating tradition and modernity. For instance, Jane Jacobs (2004) argued that tradition is inextricably linked to the modern since the imagination of modernity is predicated on tradition as the mirror image of itself. Commenting on the rampant reproduction of traditions elsewhere and the consequent obsessive quests for authentic traditions, Nezar AlSayyad (2004, p. 23) has remarked that 'what has ended is not tradition, but tradition as a place-based, temporally situated concept'. Similarly, anthropologists have observed that lamenting the disappearance of cultural traditions, or what Marilyn Ivy (1995) has called 'discourses of vanishing', is a distinctively modern phenomenon. Narratives of loss and the nostalgic view of tradition are social constructions which play upon the very modern fear of losing one's identity. Dean MacCannell (1999, p. 8) pushed the argument further, observing that 'the best indication of the final victory of modernity … is its artificial preservation and reconstruction [of a pre-modern world]'. Thus, tradition becomes a target that is constantly revisited as 'rediscovery' in order to constantly confirm one's modernity.

In contemporary South Korea, the construction of tradition as a means to rediscover an individual's identity has become particularly strong for two reasons. First, the colonial experiences have heightened the contrast between the traditional and the modern, on both discursive and perceptual levels. The political construction of Korean subjects as 'un-modern' and the unequal economic relationships between Korea and Japan have contributed to the emergence of strongly patriotic interpretations of tradition. For instance, Laurel Kendall (2011, p. 6) observed that for South Koreans the rural past 'was not so much "lost" as taken away by someone else'. Kendall (*Ibid.*, p. 3) argues that colonial legacies have generated a close link between 'the loss of an imagined rural authenticity [and] the loss of Korea itself'. Secondly, the double bind of colonial subjects, which constructed Koreans as recipients of a modernizing project yet never 'fully modern' compared to their Japanese counterparts, has resulted in an ironic phenomenon. Although Korean traditions are regarded as targets of preservation, the conditions for their preservation were constantly undermined through the rapid modernization drive of the early South Korean republic. Situated in the paradoxical position of having to prove their modernity while preserving Korean traditions, South Koreans have experienced floods of 'rediscoveries' of traditional artefacts, rituals, and sites. Thus, the strong association of globalization with reform did not result in an abandonment of the ideology of a single Korean heritage. Rather, urban planners and policy-makers have incorporated certain Korean traditions into the larger rubric of urban redevelopment. Protecting the authenticity of Korean traditions became part of the *segyehwa* drive since the effort to preserve cultural forms was part of reforms pursuing a path of balanced growth.

In addition to the aforementioned aspects, the preservation of authenticity and the invocation of common cultural traditions in South Korea has acquired another dimension. As Stephen Vlastos (1998) argued, traditions are not only the by-product of nation-states but a by-product of rising capitalism. Just as there are many versions of capitalism, the articulation of tradition in the South Korean context reflects distinctively Korean ways of dealing with crises of capitalism and threats presented by globalization. In the case of contemporary South Korea, tradition is not simply something that needs to be preserved and protected. The deeply felt sense of debt to the past, shared by many South Koreans, is the by-product of the hyper-urbanization and modernization drive of the past regime. As such, nostalgia for traditional artefacts does not stop at individually preserving and restoring artefacts. Instead, traditions become a project with the objective of reconstructing structures/objects/sites on a massive scale. In the subsequent chapters I analyze how the project of traditions has influenced the generation of urban discourses in Global Zones of South Korea. Local governments and the national government have embraced the discourse of rediscovered traditions in order to carry out 'the regeneration project', a movement to industrialize the production of rediscovered traditional forms. Such movements illustrate the historical continuity between the past development projects and the current versions which conjures up the spectre of traditions.

However, there are other kinds of traditions as well. Traditions include subtler patterns of activities that occur spontaneously. They are not necessarily a project of recovery but involve unselfconscious yet recalcitrant practices that unintentionally follow the past patterns of urban history. The chapter about Insadong will discuss such recurring activities, which have sprung up despite the opinion of many Koreans, of the place as 'having lost its former sense of place'. Although less visible, these unselfconscious traditions nevertheless find their way into the everyday landscape. In an odd way, spatial practices are also the result of dealing with changing everyday forces of life, making them simultaneously modern and traditional. This is particularly true when one considers that there is no such thing as 'pure' modernity or 'pure' representations of a singular cultural tradition. Understated traditions pick up and build on traces of ancestral uses of public space. Although such practices are rarely acknowledged as forms of tradition by the performers themselves, they share the political aspect of resistances to state regulations of space. Despite the fragile presence of such understated traditions, their presence illustrates that elements of Korean tradition defy categorization since performative aspects of tradition are messy and uneven.

Multicultural Society

As these trends converge, a mighty river of cultural change is at Korea's doorstep. In many ways, Korea has already passed the tipping point on diversification. Korea's demographics demand diversification. Korea will become multicultural. That is unstoppable.

> Josh Broward, 'Korea at the Tipping Point of a Multicultural Society',
> *Korea Times*, 12 November 2009

By 2009, the number increased another 50 percent, reaching 1.5 million, and the number of naturalized people is steadily rising… The ratio of interracial marriages is now over 10 percent. As of 2009, foreign residents in Korea were over 1.1 million people. A report estimates that by 2050, one out of every 10 people in Korea will be a foreign resident. Korea used to be the 'Land of the Morning Calm', but it is not a land of hermits anymore.

> Jae-ho Eun, 'Korea Ready to Embrace a Multicultural Society',
> *Korea Times*, 19 May 2010

In the mid-2000s, the South Korean media started to report on the increasing number of international marriages between South Korean men and foreign brides in rural areas. At the same time, an increasing number of foreign migrant workers were mentioned in Korean newspapers as cases of workplace abuse were reported by NGOs and workers. South Korea's demographic changes are partly a result of government policies since the late 1990s, such as promoting the increasing flexibility of the labour market and relaxing regulations on immigrants who obtained residency through marriage. With the start of the industrial trainee system implemented during Kim Young Sam's administration, an increasing number of unskilled workers from foreign countries were allowed into Korean workplaces (Seok, 2009). International marriages between Southeast Asian women and Korean men became common in the mid-2000s. The South Korean government was quick to respond to such demographic and economic changes. In 2005, the Ministry of Culture, Sports, and Tourism (2005) held a public debate regarding 'cultural policies toward a multicultural society' during a migrant workers' festival titled 'Migrants' Arirang'. Subsequently, a new committee devoted to supporting multicultural families was set up under the prime minister, and various studies and surveys were conducted in government branches, including the Ministry of Gender Equality and Family. Peter Underwood (2010), a descendant of an early missionary in South Korea, observed such increased attention to the issue of ethnic diversity by noting that 'the media in Korea is abuzz with the new era of multiculturalism'.

Despite much hyped discussions of 'multicultural society', there is no formal definition given to the term. One definition of 'multicultural society', given by the Korean Women's Development Institute, is 'a society where ethnic and cultural diversity is generally acknowledged as an important issue' (Kim et al., 2007, pp. 22–23). Other scholars, such as Se-hoon Park, argue that South Korean policies are not multicultural in the sense that they do not show 'consideration to acknowledge and maintain ethnically independent languages, cultures, or lifestyles' (Park et al., 2010, p. 9). Instead, they insist on using the alternative term 'foreigner policy' or 'immigrant integration policy' (Ibid., p. 10). While the state's promotion of a multicultural society was regarded as a more inclusive policy, scholars expressed concern regarding the South Korean government's use of 'multiculturalism' and 'multicultural society'. The presence of many quasi-NGOs promoting multicultural campaigns has led Han and Han (2007, p. 106) to observe that the current multicultural discourse in South Korea may have been generated as a strategic effort 'to survive in a global age rather than [a] sincere critique of the concept of single ethnicity'. Scholars remain sceptical about the effectiveness of multicultural campaigns when the current situation of a divided Korea calls for continuous use of the concept of single Korean ethnicity (Kim, H.M., 2008).

It is notable that most of the controversies regarding urban development involved the term 'cultures' or some variation thereof. In the case of Global Zones in Seoul, the project was started as a way to transform the image of Seoul from a monotonous industrial city to a versatile 'cultural' city filled with tangible and intangible resources. Changes have included the designation of global cultural zones, foreign villages, and the increasing use of English signs. Migrant workers have started forming their own communities near their workplace, and some have been named as 'multicultural streets'. However, the consensus on the need to restore cultural aspects of the city sprung out of the ambiguous status of the term 'culture'.

In contemporary South Korea, the politics of culture has gained a strategic importance as an increasing number of transnational labourers and marriages have necessitated inter-ethnic understanding and the provision of cultural resources for multiethnic families. The political rhetoric of the South Korean government's campaign of building a 'multicultural society,' however, is based on the notion of the presence of a single Korean culture. At the same time, it also assumes a linear temporal relationship by equating the 'multicultural society' with the future. This study does not accept the construction of a dichotomy between 'culture' and 'multiculture'. Nor does it accept the linear temporality implied in the current use of 'multicultural society'. There is nothing inevitable about the advent of a multicultural society. Human histories show countless examples of multicultural civilizations that have turned to the glorification of a single culture or a single ethnicity. Instead of resorting to meta-narratives of cultural politics, I engage in multiple methods of examining how cultural representations shape and are shaped by spatial practices.

Taking on Hall's notion (1989) of diversity of subjective positions, this book demonstrates that the distinction between the Self and the Others involves negotiation as different political actors seek to represent themselves in urban environments. The problem of urban cultures is interpolated not only with categorizations such as class, gender, and age, but also with historical experiences and geopolitical structures. While the term 'globalization' has been used in many societal contexts as a call for lifestyle changes, *segyehwa* in South Korea contained a strong political overtone emphasizing the reformation of Korean identities. Although the term *segye* literally means 'world', it is not a value-neutral word that contains all the societies of the globe on the same representational level. As the subsequent chapters demonstrate, diverse processes in which Korean identity is constructed and consumed cannot be understood separately from the larger global processes of economic liberalization and increasing transnational movement of labour. Thus, instead of renouncing the analysis of urban cultures, I engage in what Linda Alcoff (1991) called 'interrogatory practices', which involves critical re-examination of my own use of the term 'culture' as well as of its actual effect. The more important aspect of cultural representations then becomes examining the inherent assumptions regarding the way discussions of 'cultures' are framed.

Although the project of *segyehwa* started out as a top-down political slogan, the distinction between the Self and the Others is constantly being redrawn as the result of new subjectivities and alliances generated by changing socioeconomic forces. Changes in political economy bring opportunities as well as threats, and the discussions of 'multicultural society' even in a rhetorical sense can ignite different positions and articulations of urban cultures. Contestations with regard to what constitute 'tradition' and 'culture' have been expressed in the mass media and governmental documents dealing with the historical preservation and development of urban districts. Despite the dominant trend of mapping urban culture onto specific demographic groups or geographical areas, this tendency is mediated and confounded by different interpretations of abstract concepts and new spatial practices. This book examines how concepts such as 'tradition' and 'multicultural society' overlap with the aims of urban projects and how they are appropriated and challenged by local aspirations.

Becoming Global (Again): Ruptures and Continuities

Many people who visited South Korea in the 1950s and 1960s marvel at the speedy growth of South Korean economy since then. Whereas South Korean children in the early 1960s begged American soldiers for candies, South Korean children in 2012 play with their smart phones and Samsung tablet PCs. The memories of going outside to cold outhouse toilets are replaced with indoor bathrooms equipped with electrically heated toilet seats. South Korean society seems to be bent upon the path of continuous material growth. Political discussions in the G20 Seoul Summit in 2010 and the Free Trade Agreement with the United States abound with hopeful scenarios of South Korea becoming part of 'shared growth beyond crisis'.[4] South Koreans seem to be immersed in the vision of Benjamin's angel of history, with their eyes focused on future progress, rather than past events.

Yet the simultaneous quest to recover Korean 'tradition' and to build a multicultural society illustrates that past events and ruptures are continuously shaped by historical experiences. For instance, in *Ethnic Nationalism in Korea: Genealogy, Politics, and Legacy*, Gi-Wook Shin (2006) has argued that historical contingencies played a big role in consolidating a sense of ethnic identity among Koreans. The historical experiences under the Japanese colonial regime have cultivated a strong sense of nationalism among the minds of many Korean people. Rather than labelling nationalism as either beneficial or malignant, Shin (*Ibid.*, p. 11) concludes that it is 'a product of contentious politics' which can function as a double-edged sword. This strong sense of shared ancestry continues to exert a significant influence on contemporary Korean society when crowds cheer together for the Korean team during the 2002 World Cup which took place in South Korea and Japan.

While colonial experiences have instilled a strong sense of shared identity, they also had adverse influences. Due to the abnormal growth of capitalist economy under the Japanese colonial regime, there was barely a base for the development of liberal democracy. According to Bruce Cumings (2005, p. 193), such a thin base has induced the so-called 'interpreter's government' of the US military to ally with 'several hundred conservatives' some of whom had collaborated with the colonizers. This detrimental practice has contributed to the insufficient liquidation of the colonial past and retention of power elites who held on to colonial ties after independence. The abrupt way in which Korea was 'emancipated' from the colonial regime, and the presence of foreign powers, has led to the phenomenon of having 'no middle' with political ideologies sharply divided between liberal capitalism and communism (*Ibid.*, p. 194). This sense of having 'no middle ground' persists in the political talks in South Korea in many aspects.

It is worth noting that even the events which appear to declare a clear break with the past are in fact continuation of a similar project. For instance, the rhetoric of *segyehwa* in the Kim Young Sam administration is eerily similar to that of early reformers like Kim Ok-kyun in the 1880s. They sound anxious to get rid of the old skin and move forward, naively believing that the path will lead to a much brighter future. Similarly, recent cultural trends like *Hallyu* (literally meaning Korean wave, it refers to the popularity of Korean dramas and songs overseas) in Japan, can be traced back to the colonial time when Korean vernacular art forms constituted a part of 'the exotic, aesthetic, or affective fulfillment' (Atkins, 2010, Ch.1, Sec.1, Para 5). In *Koreana in the Japanese Colonial Gaze, 1910–1945*, Atkins argues that more innocuous appreciations of Korean arts did exist alongside more diabolic forms of art collections during the colonial period. Therefore, it would be inaccurate to consider the current talk of globalization as something which arises from a vacuum.

Contextual contingencies provide different settings in which similar impulses can take shape. The *segyehwa* drive in the 1990s has garnered substantial public support and resulted in important policy changes. On the other hand, the reform movement in the 1880s was largely a secret court affair which resulted in a failed coup. The ideals and philosophies of the reformers in the late Chosun Dynasty never reached the general populace. Likewise, *Hallyu* in the new millennium is quite different from the popularity of Korean vernacular art forms in the colonial period since it reaches a much wider audience. This book is meant to convey a sense of complexity, which arises from the coexistence of historical continuities and chance occurrences.

This book is intended as an inquiry into how the rhetoric of globalization has impacted the urban environments of Seoul. As such, the subject of this study extends beyond physical objects, and includes the political economy and cultural developments of South Korea. Several books dealing with contemporary South Korea have been published. At one end of the scholarship, there is the work of Bruce Cumings, with books titled *Korea's Place in the Sun: A Modern History* (2005) and *Parallax Visions: Making Sense of American-East Asian Relations at the End of the Century* (1999). His work analyzes the development of Korean nationalism and globalization through the lens of the Pacific Rim discourse, which centres on the role of the United States in the development of international capitalism during the Cold War. However, his work focuses largely on how American involvement has influenced the political history of Korea rather than on the reproduction of globalization and national identity discourses on the grassroots level of South Korean society.

Other books specifically dealing with the South Korean experience of nationalism and globalization include Gi-Wook Shin's *Ethnic Nationalism in Korea: Genealogy, Politics, and Legacy* (2006) and *Korea Confronts Globalization* (2009), edited by Yun-Shik Chang, Hyun-ho Seok and Donald L. Baker. The former analyzes the role and origin of the ethnic nationalism that has partly shaped modern Korean society. However, it is primarily an inquiry based on abstract political philosophy and does not relate concepts – such as national identity and ethnicity – to concrete urban experiences. Furthermore, the book does not discuss the recent political project of building a multicultural society in South Korea. The latter discusses more recent development of South Korean society after the shock of structural adjustment. However, this book is a collection of short essays on different subjects, and its format precludes the possibility of providing a deeper and more detailed account of globalization under a single theme.

On the other hand, Hong Kal's book, *Aesthetic Constructions of Korean Nationalism: Spectacle, Politics and History* (2011), examines the influence of colonial legacies and the production of nationalism by analyzing built environments including museums and expositions. Her book discusses important urban redevelopment projects that reflect changing practices of spectacle in the age of globalization. However, the primary emphasis is placed on exceptional spaces such as museums and expositions rather than ordinary places, which may tell a bigger story about urban transformations. The subject of the book is the historical construction of Korean nationalism rather than recent challenges to the very concept of the solidarity of Korean ethnicity.

This book takes on the realm where the previously mentioned studies left off. I focus on how the project of globalization has been internalized, negotiated, and resisted by the South Korean people by looking at places affected by urban redevelopment projects. Although I discuss the historical construction of Korean national identity, I focus more on the *challenges* to the project of globalization by discussing growing pressure to embrace a multi-ethnic societal structure and the reactions to related policy changes. While acknowledging the importance of colonial experiences and international relations, I aim to add another dimension to the study of the Korean experience of globalization by examining how local reactions to wider political economic changes unfold in urban settings. A chapter on Dongdaemun Design Plaza and another on Itaewon discuss local reactions, including resistance to government introduced changes. At the same time, I examine spaces of everyday and grassroots campaigns as well as high-flown urban redevelopment projects to contrast global aspirations with local needs. In addition, important changes in economic structure and policy changes are discussed in order to understand the socio-political context behind the initiation of urban construction projects.

Research Sites and Organization of the Book

This book is broadly organized according to two themes. The first part examines how the process of globalization has contributed to refashioning Korean traditions by analyzing the preservation discourse regarding Korean folk houses and pre-industrial street layouts. Renewed interest in Korean customs and 'lost heritage' is part of the reformist tendency in the *segyehwa* drive. The soft city discourse emphasizes the need to restore the 'historical quality' of Seoul that is believed to have deteriorated during the industrialization and urbanization process since the Korean War. This part of the book analyzes how the interest in Korean folk cultures, occurring in conjunction with the democratic movement in the 1980s, influenced the preservation of historical sites. Whereas the initial movement was initiated to give voices to the under-privileged and under-represented, its success has contributed to the romanticized and class-based notion of a 'timeless' Korean tradition. At the same time, the government-led project of promoting vernacular house forms has become a force for gentrifying historic neighbourhoods.

Chapter 1 provides a brief urban history of Seoul, from the time it was designated as the capital of the Chosun Dynasty in the fourteenth century to the 1980s. This chapter provides background information for the readers unfamiliar with Seoul's history as a capital city. Then it moves on to discuss current urban developments, including those in Bukchon. In Chapter 2, I focus on the architectural discussions surrounding the remodelling of urban *hanoks* (Korean-style houses) in Bukchon, a historic neighbourhood in Northern Seoul. In Bukchon, the government's attempt to reconstruct national heritage has been channelled into remodelling old and deteriorating *hanoks*. Although the project has contributed to the generation of renewed interest in *hanoks*, it has also generated gentrification and increasing commercial encroachment. Although commodification of heritage has been observed elsewhere, including Europe and United States, the Korean case is different in the sense that it is the by-product of a very condensed modernization process. As such, the commodification process has been more rapid, and also has taken the character of heightened urgency. The state's effort to construct Bukchon as the repository of Korean culture would not have been successful without the consent and aid of the local residents. I examine how the shifting relationship between grass-roots community organizations and the local government has shaped the course of neighbourhood development. Chapter 3 analyzes the urban changes in Insadong, a commercial district famous for intricate street patterns and sales of traditional paintings, artefacts, and 'authentic Korean food'. The government's promotion of the district as involving 'historic and cultural streets' involved various street beautification measures such as stone pavements and implementation of a Car Free Zone. Although the changing ambience brought by redevelopment generated a narrative of loss among professionals and historians, the effort of NGOs to save smaller shops and the use of streets by human rights activists suggest the emergence of a new kind of civic space. By tracing the continuity between the current use of public space and the March 1st independence movement in the colonial era, I conclude that invisible traditions live on despite the tendencies to channel the concept of tradition into a new development strategy.

In the second part, I move on to examine the theme of migration and the generation of new minority neighbourhoods amidst the *segyehwa* policies and the state-led efforts to build a 'multicultural society'. I analyze the historical backgrounds of existing multiethnic communities and how urban policies in the past decades unwittingly contributed to the formation of such communities. At the same time, I analyze the presence (or lack thereof) of considerations of sustaining such cultural diversity in urban environments. By examining how expressions of new subjectivities were moulded in urban environments, this part illustrates that economic policies during the *segyehwa* drive have brought unanticipated yet positive side effects such as the formation of Little Russia and the Muslim community. I question the applicability of design-oriented space to producing 'multicultural streets' and the 'world design capital'. The presence of multiethnic neighbourhoods is threatened by the city government's urban redevelopment plans when current policies regarding a 'multicultural society' do not include consideration for economic justice and housing provision.

Chapter 4 follows the urban history of Dongdaemun Market from a centre of the textile and fashion industries to the formation of an immigrant community as the result of changing economic structures and labour policies. The demolition of a sports stadium and the construction of a large-scale park in Dongdaemun Market were efforts to elevate the status of Seoul by rebranding it as the 'world design capital'. At the same time, this modernization was possible only through the negation of colonial history and selective appropriation of anti-colonial sentiments. However, the continuation of the world design capital project is operable only through hidden socioeconomic costs including poor working conditions and job instability of migrant workers. In Chapter 5, urban developments in Itaewon, considered the most exotic place in Seoul, are analyzed in order to trace the impact of changing demographics as well as diversifying consumption patterns on built environments. Although the area was initially developed due to the presence of the US military, it later became the centre of religious and sexual minority communities. Chapter 5 examines urban planning schemes to construct 'multicultural streets' in Itaewon, and the process by which a cosmopolitan consumption pattern has replaced the base-town economy of the Cold War era. Although the initial growth of the district had a lot to do with the presence of the US military base, recent commercial development of the area has been the result of the increasing transnational movement of labour. A careful examination of Itaewon's history suggests that the current cultural diversity in the area was the unanticipated by-product rather than the direct result of urban policies. On the other hand, the current plan to redevelop the larger Yongsan area, as well as the plan to build theme streets, endangers the incipient yet vibrant local multiethnic neighbourhood.

Although the government-led urban projects in the Global Zones are in large part a continuation of the growth-centred developmental framework, they have been challenged on different levels, both rhetorically and physically. While the redevelopment plan near Insadong has brought the increasing presence of large businesses and the rising cost of land, NGO-led activities to build walkable streets have stalled construction of mega-structures in the main street. The city government's effort to promote Dongdaemun Market through the construction of landmark architecture has brought a backlash from NGOs and artists who challenge the definition of 'global' by producing their own version of urban aesthetics. Since real lived experiences and urban experiments continually shape the making of Korean global spaces, the status of Seoul remains far from being defined. The effort to shift Seoul from a 'hard city' to a 'soft city' through the redesign of urban environments thus has important implications for the political role of urban planning and architecture in other fast-growing Asian metropolises. While neoliberal economic forces and state-led ambitions seek to supersize cities, grassroots movements and local activism continue to challenge such unsustainable urban visions.

Notes

1. The Cheonggyecheon Restoration Project was one of the many urban redevelopment projects that sought to pursue balanced growth by simultaneously seeking the protection of the natural environment, the preservation of history, and material accumulation.
2. The act of Real Name Financial Transaction System sought to normalize banking by making all financial dealings transparent and root out the source of corruption.
3. In the National Assembly Library in South Korea, 853 books were found to contain the word 'global' in their titles. Among them only twenty-three were published before 1997. More than 50 per cent of the books containing the word 'global' in their titles were published after 2007.
4. 'Shared Growth Beyond Crisis' was the theme of the G20 Summit held in South Korea in 2010.

Chapter 1

A Brief Urban History of Seoul

The Beginning of Seoul as the Capital City

Although records of the first settlements in what is now Seoul stretch back to prehistoric times, the history of Seoul as a capital city goes back to 1394 when Yi Seung Gye, the first king of the Chosun Dynasty, decided to make this city the capital of his new kingdom. According to *Chosonwangjo-sillok* (*The Annals of the Chosun Dynasty*), Yi asked Muhak, a Buddhist monk who later became an advisor to the king, to search for an auspicious site for the new capital. Following *feng shui* beliefs, many philosophers and leaders deemed the act of selecting a capital pivotal in determining the fate of a dynasty. Muhak thought that Seoul's landscape, surrounded with mountains and relatively flat in the middle, was auspicious in this regard (figure 1.1) (*Joseon Wangjo Sillok*, 1394).[1] The official name of the city at the time was Hansong, or Hanyang. Soon after the designation of Hansong as the capital, palace complexes and administrative units were built. Confucianism became the central political ideology of the Chosun dynasty, which distinguished the new regime from that of Koryo, the previous dynasty, which adhered to the Buddhist religion. Confucian ideology was fundamentally different from Buddhism since it is a secular ideology that emphasizes virtues such as filial piety, a value that was extended to the relationship between the king and his subjects. The ruler had to possess moral rectitude in order to guide his people and to reciprocate the loyalty of his subjects. Reflecting Confucian ideology, the city gates were named after the principle virtues of Confucius's philosophy.[2] Soon after the construction of the palaces, existing marketplaces and residential districts were expanded, making Hansong the centre of political and economic activity.

Important buildings constructed during the early days of the Chosun Dynasty include the Gyeongbok Palace Complex, the Jongmyo shrine, a memorial for deceased kings and queens; and Sungkyunkwan, the national educational facility (figure 1.2). Sited between two mountains, Gyeongbok Palace was laid out in an orthogonal fashion, similar to the layout of the imperial palace in China. A hierarchical organization of space and a symmetry of forms along the central axis characterize this main palace complex of the Chosun Dynasty. In later periods, other kings built different palace complexes, but they were less formalized in their layout. Indeed, compared to Gyeongbok Palace,

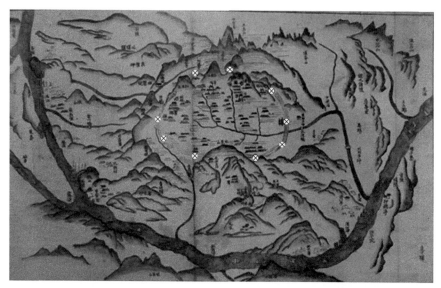

Figure 1.1. Old map of Seoul showing waterway and main gates (indicated by crosses). The river shown below is the Han River.

the Changdeok Palace Complex, built in the early fifteenth century, shows less concern for geometrical symmetry and adopts a natural landscape resembling the palaces of the previous Koryo Dynasty. Confucian ancestral rites were held in the Jongmyo Shrine, and consequently, it was designed to accommodate ancestral tablets and the necessary articles used for the rites. As the Chosun Dynasty continued, the number of tablets increased, and the structure was elongated to accommodate a total of nineteen tablets. Very large timbers and foundation stones were chosen as building materials to create a solemn and majestic ambience.

The street in front of Gyeongbok Palace was called Yuk-jo Street, where six major government ministries were located. With Gwanghwa-mun, the southern gate of Gyeongbok Palace in the centre, ministry buildings were located on either side of the street. Yuk-jo Street was connected to Jongro Street, which connected the eastern and western parts of the capital. A bit west to the Gyeongbok Palace and perpendicular to Jongro Street was Donhwamun Street which connected Jongro Street to the Changdeok Palace. Most governmental functions were centred on Jongro Street since it was close to both palace complexes. The state allowed the establishment of commercial shops on Jongro Street, and the merchants of officially recognized *sijon* (市 廛) (official markets) enjoyed market monopoly on their specialty products in return for tax payment. Since the area was close to government offices as well as the residences of high officials, Jongro area became the centre of economic activities.

The city wall which connects four major mountains of the capital, namely Buckak, Nak, Nam, and Inwang Mountains, was constructed to protect the city. About 18

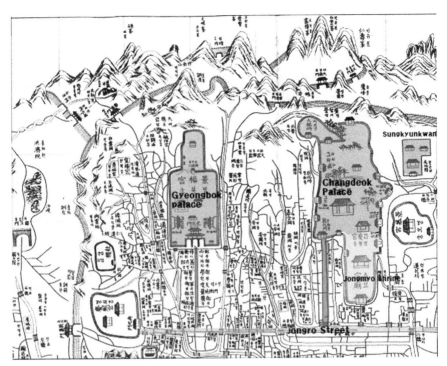

Figure 1.2. Old map of Seoul showing the Gyeongbok and Changdeok Palace complexes, the Jongmyo shrine, and Sungkyunkwan, the educational facility, Jongro Street, Yuk-jo Street, leading from Jongro Street to Gyeongbok Palace, and Donhwamun Street, leading from Jongro Street to Changdeok Palace.

kilometres long, the city wall was continuously reinforced and repaired throughout the Chosun Dynasty. There were a total of eight city gates, which controlled entry to the capital. With the Han River, the city wall built along the mountainous terrain effectively protected the city from possible threats. Initially built using both earth and stone, it was gradually replaced with boulders over the years as floods destroyed weaker parts of the city wall.

Meanwhile, less attention was given to Buddhist temples, which had occupied an important symbolic and cultural space during the Koryo Dynasty. In the Koryo Dynasty, many Buddhist temples were located in the city centre, serving as a focal point of the city and also as a landmark. By contrast, most of the Buddhist temples constructed in the Chosun Dynasty were located in the mountains or in peripheral regions. In 1510, a group of Confucian scholars set fire to the Heungcheonsa Pagoda, a famous Buddhist pagoda that was a landmark in Hansong. Although this seemed like a random act of violence, it was emblematic of the destruction of the old politico-religious order at the hands of proponents of a new order. At the beginning of the Chosun Dynasty, the preference of Confucianism as a ruling ideology was triggered by political motives, and as such, did not affect the traditionally privileged position of Buddhism in everyday life. For instance, Yi Seung Gye, the first king of the Chosun Dynasty, maintained a close relationship with Buddhist monks, being a Buddhist himself. Yet, with the consistent policy of subsequent kings to suppress the power of Buddhist priests, the end of Buddhism as a state-sponsored religion had become a *fait accompli* by the sixteenth century.

The social hierarchy at the time of the Chosun Dynasty consisted roughly of four large groups. The *Yangban* were the ruling class. They were of two types: the literati, and the military officials. In principle, a commoner could become a *yangban* after passing state examinations and acquiring an official position from the king. Although the class system, especially with regard to the literati, was in practice hereditary, the presence of the exam system based on talent has led some historians to note that the Chosun political system contained an element of meritocracy rather than being a strict aristocracy (Woodside, 2006). Below the literati were the *Jung-in*, the middle men who served as lower class officials, military, or technicians. Commoners were mostly farmers, although some depended on commercial activities or handicrafts for their livelihood. Lastly, the *Chunmin* class consisted of slaves, prostitutes, shamans, butchers, and others whose jobs were considered vulgar and low in the Confucian ideology. *Chunmin* were not allowed to take the state exams which were open to all other classes.

Learning and interpreting Confucian classical texts became a very important activity both culturally and economically, since the written state exam tested students' understanding of Confucian philosophy. Although the state exam became ineffective in the later period of the Chosun Dynasty due to corruption, it provided a very competitive system through which members of the elite class had to win the right to run the country. Primary education was usually given at the residences of local literati. The highest educational institution, which corresponded to today's national university, was the *Sungkyunkwan*. Admission was limited to about 200 students at a time, and only those who passed preliminary tests could register. The students at Sungkyunkwan were considered possible future officials of the dynasty (figure 1.3). The shrine to Confucius and the central lecture hall occupied the centre of the site, while dormitories were placed at the sides.

Residential districts were not strictly segregated according to class hierarchy. Yet the most prestigious area was the district near the palace complexes, as geographical proximity to political power was a very important marker of one's status. The area north of Cheonggye Stream and between the Gyeongbok and Changdeok palace complexes was considered most advantageous. The less well-to-do lived on the outskirts of the city or outside the four city gates. Houses for different classes used different materials, and this often resulted in different forms. Residential structures for well-to-do *yangban* usually had tiled-roofs, while commoners and the poor lived in thatched-roof houses. As they ruled a Confucian country, the leaders of the Chosun Dynasty promoted

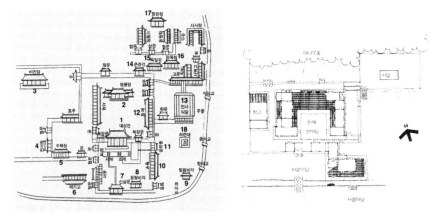

Figure 1.3. Comparison between Sungkyunkwan (*left*) and residences of elite literati named Yun Jeung (*right*) shows that both structures shared the same construction method and module system.

virtues such as frugality and moderation. Concerned about the sumptuous residential structures of the upper class rivalling palace structures, a building code that dictated the size of houses according to royal rank was formulated in the early years of the dynasty. As for commoners, they did not have the resources to afford expensive wooden bracket construction. Therefore, they turned to rammed earth and rice straw, widely available as Chosun was an agrarian country, for building materials. Unlike that of Europe, traditional Korean architecture, and by extension that of East Asian countries, did not develop different building types according to function. Palace complexes, religious complexes, and residential structures all had the same modular spatial units, with a more or less identical wooden construction method, and tiled roofs. But this did not mean architectural uniformity. Moreover, layouts of component building differed according to function. Also, subtle differences – such as the number and arrangement of modules, and details of the wooden parts of the frame – distinguished different types of spaces.

Hansong's population grew steadily throughout the five centuries of the Chosun dynasty except during the time of the Japanese invasion at the end of the sixteenth century. After the invasion, much effort was put into reconstructing destroyed palaces, houses, and some Buddhist temples. The city gradually recovered its role as the capital and prospered throughout the remainder of the Chosun dynasty. In the eighteenth century, the implementation of *daedong-bŏp*, a revised tax law which unified forms of tax payment into one product, rice, encouraged trading (Kim, D.W., 2011). Commercial activities spread outside Jongro Street, and the existing *sijon* (official markets) were extended to the edge of Hansong. Sijon was extended to Cheonggye Stream area, and the unofficial market thrived outside the city gates, including the area outside Dongdaemun (Eastern Gate) and Namdaemun (Southern Gate). Trading and

Figure 1.4. Boundary of Hansong in the late eighteenth century as seen in Gyongdo, showing that the city has expanded beyond the four gates originally demarcating the administrative boundary.

commercial activities sprung up in Yongsan and Mapo as well. In the late eighteenth century, as the residential areas outside the city gates developed, previously excluded areas were reincorporated into the administrative system (figure 1.4). Despite much destruction after the Japanese invasions in 1592 and 1597 CE, the recovering economy generated increased trading and agricultural output. In the latter period of the Chosun dynasty, some houses of rich commoners became large enough to compete with those of *yangban*. Literati, on the other hand, were divided into several factions, and factional rivalries often resulted in the purging of oppositional forces by removing them from high governmental positions. Some literati settled in rural towns, either permanently or temporarily, in order to gather local resources and strengthen their political support.

Some notable buildings constructed after the Japanese invasion are the Indeok Palace Complex and the Gyeongdeok Palace Complex. Although both of these palace complexes are gone now, they comprised a very important group of structures near Gyeongbok Palace Complex, the main palace complex. The new Changdeok Palace had a freer layout compared to Gyeongbok Palace, and halls were placed according to the natural landscape of the site rather than following an imaginary axis. During the latter half of the Chosun Dynasty, many ancestral shrines, called *sadang*, for royal families were built inside the capital.[3] Since many auxiliary rooms were required for the storage of utensils associated with ancestral rites, these shrines occupied a large parcel of land. At the same time, shrines were surrounded by wall enclosures that prohibited random visits or staring passers-by. Thus, some scholars consider the construction of many ancestral shrines in the seventeenth and eighteenth centuries as adding a solemn and stagnant urban character (Kim, D.W., 2011).

At the same time, fortifying the city walls had become another important task, as a series of foreign invasions in the late Chosun Dynasty led to a widespread feeling of insecurity among the residents. During King Sukjong 's reign (1674–1720), destroyed parts of city wall were repaired, and a new city wall near Bukhan Mountain was constructed. Along with the new wall, military posts in charge of guarding the city wall were reorganized. The fortification of the existing city wall, and the construction of a new wall signified the will of the state to defend the capital in the event of military attacks by foreign powers. Along with commercial and economic developments, increased cultural exchanges between the Chosun Dynasty and neighbouring countries brought new intellectual trends. A group of Korean scholars, who learned about Western thought through exchanges with Chinese scholars, initiated the *silhak* movement, which emphasized the practical application of knowledge. Invention and the use of pulleys in large construction projects, such as the Suwon Hwasong City Wall in 1796, show the influence of a new school that favoured practical interests over metaphysical discussions.

Opening of Ports and the Colonial Period

The political conditions in the nineteenth century would soon lead the 500-year-long dynasty into decline, eventually succumbing to Japan. After the death of Jeongjo in 1800, factional rivalries intensified, and the relatives of subsequent kings monopolized the assignment of who was appointed to important government positions. In 1863, Regent Heungseon Daewongun, the father of Gojong, a young king who was then only eleven years old, ran the country and initiated a series of reforms. Daewongun adhered to a foreign policy of isolation after a group of European traders tried to rob his ancestors' tombs. He ordered the expulsion of the Jesuits, and refused to establish diplomatic relations with the United States and European countries. But his political dominance was not very secure. In 1873, he was forced to step down. Taking advantage of the resulting political chaos, Japan sent warships to the port of Busan and demanded that Chosun open its ports for trading. Compared to his Regent father, Gojong and his wife were more open to the idea of trading with foreign nations. After signing a treaty with Japan, Chosun soon signed treaties with other nations, including the United States, Russia, and France.

The opening of ports to foreign traders in the late nineteenth century meant the introduction of different technologies, products, and architectural styles. Foreigners were allowed to engage in missionary work. Along with missionaries and ambassadors came new architectural styles. In the 1880s, a series of foreign legation buildings were constructed in Seoul. The Russian Legation Building, whose only remaining part is its tower, is one of them (figure 1.5). Built in 1890, this structure follows a Renaissance architectural style, and has a symmetrical façade with pediments. Another notable building built after the opening of the ports is Myongdong Cathedral in the Jung-gu district, built in the French gothic style. Since Chosun lacked both the construction materials and techniques needed to build such structures, workers and materials were imported. The construction was supervised by French and English engineers, and construction labourers acquainted with Western architecture were brought from neighbouring China. A French priest named Eugene Costé oversaw the construction process. Since he was not a trained architect, the resulting design shows

Figure 1.5. The Russian Legation Building (*above*) and Myungdong Cathedral (*below*) conspicuously show the growing influence of foreign powers in the late nineteenth century under the Chosun Dynasty.

a style approximating to Gothic but not fully developed so as to include typical Gothic features such as flying buttresses. Located in the cityscape, which was dominated by low single-storey houses, this Western-style building appeared very unusual, due to the height and material used. Standing over 154 feet (47 m) tall, the cathedral was in stark contrast to the single-storey dwellings nearby. Use of brick and stone was another factor that distinguished this structure from others.

Meanwhile, the king and his high officials sought to reassert political authority by engaging in reform measures and modernization projects. The Gabo Reform of 1894 brought many changes, including the abolition of the hierarchical class system. The solar calendar and a Western educational system were also introduced. A new palace structure called Seok-jo-jeon (meaning 'house made of stone') was added to the existing Deoksugung Palace Complex. It followed the neo-classical architectural style, with ionic columns on the façade. After re-establishing diplomatic relations with Japan, reform-minded government officials, such as Kim Ok Gyun, toured Japanese cities to observe their urban development. Shocked by what they saw, reformers sought to modernize the urban environment by broadening streets and improving the poor sanitary conditions. In *Chido-yakron*, the first book which discusses the need for modern city planning, Kim Ok Gyun argued for the establishment of a separate government bureau responsible for the maintenance of road systems and cultivation of a skilled labour force (Kim, O.G., 1882). A member of Gaehwa Pa (Enlightenment Party), Kim believed that the future of Chosun depended on acceptance of advanced technologies and the institutions of the West. Although the project of modernizing the streets was opposed by many whose houses were slated for demolition, it came to fruition under Lee Chae Youn, a Chosun government official who was appointed

Figure 1.6. This photo of the major thoroughfare in front of Gyeongbok Palace Complex, taken in the late nineteenth century, shows widened streets as the result of early attempts to modernize the city.

to a position akin to a present-day mayor. After his appointment in 1897, many parts of Seoul's major streets were expanded and repaired (figure 1.6). In 1899, the first street car line in Jongro Street was completed. Other efforts to modernize the country and reassert the authority of the dynasty included the construction in 1897 of Wongudan, a special shrine to heavenly gods. This was a symbolic act by King Go-jong promoting himself as an emperor, the son of heaven, instead of a king. Following the Chinese concept of the emperor being the son of heaven, King Go-jong placed himself strategically on an equal footing with a Chinese emperor. Yet such efforts were short-lived. Unfortunately, the Chosun Dynasty fell under the grip of Japanese imperial ambitions in 1910, resulting in the colonization of the country.

Despite changes in the urban environments, it was not until the twentieth century that urbanization and industrialization brought fundamental changes in Seoul's physical environment. During the time of the Japanese colonial regime, Hansong remained the central city but its name was changed to Gyongsong. As a colonial city, it became the showpiece of the modern Japanese state's newfound political and economic power. The area of present-day Yongsan and Itaewon in Seoul was developed as the site of the military command post of the Japanese imperial army and its dependents' housing. The Japanese administration concentrated on 'modernizing' Gyongsong through various measures. In 1912, a new urban master plan designed to remodel the roads and districts of Gyongsong was proposed. The population grew from about 250,000 in 1919 to 900,000 in 1945. The city expanded as the area outside the city gates, including the Mapo, Cheongryangri, and Yeongdeungpo area, were added to its jurisdictional boundary.

Persuading former subjects of the Chosun Dynasty to participate in a Japan-led project of modernization involved a visual transformation of Gyongsong's urban environment to make it a suitable colonial capital. One of the first moves of the Japanese colonial regime was to create an urban centre which culminated in the construction of the Japanese Government General Building (figure 1.7). The new government building was deliberately placed in front of Gyeongbokgung Palace, interrupting the traditional axis of spatial hierarchy established at the beginning of Seoul's history as a capital. This choice was a symbolic strike against the previous dynasty and any remaining idea of Chosun as an independent nation-state. Unlike traditional palace structures, the façade of the Government General Building established a different visual order. Whereas the inner core of traditional palaces, the seat of power, was hidden from public view, the new visual order demanded that important government buildings look imposing and regal. The Japanese Government General Building follows a neo-Renaissance style with granite finishes, with at its core a reinforced concrete structure. The central dome, while not too big in size, overwhelms the viewer through its contrasting design and materials. Behind this building, in what used to be the palace complex, various exhibitions were held to showcase the advanced technologies of the larger Japanese

Figure 1.7. Japanese Government-General Building authoritatively stands in front of the Gyeongbok Palace, seemingly asserting its supremacy over the main palace of the Chosun Dynasty.

nation. Looking formidable and authoritative, this building was emblematic of the early Japanese colonial policy which relied on military force to suppress any independent cultural movements or signs of political criticism.

However, after the March 1st (*Samil*) movement in 1919, subtler means of control were adopted. The March 1st movement was a massive resistance movement that highlighted the ineffectiveness of the Japanese colonial military regime. Initially triggered by the reading of an independence doctrine by thirty-three representatives grieved by King Gojong's death, it quickly spread to all parts of the country. As a result, in the 1920s, a new policy named *Bunka Seiji* (Culture Policy) called for a different approach, choosing appeasement instead of overt repression. Although this was only a wilier form of domination, the new approach had the effect of assimilating some of the wealthier elites of the Chosun Dynasty into the Japanese system. At the same time, the introduction of new kinds of consumer goods into Korea contributed to the formation of a new urban culture. By the 1930s, Korean intellectuals familiar with Western philosophies and cultural customs emerged as a distinct group, differentiating themselves from the older generations who still held onto traditional ways of life. Urban space became a scene for conspicuous consumption, and construction of Western-style department stores and theatres contributed to a radically different conception of urbanity. Banks and department stores were concentrated in the Namdaemun (South Gate) area, where most Japanese nationals lived and worked (figure 1.8). Among many commercial structures, the architecturally significant ones included the Mitsukoshi Department Store (currently the Shinsegae Department Store) and Chosun Bank

Figure 1.8. This photo of the Namdaemun area in the 1930s shows a radical transformation of Seoul, prompted by Japanese colonial interests.

(currently being used as a currency museum). Chosun Bank, built in 1912, exhibits neo-classical architectural features, while the Mitsukoshi Department Store, built in 1930, departed from the classicist tradition. By the 1930s, the neo-Renaissance and neo-Baroque architectural styles started to wane with the introduction of streamlined Art Deco and modern architecture.

To a certain extent, these urban spectacles served as a tool to showcase economic development under the Japanese regime. Yet not every part of the city enjoyed the same level of benefits brought by the modernization project. The flow of foreigners, mainly Japanese and Chinese, brought the development of ethnically divided residential districts. The dividing line between the Koreans and the Japanese was the Cheonggye River, separating Gyeongsong into Bukchon, where most Koreans lived, and Namchon, a town newly developed by the Japanese. According to Baek-yung Kim, this system of 'dual cities' within a city became a symbol of 'the civilized Namchon' and 'the primitive Bukchon' (Kim, B.K., 2005, p. 145). Better urban infrastructure such as paved roads, water, and sewage, were first designated for the residential area with a high concentration of Japanese, while Korean residential districts remained underdeveloped. The Jongro area, the traditional commercial area of the Chosun Dynasty, was adversely affected by the development of Honmachi, the new commercial district near Namdaemun. At the same time, examples of monumental architecture reminding Koreans of the late Chosun dynasty were deliberately destroyed. Changgyeong Palace was converted into a park, housing a zoo and a botanical garden. The large Western-style façade of the Japanese Government General Building blocked the view of Gyeongbok Palace. Such symbolic defacement and destruction of the historical urban fabric contributed to the post-liberation public perception of Seoul's historic character being distorted and deliberately undermined.

The demise of the Chosun Dynasty and colonial oppression rendered the image of Western architecture oppressive. Yet at the same time, Western architectural styles continued to attract the attention of the upper classes, since such styles were associated with political power. While traditional Korean residential structures consisted either of tiled-roof or thatched-roof houses with timber construction, newly built Western-style mansions were built of stone, which was rarely used for residential structures in Korea. As early as 1907, the Japanese ambassador built a Western-style apartment in Unhyeongung Palace for a grandson of the regent Heungseon Daewongun in order to gain the favour of the royal family. Starting in the 1920s, the theory of *munhwa juteck* ('civilized or cultural housing') put forward by Japanese and Korean architects argued that traditional *hanoks* (Korean-style houses) are inadequate due to poor sanitary conditions and an inefficient organization of space. Although advocates of the *munhwa juteck* (meaning 'cultural house') concept argued for substantive rather than stylistic changes to the traditional *hanoks*, *munhwa juteck* was often equated with Western-style dwellings. By the 1940s, many *munhwa jutecks* built along the periphery of the city showed architectural characteristics of a bungalow, as the bungalow residential type became popular in Japan. Not surprisingly, few Koreans could afford the Western-style bungalows, and they often became associated with the few wealthy Koreans and the Japanese.

Korean War and the Aftermath

The latter half of the twentieth century represented a turning point for Korea in many ways. The Japanese colonial regime, which lasted from 1910 to 1945, and the subsequent Korean War (1950–1953), left South Korea in an economically very poor and politically chaotic condition. In 1945, imperial Japan surrendered to the Allied Forces. Korea regained its independence and Gyongsong's name was changed to Seoul. Yet conflict-ridden international politics and the Cold War generated unfavourable conditions for a smooth transition to a unified post-colonial Korean republic. After a short celebratory period, Korea was embroiled in the ideological conflict between capitalism and Communism. In 1948, two Korean republics were established in the north and the south respectively. Shortly after its independence from Japan, the outbreak of the Korean War in 1950 resulted in further destruction. The Korean War brought a tremendous amount of destruction and a series of calamities left both Koreas in a very weak state. The houses of many South Koreans as well as other structures such as government buildings and schools were destroyed. Although certain projects were designed to facilitate recovery, such as the construction of rehabilitation and welfare housing, they were not comprehensive in scale, leaving most South Koreans to rely on family resources and personal connections for their livelihood.

Yet except for the brief period of the Korean War, South Korea continued with important processes that had begun much earlier, and that would determine the future trajectory of its urban and rural development. Industrialization and urbanization processes continued at an accelerated rate. The mobilization of resources in the 1960s and 1970s contributed to the development of urban infrastructure and heavy industry. Simultaneously, various modernization projects were carried out by government officials and experts who sought to lift Korea out of dire poverty, and to bring economic growth. Negative externalities, such as a housing shortage and political repression, continued to impact South Korea well into the 1980s.

One of many distinctions between the latter half of the twentieth century and other moments in Korea's history was the way in which the aforementioned historical continuities and ruptures were expressed in built environments. The modernization drive of the 1960s and 1970s was implemented under the wider project of building a society based on a concept of a single ethnicity. Also, since the South Korean state operated under the logic of capitalism, it emphasized efficiency as the way to surpass North Korea. Given these developments, the by-products of the urbanization process during the latter half of the twentieth century were very different from those under the colonial regime. Architecturally, Korean architects started to accept the International Style, which had become popular in the United States and Western Europe by the 1950s. Whereas the urbanization process in the 1930s and 1940s resulted mainly in a denser urban fabric and horizontal expansion, the same process in the latter half of the century produced a significant level of vertical expansion in urban landscapes. The discourse of efficiency dominated discussions of urban problems, and this had the effect of encouraging the development of high-rise residential complexes. To better understand this phenomenon, it is useful to examine the conditions of Seoul in the aftermath of the Korean War.

Seoul was no exception to the high level of destruction the Korean War caused. Due to its status as the capital city of South Korea, countless battles took place, and many bridges crossing the Han River were demolished to prevent the enemy forces from crossing the river. Despite much destruction, the status of the city did not change and many people returned to Seoul after the war was over. After the cease-fire in 1953, most of the urban projects focused on the recovery. Priority was given to rebuilding demolished bridges, roads, and other infrastructure. Another exigent problem the city faced was the lack of sufficient housing due to the baby boom and the increasing migration to Seoul of the rural population. Most problematic was the destruction of houses, as the urbanization process resumed and migrants from rural areas, as well as former residents returning to their homes, were looking for places to live. In 1949, the population of Seoul was 1.4 million; by 1960, 11 years later, it had increased to more than 2.4 million (Seoul Tukbyol Sisawiwonhoe, 2009, p. 323). To accommodate the growing population, its size also increased significantly, and the current city limit was reached only in the 1960s (figure 1.9). In 1963, the administrative boundary of

Seoul incorporated a significant portion of land south of Han River, including parts of the Yangju, Kimpo, Gangnam, and Siheung areas (*Ibid.*, p. 323). Many people became squatters, building makeshift homes in areas such as Yongsan, previously a site of the Japanese military base now turned into a US military camp. In the area below Nam mountain, tent houses and shanty houses made of scrap board made up most of the housing (figure 1.10). Near Cheonggye Stream, many makeshift houses built with cheap wooden planks emerged due to the severe lack of housing. Squatter communities

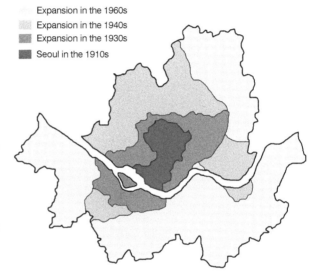

Figure 1.9. The boundary of Seoul has gone through many phases of expansion. In 1914, Gyongsong was confined to the area north of the Han River. By 1963, Seoul included a significant portion of the land to the south and east.

Figure 1.10. Shanty houses made out of cheap wooden panels were ubiquitous in Seoul in the 1960s.

were located on the outskirts of the city, yet not too far from the urban centre, which enabled most of the squatters to walk to their workplaces in the city. Although the substandard living accommodation in the squatters' communities as well as the illegal occupation of land became a big social issue, the South Korean state initially turned a blind eye to them since it lacked the resources to provide them with housing.

The population continued to grow throughout the 1970s and 1980s. By 1970, the population of Seoul had reached well over 5 million, and by 1980, it had surpassed 8 million. The population density increased, as the expansion of Seoul's boundary in the 1960s could not keep up with the rate of population growth. Prodded on by the developmental regime, Kim Hyun Ock, the Mayor of Seoul from 1966 to 1970, embarked on an ambitious project of constructing apartment buildings on sites that had been filled with illegal housing and were cleared for the new construction. Nicknamed the 'bulldozer' due to the countless demolitions under his term, Kim was akin to New York's Robert Moses in the 1930s. In 1969 alone Kim spent about 12.9 per cent of the city's annual budget on the construction of apartment houses (Kang, J.M., 2002). Although some scholars trace the first apartment building to colonial times, the Jongam Apartments, built in 1958, is generally considered the first apartment house in South Korea (Jang and Park, 2009). In 1964, the Mapo Apartments followed. The Mapo Apartments was different from previous multifamily dwellings in being of the direct access rather than corridor-sharing access type. Although the Mapo Apartments was only six storeys high, subsequent apartment buildings in Korea would become higher, and be located within large apartment *danji* (complexes), consisting of many buildings, usually ten or more storeys high.

Despite Mayor Kim's tireless efforts to promote apartment houses, most Koreans remained sceptical about apartment living until the 1970s. Although the modernization drive that had begun much earlier brought changes to traditional Korean houses, multifamily housing was not a familiar residential type for Koreans. The majority of Seoul's residents were from rural towns where extended families lived together in *hanoks*, Korean-style single-storey houses with courtyards and low-wall enclosures. Most Koreans were descendants of either farmers or landed aristocracy, and the cultural importance placed on land was very deep-rooted, making houses that 'float on air' undesirable. At the same time, many considered earlier apartments built by the Korea National Housing Corporation to be substandard public housing designed for the poor.

The continual effort by the national and city governments to brand apartment housing as a modern mode of living began to have an impact on the South Korean population in the mid-1970s. As new amenities were introduced in apartments, an increasing number of Seoul's residents moved into them. Many apartment houses were built in the area south of the Han River, and the government policy of relocating the prestigious high schools also contributed to the fast growth of the area south of the

Han River. It was in the 1980s that apartment houses became associated with middle-class status and thought of as a means of increasing one's assets.

Mayor Kim also invested much energy in the construction of broader streets and commercial infrastructure that would provide a sense of visual order to the whole city. He pushed for the construction of the Gangbyeon Expressway and several elevated highways, including the one over the Cheonggye Stream, covered up in the 1970s to make way for an elevated highway. In the Dongdaemun area adjacent to the Cheonggye Stream, discussions regarding what to do with evacuated empty land plots (called *sogae gongji*) formerly owned by the Japanese led to the construction of a market known as Saewun Arcade. Saewun Arcade was designed by Kim Soo Keun, probably the most famous of the first generation of South Korean architects to embrace modernist architecture (figure 1.11). Other architects, such as Kim Jung Up, started to design modernist-style buildings in Seoul. The Sam-il Building, designed by Kim Jung Up, was constructed in Jongro Street in 1970. Standing thirty-one storeys high, the Sam-il Building was the first high-rise office building to be built in Seoul. Although the first generation of Korean architects had aspired to follow the aesthetics of the International Style and thus join the ranks of the developed nations architecturally, South Korean construction skills lagged behind, leaving certain details of the building unsatisfactory in the eyes of architectural experts. Some claimed that the alterations made to the top

Figure 1.11. Saewun Arcade in the 1970s was a modern shopping mall designed to confer visual uniformity on what used to be a chaotic and haphazard congregation of shops.

part of the Sam-il Building were due to inadequacy in construction techniques (Park, G.R., 2005). It was not until the 1970s that technological expertise became sufficiently advanced to realize the architectural projects being envisioned.

The Developmentalist Regime and Rapid Urban Growth

During the 1970s, Seoul continued to expand. Under the developmental regime of Park Chung Hee, the expansion of the capital city and the redevelopment of the older urban fabric were in full swing. The construction of the first highway from Seoul to Busan in 1970 encouraged the expansion of the capital to the south. At the same time, the city started to actively manage the Han River area and the riverfronts. The construction of the Han River Dam allowed for the efficient use of alluvial land and the construction of waterfront parks. The development of Yeouido, a sandy island in Han River, previously considered unusable, symbolized the beginning of the ceremonial plaza as a showpiece of the modern South Korean state.

The Yeouido plan was a part of the larger Han River development project which was established in the late 1960s. It was previously used as a military airfield and racecourse in the 1920s. The island was left underdeveloped because of flooding issues. With the construction of several dams in Han River, the advantages of developing the island as a part of Seoul's urban fabric included electricity generation and provision of much needed land for housing. The development of Yeouido signalled a series of other urban projects, including the development of Gangnam, the area south of the Han River (Ahn, C.M., 2010). The plan facilitated the development of the Han River bank. Kim Soo Guen's 1968 master plan for Yeouido was based on axial organization of space with the Congress Building on the western end and the City Hall on the eastern end of the street. At the same time, it sought to maximize efficiency by separating pedestrian and automobile traffic vertically. Some scholars, such as Jung-in Kim (2008), argue that the huge scale and modular units used in the project resemble the Japanese metabolist project of Tokyo Bay Plan.

In addition to the construction of roads and houses, there was extensive industrial and commercial development in the 1960s and 1970s. In the 1960s, most South Korean exports were light manufacturing products such as apparel and shoes. Manufacturing and light industry were concentrated in the Dongdaemun area, and the presence of many sewing factories near the major market provided steady consumer demand and workers at many sewing factories. Another industrial district in Seoul was Guro, a district located in the south-west of the city. Light industries such as clothes manufacturing, publishing, and other labour-intensive businesses prospered in this area since it was incorporated into Seoul relatively late. Many rural migrants without education or special job skills found employment in these industrial districts as factory workers. A significant part of the growth of the South Korean economy was based on the low wages of labourers who worked long hours without benefits. As the South Korean economy grew, the state began to shift its focus from light to heavy industry.

Such a rapid pace of development and urbanization did not proceed entirely without resistance or criticism. There were cases of corruption and shoddiness as a result of the rushed pace. As early as 1970, the collapse of the Wawu Apartments sparked sharp criticism of the rushed and often corrupt construction practices, culminating in the resignation of 'the bulldozer' Kim. Residents of slum dwellings in the area slated for demolition also resisted the authority's plans to destroy their homes. Yet early cases of resistance were episodic. They came mostly from those whose living environments were directly threatened, rather than from professionals such as architects and planners. Most practitioners saw the developmental regime's emphasis on urban redevelopment as an opportunity to exhibit their design aesthetics. For instance, the design of a master plan for Yeouido was entrusted to a group of architects, including Kim Soo Keun, who had received his architectural training in Japan. Though his plan was not realized, it reflected the ambitious idealism of the modernist architecture popular at the time. Despite expressing belief in material progress, the experts rarely challenged the undemocratic and authoritarian connotations conveyed by large urban projects like the Yeouido plan.

Even though Seoul's territorial boundary had been fixed by the 1960s, in the 1970s the city still contained a large amount of undeveloped land, including a significant part of Gangnam (the area south of the Han River). Yet beginning in the 1970s, this area began to be radically transformed as a result of state policy redirecting the urban development previously concentrated in the older districts. While the term Gangnam refers to the south of Han River, it usually means three districts of Gangnam, Songpa, and Seocho. As late as the 1970s, most of the Gangnam area was rice paddies or agricultural fields. But it did not remain undeveloped for long. The policy direction of the South Korean government was to suppress further development of the centre of Seoul, located to the north of Han River. With the development of Han River riverfront and Yeouido, and relocation of elite high schools to south of Han River, the Gangnam area began very rapid development.[4] The South Korean state encouraged the development of the three districts by providing various tax incentives to real estate sales in the area. As a result, many large-scale apartment complexes, such as Hyundai Apartments in Apgujeong-dong, an area in Gangnam district, were built during the 1970s and 1980s. As Gangnam became the favoured place of residence, average housing and land prices there skyrocketed, producing numbers of nouveau riche who became rich through real estate speculations. While land prices in Gangbuk (the area north of the Han River) increased 2,500 per cent from 1963 to 1979, those in Gangnam increased between 80,000 and 130,000 per cent over the same period (Kang, J.M., 2006, p. 74).

As the rich relocated to Gangnam, various commercial developments followed, including the construction of department stores and boutique shops. These commercial venues catered for the tastes of the rich, and consequently, Gangnam became the centre of consumption and a symbol of upper class lifestyle. Seokjae Lim (2005, p. 82), a professor of architecture at Ewha University, has noted that the presence of a department store is welcomed by residents not only because it provides shopping opportunities but also because it contributes to the increase in housing prices. Furthermore, the concentration of elite high schools and other private educational institutions in Gangnam has resulted in a disproportionate number of students from the area getting admission to top universities. Such a phenomenon, in turn, reproduced and strengthened the high socioeconomic status of Gangnam residents.

Certainly the real estate bubble produced by the high growth economy was not unique to the Gangnam area. During the 1980s and early 1990s, many other areas, such as Mokdong and Sanggyedong in Gangbuk, and new satellite cities such as Bundang and Ilsan went through a similar process of development. Housing and land prices in Seoul in general increased very fast.

The phenomenon of skyrocketing prices of apartment houses, which started in the Gangnam area, spread to other areas of Seoul such as Oksu-dong Hyundai Apartments sold in 1989 (Jeon et al., 2008, p. 283). Many residents of Seoul outside Gangnam also profited from sales of apartment homes. The expansion and development of Seoul reached a pinnacle in the 1980s in preparation for the Seoul Olympic Games in 1988. The continuous growth of the city necessitated the development of several satellite cities near Seoul, including Ilsan and Bundang. To connect the ever-expanding periphery of the city to the central area, the number of Seoul's subway lines increased from four in 1985 to nine in 2001.

Seoul's rapid economic growth was possible due to both external and internal factors. Externally, the Cold War political structure made possible a mixed and rather protectionist economy. Many forms of foreign aid were available as US international policies were designed to prevent the further spread of communism into South Korea. In terms of international trade, South Korea was in an advantageous position since labour costs remained very low throughout the 1960s and 1970s. Furthermore, the outbreak of the Vietnam War and the increasing demand for war-related industry contributed to the rapid economic growth. Internally, labour repression and the government-led planned economic system meant that there was less room for dissent or time-consuming discussion regarding policy directives, whether economic or political. The shift from light manufacturing to heavy industry in the 1970s, combined with the emphasis placed on higher education and individual competition, produced many skilled workers in the late 1970s and 1980s.

The criticisms of architectural professionals about the recklessness of urban redevelopment coincided with the rise of the democratic movement in the 1980s. The authoritarian military regime of Park Chung Hee, who was the President from 1963 to 1979, came to an abrupt end when he was assassinated by a close aide. With the increase in the educated middle-class population, repressive political moves, such as the bloody suppression of the Gwangju Uprising and the torture of political dissidents, had become intolerable. Many South Koreans, including corporate employees and college students, took to the streets to demonstrate. In 1987, a series of democratic measures, including direct suffrage for election of the presidents, were declared. At the same time, the labour movement, which had begun much earlier, in the 1960s, gained traction, resulting in the formation in 1995 of the Korean Confederation of Trade Unions (KCTU).

Beginning in the mid-1980s, more people were willing to speak out against the dictatorial practices, including construction projects that ignored environmental and historical costs (Lee, Y.I., 1987). The criticism of efficiency-driven projects became more poignant when events like the sudden collapse of the Sampoong Department Store and of Seongsu Bridge in the mid-1990s highlighted the ineffectiveness of a developmentalist regime. Criticism of this regime coincided with the decline of manufacturing businesses in Seoul as labour costs increased due to the improved conditions of the labourers. Manufacturing plants started to relocate elsewhere, mostly overseas, where the cost of labour was much cheaper. As soon as Seoul reached the zenith of its success as an industrial city, as such it was already on the way to its demise. Furthermore, the onset of the Asian Financial Crisis in 1997, despite the Kim Young Sam administration's efforts to reform the economic structure, facilitated discussion of the need for change, which included both physical and mental dimensions.

In such a socio-political context, the rapid development of the Gangnam area also produced criticism. Increasing socio-economic polarization in the 1980s and onwards was viewed as the result of predatory real estate speculation. Many residents of Seoul who did not own their homes due to the high price blamed the housing price bubble on the speculative apartment sales. Although the average housing price increased throughout Seoul in the 1970s and 1980s, the most dramatic rise was in the Gangnam area. In the media, including TV dramas and movies, many newly rich residents of Gangnam, who profited from the real estate sales, are portrayed as vain and materialistic individuals who did not care for others such as the poor or marginalized. The abrupt environmental changes introduced in the area, characterized by high-rise apartments and commercial establishments, also became a target of criticism. Many city planners, historians, and public intellectuals view Gangnam and its development as a symbol of greed and insatiability which destroys anything in its developmental path.

Some scholars, such as Junman Kang (2006) of Jeonbuk University, argue that labelling all residents of Gangnam as 'immoral and greedy' speculators is not accurate since there are many middle-class residents there who had slowly and steadily accumulated wealth. Yet the sense of relative deprivation continues to shape the critical discourse against the perceived culture of Gangnam. With the structural adjustment and slow growing economy which emerged in the late 1990s, making easy money through real estate speculation became more and more difficult. The Gangnam model which once represented 'the engine of Korean capitalism' does not seem as viable as before (Kang, J.M., 2006, p. 324).

In contrast, a series of urban redevelopment projects in Gangbuk, including those which are discussed in subsequent chapters, show that the Gangbuk area, with a longer urban history and historical artefacts, contains much potential for further development, especially by deploying concepts such as 'culture' or 'history'. If Gangnam can be imagined as symbolizing the recent material growth of Seoul, Gangbuk, especially the historic part, represents spiritual maturity and cultural richness. Certain parts of Gangbuk just needed remodelling in order to make them suitable for contemporary sensibilities including environmental and cultural consciousness, and a contrast to the 'soulless' sprawl of Gangnam area. Policy-makers concerned about unequal regional development, NGOs whose goal is to raise awareness of cultural heritage, and residents of Gangbuk with a sense of relative deprivation welcomed new urban projects. The so-called Gangbuk Renaissance involved remaking various urban parts of Gangbuk in order to shift the image of Seoul from that of an industrial city to a post-industrial service-oriented city.

Thus, the period of the decline of Seoul as an industrial city overlapped with new types of urban development. At the same time that Seoul was transforming into the most wired city in the world many of its residents were longing for a slower mode of living. Seoul's urban landscape was frequently likened to a concrete forest devoid of emotional fulfilment. High pollution levels, uncommunicative architectural designs, and the lack of traditional ambience in Seoul were highlighted as major problems. Disappointed with the developmentalist regime's disregard for the historical value of older structures and urban fabric, many residents of Seoul started to yearn for a place to which they could feel emotionally connected. The desire to rediscover the non-economic aspects of cities such as Seoul's 'cultural heritage' and 'historical character' was reflected in the formation of historical societies and preservation organizations with the aim of preserving objects and sites of historical importance. Others focused on ecological issues and the high pollution levels in Seoul, and pointed out the need to control the environmental impact of industries.

The new direction of urban development plans is perhaps best captured by the concept of 'soft city' in contrast to 'hard city', which the Seoul Design Foundation posited as opposing urban imaginaries (Kwon, 2010). Whereas the 'hard city' model, making economic growth and efficiency priorities, is meant to describe the industrial societies of the past, the 'soft city' model, emphasizing values such as communication and understanding, is a model fit for a post-industrial society. According to this theory, Seoul in the past was a 'hard' industrial city that was preoccupied with the construction of factories and efficient high-rise structures. But recently, the city has instead been undergoing a transition to an economy based on service and information-based industries. While this dualistic conceptualization may not accurately portray the complexities of Seoul, such a division serves as a rationale to introduce change in certain parts of the city, in order to make the transition to the post-industrial age possible. What this new urban discourse signals, in terms of Seoul's visual landscape, is that the city needed to transform its image from a city dominated by conventional concrete boxes to something else. If the urban redevelopment plans in colonial times and during the early period of the South Korean republic emphasized 'sanitation' and 'health' as quantifiable and measurable values, now the emphasis was placed on more ambiguous qualities such as 'emotional well-being'. Similar attempts have been made in other cities in different countries, yet what distinguished Seoul from other cases is that the introduction of one architectural style and its displacement occurred in a very short time period. Many pre-industrial structures and parts of the urban fabric have disappeared due to the high rate of growth in the latter half of the twentieth century. In such a context, a new aesthetic, which emphasizes the emotional and affective impact of urban environments, seeks to re-establish the link between the pre-industrial past and the industrialized present.

In more ways than one, architectural design was considered to be the trigger of further urban transformation, imagined as destined to bring larger changes along with aesthetic ones. The designation of global cultural zones and 'culture streets' in several parts of Seoul was a means to promote the idea of Seoul as a site of tourism both on the local and global scale. The following chapters analyze how specific urban projects and architectural works in Seoul reflect the changed attitude articulated in the 'cultural city' or 'soft city' urban discourse. Despite Seoul's radical transformation since 1945, the historical legacies of the Confucian past and the colonial period continue to exert influences on the shaping of the urban environment. Each chapter will examine why and how, despite critique of the past development regime, traces of its practices remain in the urban imaginary and in architectural expressions in contemporary Seoul.

Notes

1. *Chosonwangjosillok* [*The Annals of the Joseon Dynasty*]. Taejo 3-nyon, August 13, Kyungjin. Digital version available at: http://sillok.history.go.kr/main/main.jsp.
2. The five virtues of Confucian philosophy are humaneness (仁), righteousness (義), propriety or etiquette (禮), knowledge (智), and integrity (信). The city gates were Eastern Gate (Heunginji Mun 興仁之門), Western Gate (Don-ui Mun 敦義門), Southern Gate (Sungrae Mun 崇禮門), and Northern Gate (Soji Mun 炤智門). At the centre was Boshingak (普信閣), a belfry.
3. Sadang for royal families were called *Sachinmyo*.
4. In Autumn 2012, Korean pop singer Psy's music video titled 'Gangnam Style' went viral on the internet. While many people watched his video which showed different parts of Seoul, those unfamiliar with Korea could not see beyond his comical gestures to grasp the deep socioeconomic chasm implied in the song. Since its rapid development in the 1970s the Gangnam area south of Han River has become a keyword which differentiates Seoul's socioeconomic classes. As 'gangnam style' became associated with chic and affluent lifestyles, Gangbuk (north of Han River) came to mean relative backwardness.

Chapter 2

Rediscovered Traditions: Remodelled *Hanoks* in Bukchon

'*This looks marvelous. Very snug, but isn't it still a bit uncomfortable to live in?*' This is the typical response of people who visit a *hanok*. For us, a *hanok* is largely recognized as an uncomfortable and inefficient form of residence despite its stylistic elegance. However, newly remodelled hanoks have changed significantly from conventional hanoks… Renovations, which revive the traditional appearance of a hanok while sparing the advantage of modern living, are taking place in areas such as Bukchon.

Herald Media, 16 November 2007

Life in Seoul, characterized by traffic jams, uninterrupted routines, and getting off work and emerging into a gray forest of apartments, contains room for enjoyment of leisure just like life in the countryside. The convenience of urban life and the relaxing composure that suburban life offers can be enjoyed in urban hanoks.

Munhwa Daily Newspaper, 3 July 2003

Beginning in the early 2000s, there was a surge of interest in remodelling *hanoks*, traditional Korean-style houses, in various urban landscapes, including residential and commercial structures. Often described by the popular media as the '*hanok* renaissance', the increasing popularity of remodelled *hanoks* in the early 2000s included commercial adoption of the vernacular form in restaurants, cafés, and hotels, as well as unlikely applications, such as offices and dental clinics.[1]

Remodelled *hanoks* generated favourable responses from the popular media, which described the phenomenon as a novel approach of reviving *hanoks* while not neglecting the practical aspects of domestic life. The combination of a modern facility and traditional aesthetics, one of the crucial characteristics of the remodelled *hanok*, is celebrated as a sign of the diversification of lifestyles. The portrayal of residences in remodelled *hanoks*, as reflected in popular magazines and newspapers, hinges upon the

Figure 2.1. The old map of Seoul showing Bukchon. Living in Bukchon meant having more political opportunities as well as geographical advantages. (Text added by the author.)

idea of a dialectic between two opposing forces, such as the material vs. the immaterial, technology vs. spirituality, and fast-paced urban life vs. leisurely slowness.

The increasing popularity of the *hanok* is perhaps best reflected in government efforts to reconstruct and remodel the vernacular houses in Bukchon (North Village) (figure 2.1) of Seoul. Bukchon, located in the historical centre of Seoul, refers to an area between the Gyeongbok Palace and Changdeok Palace Complexes. Its name comes from its location being north of the Cheonggye Stream, which divides the historic part of Seoul into two parts. The relative concentration of vernacular dwellings in the area has prompted the city government to remark that 'the area can be called a "street museum in the urban core" with many historical spots, cultural heritages, and folk materials'.[2] Efforts to remodel deteriorating *hanok* dwellings in the area in order to restore the historical character of Seoul were realized in the Bukchon Hanok Regeneration Project in 2000, which received the UNESCO Asia-Pacific Heritage Award in 2009.

Analyzing the process of the Bukchon Regeneration Project is crucial for understanding the wider processes of rediscovering 'traditions' in the South Korean context of globalization. The process of remodelling *hanoks* in Bukchon illustrates that the status of the *hanok* is closely linked to the effort to transform Seoul from an industrial to a post-industrial city. In the 'cultural city' discourse, it is often emphasized that the cultural and historical aspects of the capital city in past decades were neglected due to the heavy emphasis on economic efficiency. In other words, Seoul needed its own repository of artefacts and historical landmarks in order to become a truly global city. The Bukchon Regeneration Project is a part of the wider urban rubric of creating several Cultural Districts to transform Seoul into a global city by marketing the *hanok* village as a source of local and global tourism. While changes in *hanok* preservation policy reflect the changing attitude of the government with regard to residents in Seoul, they also stem from the need to make Seoul 'the soul of Asia', where a visitor can simultaneously enjoy modern conveniences and indulge in the exploration of historical artefacts.

On another level, the increasing construction of remodelled *hanoks* challenges the unspoken assumptions about vernacular houses in developing countries in general. Vernacular houses are often viewed as the opposite of highbrow architecture and defined as structures built for the common people. They are imagined as the dwellings for the indigenous or the poor, who cannot afford to live in contemporary houses. While such a premise holds true in many cases, the case study of Bukchon illustrates that vernacular houses can be incorporated into a highbrow consumptive pattern through the process of reinvention. In the case of the *hanoks* in South Korea, the rapid process of modernization has resulted in the flattening of different types of *hanoks* into one representational type based on the *yangban* (Confucius *literati*) residence with wooden post-and-beam construction. In this chapter, I argue that remodelled *hanoks* have become an example of blurring the line between the vernacular and high architecture, although *hanoks* are hailed as the epitome of Korean 'tradition'. Remodelled *hanoks* represent a significant level of both symbolic and tangible capital. They are symbolic due to their association with an upper-class lifestyle. They are also tangible since the presence of *hanoks* brings in more profit by increasing real estate prices and the number of tourists who visit the area.

The so-called '*hanok* renaissance' reveals complex patterns of development impulses and moral values intertwined to produce a powerful driving force behind urban renewal. The association of remodelled *hanoks* with a rediscovery of virtues, and the large amount of symbolic capital attached to *hanoks*, has important ramifications for the politics of aesthetics. Partly generated by criticism of state-led modernization, the increasing popularity of *hanoks* shows that the vernacular has become closely associated with cultural modernity, as well as with the greatness of Korean civilization. As the feeling of deprivation resulting from colonial experiences had the effect of conferring a sacred status on 'Korean tradition', most attempts to revive or allude to traditional forms have garnered public support (Kendall, 2011). Ironically, such historical experiences allow gentrifying forces to take diverse forms without appearing to threaten local communities. While the state-led project to remodel *hanoks* may help to relieve doubts about an unstable Korean identity in the era of globalization, it also poses a danger of erasing important issues regarding class, colonial history, and cultural representations. The government's rhetoric of protecting the 'historic character' of Seoul sometimes becomes a pretext for subsidizing the rich by providing tax breaks for the maintenance costs of *hanoks*. This chapter demonstrates that the subordination of preservation under the state's goal of promoting global and local tourism not only resulted in gentrification but also in highlighting a cleavage within neighbourhood organizations established for the cause of protecting and supporting urban *hanoks*.

Hanok Village as a Commodity in the Global Heritage Market

The North Village Hanok Regeneration Project began to be implemented in 2001 when the first comprehensive plan by the city government was carried out through policies such as a *hanok* registration system and governmental aid for remodelling registered *hanoks*. While the project is primarily funded by the city government, the initiation of the project was the product of collaboration between Jongro North Village Keepers' Association (JNVKA) and the city government. Such collaborations with local associations marked an important break from the previous authoritarian planning approach of the government. The neighbourhood association was formed in order to protect the community from the imposition of restrictive laws that sometimes threatened residents' safety. On the other hand, the subsequent development of the *hanok* village illustrates how the process of preservation can result in the subordination of a community movement to the state's ambitions and private interests in boosting tourism. In the case of South Korea, the deep sense of an historical crisis and the cultural customs shared by the *Minjung* movement have been appropriated by the state to enable remodelled *hanoks* in Bukchon 'to serve as "banks" of national memory and pride and to ward off the subversive effects of historical changes' (AlSayyad, 2001, p. 9). In other words, many remodelled *hanoks* in Bukchon have become visual statements to deflect possible criticisms of urban redevelopment projects hiding under the name of 'preservation'.

During the 1970s and 1980s, residents of North Village were vehemently opposed to the government *hanok* preservation policy that strictly limited any form of repairs and renovations. Although such a draconian measure restrained demolition of many vernacular dwellings, worsening housing conditions produced a significant level of objections from residents unable even to replace rotting wooden columns.[3] At the same time, governmental preservation policy was inconsistent and opportunistic since it precluded a site planned for governmental functions. Demolition of many vernacular dwellings in the late 1980s to clear the site for the Constitutional Court contrasted sharply with the inability of residents to make simple improvements to their own homes (Lee, S.Y., 2006, pp. 99–130). Ironically, the formation of the Jongro North

Village Keepers' Association can be traced back to 1988 when the Committee for the Revocation of the Hanok Preservation District was established to protect residents' rights and to protest against the inflexibility of government preservation policy (Jeong, S., 2000, p. 96).

However, changes in the political climate after the democratic movement of the late 1980s made the implementation of autocratic policy seem unwise. At the same time, relaxed regulations in the early 1990s resulted in 'reckless developments of multiplex housing' and worsening living conditions (*Ibid.*). Close collaboration between the Seoul city government and the JNVKA led to a consensus between the two parties in 1999. In the new plan, the government provides aid to repairs made to a *hanok* as long as it meets the guidelines designed to maintain the historical ambience of the neighbourhood. In official policy, the city government supports up to two-thirds of the exterior repair cost (to a maximum of $25,000) and up to one-third of the new construction of a *hanok* (to a maximum of $50,000) (*Ibid.*). The plan not only encourages residents to register their *hanoks* by providing financial aid for the renovation of existing *hanoks*, but also encourages the construction of new ones. The city government also purchased several urban *hanoks* in the North Village in order to regenerate them according to the traditional aesthetic guidelines. At the same time, many existing construction limitations, albeit somewhat relaxed to give more room for interior repair, continue to be effective. For instance, a limit on the maximum height of the structures allowed in the area regulates the scale of a residential complex. By implementing such a double strategy of promoting *hanoks* and discouraging large-scale constructions, it is hoped that the proliferation of extraordinary and exotic architecture will be curtailed to a certain extent.

Notwithstanding the earnest concern for the disappearance of vernacular spatial forms and the need to incorporate residents' voices, the North Village Hanok Regeneration Project included the marketing of the neighbourhood as a desirable tourist destination for experiencing 'Korean culture'. Contrary to the *hanoks* in earlier times, defined by their agrarian socioeconomic structure, remodelled *hanoks* serve multiple functions in an ever-fragmenting South Korean society. While the *hanok* was primarily considered as a residence, the remodelled *hanok* village is imagined as a tool to achieve more specific goals than a residential purpose. For one thing, an increase in global tourism means that the city government can regard remodelled *hanoks* as a possible source of tourism. Although a single remodelled *hanok* does not amount to much, a group or a town made up of *hanoks* certainly becomes a new urban spectacle in the forest of buildings and other familiar forms of consumerism.

The state's effort to promote Bukchon Village as a repository of Korean history and cultural traditions can be detected in various official documents, including *Bukchon Gakugi Gibon Gyehoek (Basic Plan to Tend Bukchon)*. The plan states that the two components of the project are resident-driven 'community building' and the state-driven 'model undertaking/project' to conserve Seoul's historic districts (Seoul Metropolitan City, 2001*b*). In a study conducted by the Seoul Development Institute in 2001, Bukchon was acknowledged as a place of cultural tourism where foreign visitors during the 2002 World Cup could be directed to get in touch with the local customs (SDI, 2001*a*). It is emphasized that the 'cultural tourism' promoted in Bukchon is unlike an existing large-scale tour, in the sense that it encourages intimate cultural contacts and cultivation of 'a sense of place' (*Ibid*., p. 40).

The 'regeneration' part of the project includes not only the preservation and remodelling of older *hanoks* but also the development of various programmes associated with Korean customs. Policy documents point out that simple 'restoration' or 'preservation' is not enough to guarantee increased tourism. Rather, policy planners argue that it is important for the government to develop many new cultural features that fit the historical ambience generated by the presence of the *hanok* village (Baek, 2007). To achieve this effect, many *hanoks* that the city purchased were converted into guesthouses and museums, where foreign and domestic travellers can stay and participate in various cultural activities, such as calligraphy and tea drinking. Multiple brochures published by the Seoul Metropolitan Government contain not only travel journals of foreign travellers with explanations of each place of interest, but also detailed maps showing 'cultural exploratory routes' around the neighbourhood. Promotion of the place starts at the two tourist information centres, where one can obtain not only information booklets in English and Japanese, but can also rent bicycles and Korean costumes in which to be photographed. For domestic visitors living within Seoul, many classes teaching Korean arts and crafts are provided at the Bukchon Culture Center. Designation of several 'open *hanoks*' within Bukchon, private residences of artisans and craftsmen open to the public during certain hours, reflects the attempt to integrate the concept of residence and tourism. However, many of these residences remain closed to outsiders or are uninhabited.[4] Notwithstanding that 53.2 per cent of the domestic tourists in Bukchon described the purpose of their visit as 'to take a look at traditional houses', their experience is often confined to the exterior of the *hanoks* (*Ibid*., 2007).

Full-scale initiation of the project was soon followed by the opening of many cafés, boutiques, art galleries, and restaurants in the village. The media were quick to note the changing characteristics of the village. One news magazine noted that '[Bukchon] provides a one-stop place for cultural experiences' and that the presence of museums, *hanok* villages, restaurants, boutiques, and craft shops has the potential to make the place 'Korea's Montmartre' (Cho, S., 2005, pp. 6–25). Geographers have also commented that while the older generation associates the place with the house of the prime minister and Korean noodle shops, youngsters associate the place with 'trendy wine bars, contemporary art galleries, and fashionable shops' (Kim, H.H., 2007, p. 129). The rapid pace of commercial expansion continues to be a source of concern for residents who worry that the serenity of the residential area will be compromised by excessive place marketing.

In this new policy phase of Bukchon's urban development, it seems inevitable that some of the remodelled *hanoks* would contain eclectic architectural elements. Not only wine bars, art galleries, and museums, but also other highly specialized services such as dentists' offices, use *hanok* motifs as a way of differentiating their establishments (figure 2.2). Whereas certain shops have recycled existing *hanok* fabrics while adding contemporary materials, other shops have constructed new *hanoks* from scratch. Several art galleries, entertaining a more adventurous design, have integrated the features of the *hanok* with elements of pop art to draw the attention of pedestrians. To borrow Elizabeth Outka's words, the appeal of the place is based on '[the] contradictory move, to recognize the value of continuity while foregrounding the constructed and commodified nature of this continuity' (Outka, 2009, p. 19). It may be argued that the

Figure 2.2. Remodelled urban *hanoks*. From top, clockwise: an Italian restaurant, an art gallery, and a café with a 'coffee take out' sign all either use *hanok* forms or allude to *hanoks*.

commodification of tradition is not always a negative phenomenon. Some scholars, such as Michel Picard, argue that tourism is not always inimical to the 'authenticity' or traditional character of a place (Picard, 1996). In fact, he argues that increased international tourism in Bali functioned to encourage protection of the various forms of local cultural traditions (*Ibid.*).

The premise that touristic culture and local culture can mutually reinforce each other is a very attractive notion for the Seoul city government, aiming to achieve the status of a 'soft city' by boosting the tourist industry. The policy documents prepared by the Seoul Development Institute on the Bukchon Regeneration Project quote Picard's research on Balinese tourism to argue that the promotion of cultural tourism is not antithetical to the preservation of the neighbourhood's historical ambience (Baek, 2007, p. 24). However, not all local customs are regarded as worthy of 'preservation' in the sphere of touristic interests. More importantly, the argument that tourism can encourage the protection of cultural traditions ignores the opportunity cost of the regeneration project. In other words, the current emphasis on a synergistic relationship between preservation and tourism begs the question of 'at what cost?'.

The *Hanok* Boom as a Rediscovery of Korean Cultural Traditions

The current remodelling boom of urban *hanoks* in South Korea illustrates the process in which *hanoks* and Korean identity become essentialized. *Hanoks* are reinvented as the cultural representation of the collective Korean past without a trace of cultural hybridization and class conflict. Although the concept of the *hanok* implies the timeless presence of the building type, stretching more than a millennium, the term itself is new. The term *hanok* was included in Korean dictionaries in the middle of the 1970s in order to distinguish between Western-style houses and conventional ones (Kim, K.Y., 2003). Although the built forms associated with *hanoks* were not the products of 'invented traditions' in the sense that they did not derive from fictitious rituals, the process of positioning *hanoks* as the antithesis of modernization indicates that they were reinvented as a new category of housing. Thus, notwithstanding the diverse prototypes and construction styles of the *hanok*, it is easier to grasp the notion of the *hanok* when it is imagined as the opposite of contemporary dwellings.

One of the factors behind the recent *hanok* renaissance is the mounting criticism of the monotonous urban landscape of Seoul, or 'apartment forests', consisting of endless rows of rectangular concrete boxes. The proliferation of apartments as the popular residential choice goes back to the modernization drive of the early Korean republic. Beginning in the 1960s, individual detached houses, including *hanoks*, began to be associated with inefficient land use and an underdeveloped lifestyle, whereas apartment residences were deliberately promoted by the state as part of a wider modernization project. One of the reasons for the government's promotion of apartment houses was the urgent need to provide housing to accommodate a rapidly urbanizing population, including migrants from rural areas (Jon, S.I., 2009). The city government battled against the rising number of squatter settlements in Seoul. Already in the 1960s, Hochul Lee's popular novel *Seoul un Manwon Ida* (*Seoul is Full*), described the explosive population growth of Seoul as well as various social maladies arising from rapid urbanization and lack of economic opportunities.[5] However, the initial reactions to the government-led construction were sceptical due to poor construction quality and the collapse of the Wawu Apartment in 1970.[6] The public perception of apartment houses was that of 'modest-sized dwellings designed for the low-income bracket residents' (Gelezeau, 2007, p. 34). Even the Mapo Apartments, constructed in 1964 and mainly targeting middle-class residents, suffered an initial lack of prospective residents due to scepticism regarding safety, which included the danger of carbon monoxide poisoning (Kang, J.M., 2006, p. 22).

However, the low status associated with apartment housing began to change as the South Korean state changed its strategy and started to market apartment houses to middle-class consumers rather than utilize them as relocation sites for squatters (Park, C.S., 2006). While most South Koreans were initially sceptical about living in apartments, improvement in infrastructure, which included upgraded central heating systems, elevators, and flush toilets, began to attract the middle and upper-middle classes.[7] The new apartments marketed for these groups were often called 'demonstration apartments' by the state, using them as a showcase of modern living (figure 2.3). In addition, the South Korean state aggressively promoted the apartment lifestyle as desirable by portraying it in advertisements, movies, and other popular media. In *Ju-teck* (*Housing*), a magazine owned by the Korea Housing Corporation,

Figure 2.3. This 1970 advertisement of 'demonstration' apartment houses in Yŏ-ŭido, of Seoul, was promoted by the Mayor of Seoul. In a smaller font, the advertisement reads 'new village with good atmosphere, apartments with dignity'.

interviews with residents of new apartment houses were published in 1968. Most interviewed praised the lifestyle of the apartments as 'revolutionary' and 'convenient' (Kang, J.M., 2006, p. 38).

Not only did residence in apartments become associated with higher socioeconomic status, but the rising prices of apartment units also meant that it was more profitable to purchase an apartment, if one could afford it. Government policies included not only the preferential provision of urban services to apartment complexes but also various tax breaks (Cho, M.R., 2004, p. 28). As finding new sites for large apartment complexes became more difficult in the historic part of Seoul, the state encouraged the development outside the historical boundary of Seoul. Coupled with the policy recommendations and increasingly favourable public perception of apartment houses, the newly constructed apartment houses in Gangnam became hot commodities. As Gelezeau (2007, p. 143) succinctly put it, apartment complexes became 'factories manufacturing middle class citizens' by almost ensuring that buyers would make a profit when they resold the apartment units.

On the other hand, there was a general lack of effort to improve the quality of life in the *hanoks*. In the context of the rapid urbanization and modernization drive, living in a *hanok* became less attractive, as the deteriorating conditions of the urban *hanoks* were considered a symbol of poverty and lack of progressiveness. Such a notion was furthered when President Park, the military dictator in the 1960s and 1970s, issued a presidential decree to replace thatched roofs with tiled roofs, which were considered more advanced. Not only were outside toilets and conventional kitchens denounced as inferior, but the buildings were also regarded as a threat since architectural features such as raised door thresholds were believed to contribute to bad posture. The association of *hanoks* with underdevelopment went hand in hand with the promotion of high-rise apartment housing as the only solution for the increasing density of Seoul. Although older architectural forms and craftsmanship were revered even during the time of industrialization, the end product was considered unsuitable for contemporary urban lifestyles. The horizontal organization of spaces and courtyards was regarded as wasteful in the rapidly urbanizing city of Seoul. In addition, the rising values of apartment housing induced the relocation of many Seoul residents to high-rise apartments.

However, the significance attached to modern living in apartment houses began to be challenged in the late 1980s. Invigorated by the successful democratic movements, urban theorists and intellectuals began to claim that the urban landscape of Seoul had become barren and uninteresting due to the disregard for cultural and historical artefacts. In the context of a shared feeling of political oppression and historical subjectivity, criticism of apartment housing was focused on its methods of production and consumption as well as its aesthetics. Beginning in the 1980s, the portrayal of apartment housing in popular literature discussed social alienation and distorted relationships among neighbours.[8] However, even sharper attacks were made on the economic aspect of apartment housing, representing a deeper socioeconomic critique of unrestrained capitalism. Rising prices of high-rise apartment housing units, reflecting the commercial success of this residential type, encouraged a high level of real estate speculation. The very commercial success of high rises also generated social controversy, as the continual increase in apartment housing prices rendered the purchase of homes in Seoul extremely difficult for the majority of the population. While the ownership of multiple apartment units in Seoul, especially in the Gangnam area, is a source of envy for many South Koreans, it has also become associated with the ills of modernism and capitalism.

Stylistically, apartment houses were also criticized. Yim Sokchae argued that while the origin of modern architecture in the West goes back to philosophical and multidisciplinary debates regarding the human condition, Korean perceptions of modern architecture were confined to technological advances associated with International Style glass boxes (Yim, 1995, p. 136). In a similar vein, Kim criticized the 'violent production method' of modern Korean architecture that exhibited characteristics of high-energy consumption, large-scale developments, and high density (Kim, H.S., 2004, p. 89). In this sense, the influence of 'postmodern' architecture in the Korean context was evaluated by scholars as stopping short at 'indulgence in morphologic amusements' (Song, I.S., 1995, p. 145). However, the Western debates about modernism/postmodernism had a bigger influence since they functioned as the opportunity to 'dispel [Koreans'] general tendency to perceive modernist architecture as the only representation of Western architectural thoughts' (Lee, D.H., 1988).

The renewed interest, or the so-called 'rediscovery', of *hanoks* should be understood in the wider context of a general surge of interest in pre-industrial artefacts and things considered part of the 'Korean heritage'. As part of the critique of reckless developmentalism in the past, the insufficient maintenance of cultural artefacts and heritage sites became the source of constant attack. Perhaps the most notable literature on this within the academic community was a book *Na ŭi Munhwa Yousan Dapsagi* (*My Survey of Cultural Heritage*) by Hong-jun Yu (1993), which sold more than two million copies. Yu was trained as an art historian.[9] His argument was that cultural judgment based solely on the scale of artefacts is inappropriate and that South Korea contains many subtler yet important cultural artefacts. The surge of public interest in cultural artefacts and the national heritage was followed by the establishment of various historical societies and organizations aiming to preserve and protect historical artefacts and rituals. The popularity of remodelled *hanboks* (Korean-style clothes) as well as increased local tourism, including temple stay programmes, reflected the desire to recover and validate South Korean identities in the context of an increasingly competitive modern world. One resident in a remodelled *hanok* echoed such sentiment when he explained that he decided to move to a *hanok* after looking at the sketch of his child depicting his home as a cold concrete box (Cho, H.S., 2007, p. 18). It is feared that while members of the older generation, with the memory of *hanoks*, can manage to retain their Korean identity, the younger generations with no such prior experience would lose the sense of who they are if they continued to live in high-rise apartments.

Interestingly enough, the start of the tradition boom in South Korea was simultaneous with the globalization drive of the Kim Young Sam administration in the early 1990s. It is important to note that the re-evaluation of national culture and history went hand in hand with that of other nations. Yu's argument appealed to South Koreans, who started travelling abroad in increasing numbers after the liberalization of international travel in 1989. The increased recognition and maintenance of cultural artefacts became the sign of becoming a developed country. Thus, the 'tradition boom' in the 1990s and the subsequent '*hanok* renaissance' simultaneously reflected the desire to recover 'lost histories' as well as the desire to be associated with higher cultural accomplishments and higher rank in the international community.

In particular, remodelled *hanoks* appealed most strongly to middle-aged South Koreans – those tired of living in apartment houses, and who had limited childhood memories of living in a *hanok*. According to news articles, most people who prefer living in a *hanok* are Koreans in their forties who seek to re-enact childhood experiences (Jung, B.H., 2010). Older residents fully aware of the inconvenient aspects associated with residence in hanoks were less enamored with the idea of living in one. Sunjoo Kim, a columnist for the Korean newspaper *Hankyoreh Shinmun*, noted that she decided to move to a hanok, although her husband, 'who had been living in a hanok until he got married,' was opposed to the idea (Kim, S.J., 2009). An architect working on remodelling *hanoks* has observed, 'Some old-timers who have memories of all the inconveniencies [associated with *hanoks*] still have trouble "forgiving" the *hanoks*' (Hwang, D.J., 2006, p. 50). For the younger generation in an urban area who grew up in apartments, *hanoks* feel exotic, just like the houses that appear in television history drama series.

The rising popularity of *hanoks* and the romanticization of a pre-industrial lifestyle among middle-aged Koreans are reflected in a series of publications regarding *hanoks*. For instance, in a book titled *I'll Trade My Apartment for a Hanok* (2008), the authors argue that apartments are a thing of the past industrial era while *hanoks* are the new solution for contemporary life. Other books, such as *Going Back to Earth House: A Study of 52 Earth Houses* (2009), *True Life: Hanok* (2006), and *Yuri's Home: A Story of Housekeeping in a Small Yet Sufficient Hanok* (2009), all refer to life in *hanoks* as a way to appreciate the true meaning of life by being in close contact with nature. As we shall see in the remainder of this chapter, the rediscovery of *hanoks* was followed by repercussions including conflating various housing types into an elite version of tiled-roof houses.

Imagining Korean Life in a *Hanok*:
The Blurred Line between Vernacular and Modern

In South Korea, academic discussions of vernacular houses centred on the term *minga*, equivalent to the English term 'folk houses' rather than the ambiguous and elusive term *hanok* (Chang, P.U., 1996, p. 44). Although there is no exact definition of *minga*, most Korean scholars argue that *minga* are ordinary people's houses that retain traditional qualities. For instance, Chang argued that *minga* are 'houses of the low-income people with traditional characteristics rather than houses exhibiting contemporary and universal characteristics' (*Ibid.*, p. 22). Young-hwan Kang noted that *minga* belongs to '*minjung*' or 'the subjugated class' (Kang, Y.H., 1992, p. 56). Mentioning Amos Rapoport's concept of pre-industrial vernacular, Kang argued that there is no fundamental difference between Korean *minga* and vernacular houses despite some differences in their focuses (Kang, Y.H., 1989, p. 31). Cho, on the other hand, acknowledged the difficulty involving academic categorizations of housing types. However, he reaffirmed the boundary of *minga* by noting that 'upper class residences tend to exhibit standard elements due to the same social norms, while *minga* exhibit stronger regional characteristics' (Cho, S.G., 2006).

The notion that vernacular houses are 'traditional architecture' was prevalent among Korean scholars until in very recent academic discussions the question started to be asked whether apartment houses should belong to the category of the 'new Korean vernacular'. For instance, Valerie Gelezeau (2007) has argued that while South Korean lifestyles have changed during the modernization drive, apartment houses have also gone through changes to suit uniquely Korean socio-cultural norms. In the South Korean context where a heightened modernization drive has resulted in the rapid spread of modernist architecture, housing does not always follow Bernard Rudofsky's descriptions of typical vernacular houses, which are 'anonymous, spontaneous, indigenous, [and] rural' (Rudofsky, 1964, p. 1). Nor is Paul Oliver's observation – that buildings designed by professional architects do not 'come within the compass of the vernacular'– adequate to describe South Korean apartment houses (Oliver, 2003). Most Korean apartment houses are designed by professional architects hired by large construction companies, although they are not necessarily as bent upon making strong visual statements as star architects. In fact, the rapid urbanization process of South Korea has made it extremely difficult to find examples of vernacular houses, if one takes the definition of Rudofsky or Oliver.

On the other hand, for various reasons many South Koreans do not live in apartments despite the rapid increase in apartment houses. At the same time, more 'traditional' houses built by local residents continue to exist, albeit in small numbers. Therefore, the renewed interest in *hanoks* should be regarded partly as an effort to diversify the scope of 'Korean vernacular houses' in the context of increasing criticism of modernist architecture. Notwithstanding the close association between the vernacular and a lack of sophistication, the case of the remodelled *hanoks* in South Korea illustrates that vernacular houses can become a form of symbolic capital and a sign of aesthetic superiority. Living in a remodelled *hanok* is far from having an anonymous, spontaneous, or rural lifestyle. Rather, one can enjoy all the urban amenities while at the same time visibly marking one's socioeconomic position with very clearly stated aesthetics. At the same time, aesthetic ideas are often given more importance than the devices or physical aspects of remodelled *hanoks*. The consumption of the house form becomes not the act of 'noble savages' but the symbol of being 'nobler Koreans'. In other words, urban *hanoks* have become an example of the blurring between the vernacular and modern architecture, or what Bernd Huppauf and Maiken Umbach (2005) called 'vernacular modernism'. The high level of cultural sophistication associated with living in remodelled *hanoks* in contemporary South Korea shows that appreciation of the vernacular practices and being culturally modern are interdependent of each other.

Although many middle-aged South Koreans fantasize about living in *hanoks*, not many can realize their dreams. The construction cost of a *hanok* is twice that of a detached single-family house with steel frames. Not only is the construction expensive, but finding a carpenter and artisans with the skills to build a *hanok* is challenging because of the shortage of such specialized labour. Finding the right materials, such as the timber and *hanji* (Korean rice paper used for paper screen walls), is also very difficult. In *Arumjigi's Story of Building a Hanok*, Minja Kim, owner of a remodelled *hanok* and a member of the Hanok Advisory Committee for Seoul Metropolitan City, describes her involvement in the complicated 3-year design process as arduous, yet 'offering a chance to learn many aspects of life, such as the value of patience' (Jung, M.J., 2003, p. 122). Moreover, becoming a resident of a remodelled *hanok* requires a considerable expenditure of both time and money, which the average South Korean cannot afford. As more upper-class South Koreans began living in remodelled *hanoks*, they soon became a status symbol and evidence of cultural sophistication. For instance, recent media interviews with people living in remodelled *hanoks* portrayed their lifestyles not as underdeveloped but as heroic and elegant. In an interview with a resident in the Gahoe-dong section of Bukchon who had recently moved into a remodelled *hanok*, the reporter noted that 'while it was necessary to get rid of the enormous furniture, which she used to have in an apartment, it did not particularly feel uncomfortable. Rather, she remarked that it felt refreshing and light to have simplified housekeeping'.[10]

Although a positive portrayal of living in *hanoks* has come mostly from the popular press, there has been a tendency to romanticize *hanoks* and their aesthetics in academic literature as well. Influenced by the 'heritage' discussions that began with Yu Hong-jun's work, many architectural historians started writing about the rediscovered beauties of *hanoks* and how they might become relevant in contemporary contexts. For instance, Kim Bongryul, a professor of architecture at the Korean National

University of Arts, has published three books under the series title 'Rediscovery of Korean Architecture' that became very influential among both architects and general public (Kim, B.R., 1999*a*, 1999*b*). In another instance, Kim Gaechon, a professor of architecture at Kookmin University, published *Myŏngmuk ui gŏnchuk* (*The Architecture of Light and Calm*), which celebrated the structural characteristics of the *hanok* as embodying an aesthetic of emptiness. The lack of colour and absence of decoration on the paper-screen walls and doors have been hailed as reflecting the core Taoist belief in 'non-action' (Kim, G.C. and Jo, 2004, p. 231). Instead, features of natural beauty were framed and emphasized in a very purposeful way by surrounding the house with emptiness and accentuating it. Too much artificiality or construction is discouraged as interfering with meditation or a study of one's mind. Such harmonious coexistence of design and non-design within the architectural language of the *hanok* was praised as a philosophical statement that 'simultaneously sought to overcome the limits of artificiality and inactivity' (*Ibid.*, p. 7).

Scholars argue that the minimalist aesthetics believed to be inherent in the *hanok*'s structural form possess a moral dimension. For instance, a book published by the Society of Hanok Space notes that simplicity as a rejection of extravagance is 'an expression of *yangban* class philosophy, emphasizing a graceful and restrained lifestyle rather than a luxurious or indulgent attitude' (Society of Hanok Space, 2004, p. 259).

Figure 2.4. Most of the remodelled *hanoks* in Bukchon, like the one shown in this photo, are wooden post-and-beam structures.

In another case, the book observes that use of naturally curvy wooden members for columns and beams represent a 'tolerance of nature' and a 'generous spirit characteristic of Taoism' (*Ibid.*, pp. 244–245). Most remodelled *hanoks* are wooden post-and-beam structures reminiscent of *yangban literati* residences from the late Chosun Dynasty (figure 2.4). According to the Hanok Aid Ordinance prepared and implemented by the Seoul city government in 2002, *hanoks* are defined as 'wooden post-and-beam structures' (Seoul Metropolitan City, 2002).

The *hanok*'s strong association with a supposedly higher moral standard has been challenged by several architectural critics and historians. For instance, Seoh noted that the use of naturally curved wood in the *hanok* merely reflects the lack of timber due to the increasing housing demand of the late Chosun Dynasty (roughly from the seventeenth to the late nineteenth century) (Seoh, 2007). However, romantic interpretations of the *hanok*'s structural characteristics were reproduced and often exaggerated by the popular press. A willingness to endure small inconveniences is celebrated as evidence of independence and mental fortitude. The maintenance of the existing *hanok* structure, notwithstanding the new construction of the *hanok*, involves much more work than living in an apartment complex with a twenty-four hour security guard/handyman. New meaning is attached to the more specific architectural features previously regarded as irksome. A newspaper article introduced a journal written by a mother who noted that while her children tripped at the high door threshold in the beginning, 'they soon learned to avoid falling, which reminded me of a story that living in a *hanok* is conducive to a child's physical development and cultivation of careful behaviour' (Kim, J.M., 2009). In another case, handling the paper sliding doors of the *hanok*, which often requires a slow and careful manoeuvre, is cited as teaching children to seek a roundabout solution rather than using sheer force (Cho, H.S., 2007, p. 21). Individual tenacity to adhere to design integrity is associated with upper-class culture as well as with the expression of environmental consciousness. Overcoming minute annoyance is rendered as a heroic attempt to break out of the banal modern life in which people are enslaved by addiction to technology.

Whether the decision to move to a *hanok* is based on criticism of living in high-rises or the simple desire to find alternative housing, the moral discourse surrounding remodelled *hanoks* suggests that 'Korean culture' is imagined to be inherent in the formal characteristics of the *hanok*. Although the high door threshold of the *hanok* is not intended to promote careful behaviour, it is imagined to instil in children fastidiousness. Regardless of whether the 'inconvenient aspect' of the *hanok* is appreciated as the wisdom of the ancestors or minor nuisances to be overcome, both discourses imagine *hanoks* as the antithesis of artificiality. The confusion between the intentions behind and consequences of design remains prevalent due to the mental construction of an insurmountable dichotomy between the natural and the artificial. In this case, the construction of the *hanok* as traditional architecture contains an element of cultural essentialism which, despite the mostly positive evaluation of Korean culture, can work to conceal existing structural socioeconomic problems.

The Bukchon regeneration project first initiated by the neighbourhood association has brought deepening internal divisions within the organization as the result of the increasing prices of land and remodelled *hanoks* in the area. At the same time, the establishment of other NGOs designed to protect urban *hanoks* in the area has highlighted growing conflicts between local residents and those outside interested in purchasing older *hanoks* to convert them into modern residences. Although such conflicts and debates have revolved around the definition of 'preservation' and also the proper ways to remodel older *hanoks*, they are in fact rooted in economics.

From the real estate developer's point of view, *hanoks* in Bukchon are considered hot commodities, which, when combined with the rising price of land, become a source of profit. Lee Ju-yeon, the director of the Bukchon Culture Forum, has commented that after the initiation of the city's project, the average price of land per *pyung* (approximately 3.3 square metres) rose from 5 million won (about $4,400) to more than 10 or 20 million won' (Lee, J.J., 2008). While Minja Jung noted in her book that land cost about 6 million Korean won (KW) per pyung in 2001, my field research conducted in 2009 revealed that it cost about 20 to 40 million KW per pyung. Kum-Ock Choi, a long-time resident of Bukchon, has argued that certain NGOs have participated in real-estate speculation rather than focusing on preservation (Jung, W.S., 2009). The change in the city government's regeneration policy, which increased the amount of financial aid to new *hanok* construction from 30 million KW to 60 million KW, contributed to inflation. With the rising prices of urban *hanoks* and the land they occupy, many previous residents in the Samchung-dong part of the village sold their houses to rich outsiders after the sharp rise in land prices (Lee, J.J., 2008). In an interview with *Weekly Kyunghyang*, one real-estate agent observed that many of the *hanoks* in the 31st district of Gahoe-dong are empty because they are second homes and used primarily during weekends. Compared to land prices in other parts of Seoul, such a sharp rise in land prices illustrates that the regeneration project has contributed to the gentrification of the neighbourhood.

Even for those residents who decided to remain in the neighbourhood, problems arising from new construction have contributed to mounting friction within the community. The repair standards stipulated by the Seoul city government only specified design guidelines for tiled-roof *hanoks*, with even more specific guidelines for the treatment of outside walls adjacent to streets. According to the guidelines, outside walls are to be divided into three parts, with the upper part consisting of paper screen windows and plasters, the middle part being either red brick or cobblestone, and the lower part consisting of larger granite stone (figure 2.5) (Seoul Metropolitan City, 2001*b*). *Hanoks* depicted in the repair guidelines show a wall with moderate height, with the lower part of the rusticated foundation occupying a small portion. It

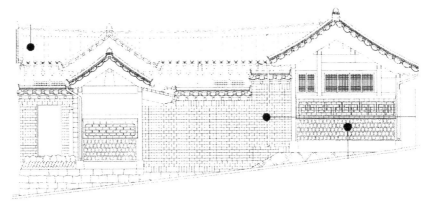

Figure 2.5. Repair guidelines showing the elevation drawing of a remodelled *hanok* were prepared by Seoul Metropolitan Government to promote safety and contextual conformity. Many *hanoks* in Bukchon follow these guidelines as the photo shows.

is recommended that the height of the outside wall be about the middle height of the neighbouring wall, with the main structure of the *hanok* appearing over the wall.

While this was stipulated to encourage residents to take context into consideration, it has been manipulated in several cases to raise the embankment in advance and enlarge the foundation disproportionately. Since architectural guidelines put forward by the city government are not compulsory, residents can make structural changes according to their tastes. Insuk Cho, the vice-chair of the Seoul Hanok Preservation Committee, noted that attempts to remodel *hanoks* face a double bind: while there is a general lack of expertise in traditional wooden constructions, most *hanok* experts only know the preservation techniques suitable for cultural artefacts rather than for ordinary houses (Cho, I.S., 2008). An absence of clear guidelines for remodelling, when combined with the reckless pace of redevelopment, has resulted in the appearance of a new *hanok* archetype. The location of several residential *hanoks* on a sloped hill allowed the construction of huge walls as well as garages underneath (figure 2.6.)

The unconventional construction method produced friction between the existing

Figure 2.6. Although contemporary *hanoks* in Bukchon maintain the tripartite wall composition described in the design guidelines, they are far from the imagined lifestyle of restraint and simplicity.

residents, who suffered from the high level of noise from the construction sites. Kum Ock Choi and David Kilburn, residents of Bukchon for more than 20 years, have argued that new construction by their neighbour caused not only a high level of noise but also damage to their house due to an 'unauthorized use of fork lifts'

(Moon, J.M., 2009). In interviews with the media and in public debates about *hanok* preservation policy, Kilburn repeatedly criticized the current city government's project, which subsidizes the rich while ignoring the rights of local residents. The dispute between Choi and her neighbour remains unsettled, as the case has been elevated to conflicts of interest. It is difficult to conclude that the city government's policy is the sole cause of friction. However some neighbourhood organizations, such as Hanok Jikimi, which was established after the government's regeneration project began, have been accused by local residents of failing to take care of the *hanoks* they had purchased (Lee, S.Y., 2006). While some groups continue to function as models of civil society, others opportunistically pursue various members' private interests under the mantle of community activism.

The history of the *hanoks* reveals important divergences from the aforementioned romanticized readings of their physical qualities. Dwellings of the *yangban literati* were far from being minimal and simple. Conforming to the numerous requirements specified in Confucius's teachings meant that the ruling elite's homes had to be large enough to contain separate functional spaces. For instance, women's quarters had to be separate from men's quarters since one of the five basic tenets of Confucianism is the 'separate roles of the sexes'. Upper-class residences also featured a separate quarter near the main gate reserved for servants to answer calls from visitors and to tend to household animals. In addition, an extra space dedicated to ancestor worship was needed in order to uphold filial duties specified in Confucian ethics. Observing such an emphasis on spatial hierarchy was critical in defining the identity of *yangban literati* since their formal status was not determined simply by the inheritance of the title. One had to earn the status by passing the national examinations as well as by observing Confucius's rules in every aspect of daily life.

Contrary to the strong association of *hanoks* with absence of artificiality, many aspects of their architectural elements show that each design element is very deliberately placed. Not only are the locations of the *Ahn* (the inner independent building) and *Sarang* (the outer independent building) complexes in relation to the heating system very deliberate, but the slope of the staircases is designed so that land is used more efficiently while reducing the danger of structural failure. In another instance, it has been pointed out that the location of the wife's room is strategically placed within the Ahn complex in such a way that it can easily be observed from the mother-in-law's room (Kim, B.R., 1999a, p. 251). The difficulty of household labour associated with low fire stoves is regarded as a common burden for women, although such an architectural feature disproportionately affected servant-class women. A typical *yangban* male did not feel the inconveniences of *hanok* life since servants carried portable tables of food to his room and regularly emptied his chamber pot. Although the influence of class hierarchy in the layout of the *hanok* is acknowledged, specific experiences associated with them are rarely discussed both due to historical distance and a strong tendency to romanticize them. Thus, the negative realities associated with the elitist tradition are downplayed while abstract spiritual meanings are emphasized.

What in fact has contributed to the popular notion of *hanoks* embodying a minimalist mode of living are the physical qualities of the urban *hanoks* in Bukchon, resulting from an intense urbanization process during colonial times. During the Chosun Dynasty, Bukchon remained a desirable residential quarter for high officials of the *yangban literati* class since its proximity to the monarch meant more political opportunities. However, older *hanoks* began to disappear due to the declining socioeconomic status of the *yangban literati* class as well as the weakening of the national economy as a whole. At the same time, the increasing pace of urbanization in Seoul pressured the colonial administration to readjust and divide the existing lots into smaller and standardized subdivisions. The establishment of many housing companies in the 1920s, such as Gun-yang Company, facilitated the process of the industrial production of *hanoks* (Cho, J.B., 2003, p. 112). The process of demolition of *hanoks* was described in an article written in 1935, as follows:

Elegant Chosun Dynasty-style buildings are destroyed one by one while two-, three-, or five-story brick houses and stone houses replace them. Streets in Seoul are always under construction with an increasing number of paved streets with cars, bicycles, and motorcycles passing on top of them.[11]

Also, the unprecedented migration of the rural population to Seoul, the rising cost of land, and sociopolitical pressure to adopt a new lifestyle inhibited the construction of *hanok* complexes, which required a substantial amount of land.

Housing shortages in Seoul and the beginning of the capitalist housing industry contributed to the birth of a new type of *hanok* suitable as urban residences. Changes

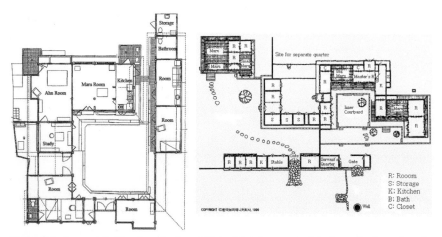

Figure 2.7. A remodelled *hanok* at Gyedong 135-1 of Bukchon on the left shows the floor plan of a simplified version of an urban *hanok*, while the floor plan of Sungyojang, a *hanok* complex originating from the eighteenth century, on the right, exhibits a series of courtyards and multiple complexes.

in street layouts, instituted by the colonial administration in 1934, resulted in the rectilinear street grid, necessitating that *hanoks* adapt to standardized subdivisions. Reduced house size as well as the standardized construction methods rendered the *hanoks* much less glamorous. The stylistic changes reflected in new urban hanoks were similar to the housing of the *jung-in* class, mostly technicians and government clerks situated between the *yangban literati* class and the common people.[12] The floor plan of a *hanok* at 135-1 Gye-dong in North Village exhibits the characteristics of an urban *hanok* (figure 2.7).

Although the house was a part of a larger complex with an additional Sarang complex, it was subdivided into two housing units in 1924 (Seoul Metropolitan City, 2001*a*, appendix 45). Currently used as a guesthouse, it presents a radical departure from the older *hanok* complexes. Due to the shortage of land, the two building compounds were combined into one building mass, which also meant that instead of the conventional system of multiple courtyards, the new urban *hanok* contained only one courtyard. In general, a decrease in the lot size was complemented by the introduction of Western furniture and the enlargement of individual rooms (Kim, E.H., 1995).

The urban *hanoks* that emerged in the 1920s were generally despised due to the use of cheaper materials and lack of proper functional spaces. Industrially-produced *hanoks* were often derogatively called *jipjangsa-jip*, meaning houses of home sellers, which implied that they lacked any sense of individuality. The low status associated with urban *hanoks* can be detected in the following remark made by an individual who worked as a city planning official in the 1970s:

It was already too late to save the hanoks worth preserving. Most hanoks in [Bukchon] were not hanoks from the Chosun Dynasty but houses mass-produced in the late colonial period by *jipjangsa*. They were not even properly maintained, looking shabby and vulgar. Therefore there was no need for preservation. They were just evidence of poverty, and we hoped they would disappear.[13]

Such controversy regarding what *hanoks* should look like shows that that there is no *a priori* category of *hanok*, and that what constitutes 'Korean' is not always clear.

The tendency to essentialize the definition of *hanoks* overlooks changes in residential patterns during the urbanization process and increasing socioeconomic polarity. Although the servants who guarded the main gate and cooked food in the fire stove are gone, they have been replaced with security cameras and housekeepers. In addition, the cultural capital necessary to afford the high construction costs of the *hanok* distinguishes modern-day *yangban* from the rest of society; their material benefits generated by the industrial mode of life outweigh the cultural benefits. More importantly, reverence toward the '*hanok* tradition' shared by most South Koreans has been appropriated by the government as a means to redevelop a *hanok* village and promote local and international tourism. The governmental project of marketing the 'historical character' of Seoul has tapped into the desire of middle- and upper-class South Koreans to own an ideal (often second) home. Ironically, urban redevelopment capitalizes on the strong association of *hanoks* with minimalist and modest households in order to bring further economic growth of the Gangbuk (North of the Han River) area. The dominance of commercial interests and the speculation process are not unique to forms of modern architecture and apartment houses. Contrary to common assumptions, the remodelling process of *hanoks* in Bukchon shows that they can also function as profit-generating machines.

Despite the Seoul city government's ambition to utilize hanok preservation in Bukchon as a 'model undertaking' to restore the historic character of Seoul, such a process of tourist-oriented development cannot guarantee consensus on what counts as 'historic' or 'traditional' and what does not. At the same time, idealization of *hanoks* as 'virtuous living' shifts attention away from structural problems in the current real-estate market of Seoul. The popularity of apartment houses among South Koreans was primarily due to socioeconomics rather than aesthetic considerations. Simply changing policy orientation to promote residence in remodelled *hanoks* without considering who is benefiting does not help to safeguard endangered forms of 'Korean-style houses'. Rather, a fusion of preservation and redevelopment interests threatens to undermine other values such as community solidarity and socioeconomic diversity. Similar to Harvey's notion of a spatial-temporal fix, the state's project of manufacturing a *hanok* village becomes a quick 'spatial fix', on a large scale, to existing socioeconomic problems (Harvey, 2001).

Conclusion: The Future of *Hanoks* in the Era of Globalization

The future of the *hanok* remains uncertain. Despite the state's appropriation of the public interest in Korean folk houses, the *minjung* movement triggered various efforts to conserve cultural items which might have been forgotten in the heightened pace of the modernization drive. Within the architectural profession, many individuals outside the government continue in their efforts to protect local construction methods and craftsmanship. Various NGOs and historical societies, including the Contemporary Hanok Society, are conducting research into lowering the construction costs of *hanoks* and making them accessible to greater numbers of people. Admittedly, the recent surge of interest in *hanoks* reflects a social phenomenon beyond the simple longing for a bygone era. Desire to recover a lost historical agency and to relieve doubts about an unstable Korean identity do play a part in the current boom of remodelled *hanoks*.

However, the current idealization and increasingly high profile of the notion of the 'Korean house' can bring negative results. Some cases of remodelled *hanoks* are far from generating idyllic village life, with shared values and communitarian attitudes, because of the high environmental impacts some have had. The strong association of *hanoks* with 'the nobler lifestyles of the *literati*' has made discourse regarding *hanoks* dominantly positive without reflecting upon historical realities or assessing real-life consequences. At the same time, the romanticization of *hanoks* goes hand in hand with the romanticization of the Korean past, which obscures traces of class conflicts and cross-cultural hybridization. Architectural representations of different classes as well as of different regions become representations of the 'Others', who are excluded from the scope of Korean cultural heritage. Just as there is no *a priori* 'Chinese house', so there is no single Korean house. Rather, architectural forms of *hanoks* are diverse and flexible just as Korean identities are. Current discussions about mass-producing *hanoks*, therefore, raise concern regarding which types of *hanok* will be preserved and which will be forgotten.

On another level, the idealization of 'Korean traditions' without critical analysis can contribute to preservation becoming a pretext for large-scale urban redevelopment. The Bukchon Hanok Regeneration Project is closely related to the marketing of cultural heritage in order to boost the local economy in the context of increasing competition in the global tourist industry. As a part of a bigger scheme to elevate the status of Seoul from an industrial city to a post-industrial global hub, the aesthetics of the *hanok* become a tool to attract more tourists and more capital investment. While the *hanok* is imagined as the physical manifestation of a common cultural heritage by invoking the concept of Korean ethnicity, not everyone enjoys the same level of benefits generated by the remodelled *hanoks*. Under the strong aura of sacred 'tradition', the gentrification resulting from the project has received little attention. The current regeneration project is stongly benefiting moneyed middle-aged Koreans at the expense of public funds, and this is obscured by the notion that *hanoks* are part of a Korean tradition that needs to be 'rescued'. Despite positive reactions to the project, the increasing level of socioeconomic polarization makes the *hanok*'s continuous functioning as a social adhesive in the community very unlikely.

Notwithstanding the strong influence the notion of *hanoks* as 'rediscoveries' has in obscuring structural problems, not every urban project and architectural representation is constructed without encountering challenges. In many cases, the very definition of tradition is challenged when the livelihood of people is affected by an abstract concept. In the next chapter, I turn to the case of Insadong, where the conflicting interests with regard to the direction of urban transformation have rendered the discussion of cultural heritage more convoluted. Although nicknamed 'the most Korean place in Seoul', current urban developments in Insadong have generated criticism and concern regarding 'the loss of identity'. Despite efforts to market the area as representative of 'authentic Korean culture', the everyday spatial practices of occupants continue to challenge the established notion of 'being Korean'.

Notes

1. For instance, *JoongAng Ilbo*, one of the three leading newspapers in South Korea ran an article titled 'Hanok Runaesangsu Yolrynda' ['Hanok renaissance is beginning'] on 17 March 2007.
2. From the official homepage of North Village (http://bukchon.seoul.go.kr/eng/index.jsp).
3. Such an inflexible prohibition on any form of repair contributed to the collapse of a *hanok* in the 1990s, resulting in the deaths of a whole family.
4. During the fieldwork conducted in 2009, most of them were inaccessible during the weekdays and weekends. Certain places only displayed phone numbers on which the owner could be reached.
5. In the novel, Kil-nyŏh moves from a rural village to Seoul only to end up as a prostitute. Sang-hyun, a male character from the same village, comes to Seoul to find her. They return to the village together after realizing that there is no place for them in Seoul (see Lee, H., 1966).
6. The collapse of Wawu Apartment, constructed by an unlicensed construction company, was due to the sparse use of construction materials. During the trial, it was revealed that the company offered a bribe to government officials to get the construction job. This practice drove the construction cost higher, which in turn led to the company spending less money on the construction materials.
7. Gelezeau writes that the central heating system using an oil boiler was revolutionary for the majority of Koreans, who at the time used charcoal briquettes, which sometimes caused fatalities due to carbon monoxide poisoning.
8. In Song-ran Ha's 1999 novel titled *Gompang-yi Ggot* (*Mould Flowers*), apartment residents were described as finding out information about their neighbours by rummaging through garbage instead of by engaging in normal social interactions.
9. After studying aesthetics at Seoul National University, Yu went to Hong-ik University to do graduate work in art history. His interest in Korean ethnic arts was expressed when he joined the Minjok Misul Hyŏp ŭi Hoe (Council of Korean Ethnic Arts).
10. Gahoedong Adamhan 29 Pyeong Hanok. Available at: http://article.joinsmsn.com/news/article/article.asp?total_id=2729391.
11. Yu, G.Y. (1935), quoted in Kim, J.S., 1999, p. 284.
12. According to Professor Song, the characteristic of the urban *hanok* is the simplified U shape of the floor plan instead of the traditional composition of an L + I structure with more open space between the two building masses (Song, I.H., 1990).
13. Quoted in Song, D.Y., 2004, p. 186.

Chapter 3

From Mary's Alley to a Culture Street: Contested Traditions in Insadong

To be honest, attempts to find tradition are ridiculous. We are doing this since it is our job. We can only make a living if we search for tradition. So we follow that path. There isn't any one who consciously tries to maintain a tradition. We only keep it since it is profitable to mention tradition. What is the tradition of Insadong? As long as people use hanji [Korean rice paper], it will be a tradition and as long as people look for antiques there will be those trying to make money by selling antiques. That's the way it is.

Interview with a shopkeeper in Insadong, quoted in Kang, S.M. *et al.*, 2003, p. 260

Although the above comments by a shopkeeper in Insadong, published in *Discovery of Life in Seoul*, are hardly new philosophical revelations, they contrast sharply with travel brochures and tourist guidebooks that promote the idea of 'timeless Korean tradition' in Insadong. Commonly accepted as one of the historical places of Seoul, Insadong is a commercial district with many Korean restaurants, crafts shops, and art galleries (figure 3.1). Insadong refers to the area south of the North Village (Bukchon) and surrounded by two palace complexes and Jongmyo, the royal ancestral shrine during the Chosun Dynasty from the fourteenth to the late nineteenth century. The area was adjacent to the administration office that oversaw artworks and paintings, and the concentration of artists in the area resulted in a large number of shops specializing in brushes, paints, and other supplies. Nicknamed 'Mary's Alley' by foreign residents due to its many curvy and dead-end alleyways, Insadong has long been synonymous with Korean art and culture, and, since 1987, it has increasingly served as a stage for numerous festivals and exhibitions. Furthermore, the increasing popularity of Insadong as a tourist destination has prompted the city government to designate the district as a Global Cultural Zone and as the site of one of Seoul's Culture Streets.

The shopkeeper's observations about 'Korean tradition' are partly a response to recent discussions regarding a lost 'sense of place' in Insadong. Although older residents

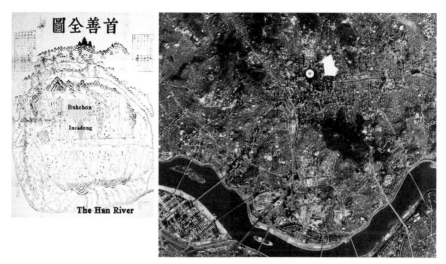

Figure 3.1. On the left is Susŏnjŏndo, the historical map drawn by Jŏngho Kim in the mid-nineteenth century showing the location of Insadong and Bukchon within historical Seoul. On the right is a contemporary map of Seoul showing the Insadong area in white. (English text added by the author)

of Seoul interested in calligraphy and pottery have frequented Insadong in the past, the implementation of several new policies, such as prohibiting car traffic at the weekend, has changed the neighbourhood's demographic composition. The decreasing average age of visitors and the changing commercial ambience – partly brought about by implementation of the Car-free Zone – have led members of the older generation to lament that 'the end of Insadong is near' and that 'merciless redevelopment and commercialization will erase the smiles of the streets' (Yu, S.O., 2001, p. 8). Sung-tae Hong (2004) highlights the widespread concerns about the 'loss of urban identity'. He observes that 'the rapid rate of change in Insadong, which began in 1999, has wounded Insadong's identity significantly'. Some are worried that the current rate of increasing crowds in Insadong may permanently eliminate the area's quiet ambience while others lament the invasion of foreign commercial interests. The 'authentic identity' of Insadong is threatened not only by a proliferation of contemporary art galleries but also by cheap souvenir shops and an overload of restaurants. Another study notes that the decreasing number of antique shops and reputable galleries, along with the parallel increase in souvenir retailers and liquor shops, is 'destroying Insadong's intrinsic physical environment' (Cho, J.S. and Kim, 2002, p. 20).

This chapter continues to discuss the theme of 'tradition as rediscovery' by analyzing the narrative of loss that has emerged in conjunction with Insadong's recent transformation. In the previous chapter on the '*hanok* renaissance', I argued that remodelled *hanoks*, despite being constructed as 'rediscoveries', were part of a broader development project to reconfirm the modernity of Seoul. In Insadong, the combined efforts of the city government and an NGO to promote 'rediscoveries' have backfired, producing instead a narrative of loss. While concerns regarding Insadong's fading urban identity reveal a conflict between the desire to preserve the area and the economic imperative to promote it, they also involve deep-seated assumptions about what comprises 'Korean culture'. This chapter argues that nostalgia-fuelled resistance to change can be detrimental to cultural diversity, although nostagia was, in part, generated by past forms of urban redevelopment that threatened such diversity. While indignant attitudes towards the current transformation are partly the result of a 'culture policy' perceived as a tool for global place marketing, placing the blame on 'poor cultural taste' may inadvertently marginalize the burgeoning spatial practices associated with the right to walkable streets. Despite the close association between increased pedestrian numbers and global cultural homogenization, this viewpoint fails to consider diverse manifestations of global cultural flows. At the same time, it takes a narrow definition of Korean tradition and culture, and neglects the inherent fluidity within these terms.

Controversy surrounding the implementation of the Car-free Zone policy in Insadong during weekends highlights the interlocking relationship between the state and civil society. The alignment between the government project of promoting Insadong as one of the Culture Streets and the mobilization of the NGO Dosi-yŏndae (Urban Action Network) for the idea of walkable streets has broadened the area's accessibility to new urban crowds by prohibiting automobile traffic. However, their respective primary focuses differed tremendously. While Dosi-yŏndae was more interested in preventing large-scale development, the city government's focus was on improving the physical environment to attract more visitors and to promote the economic growth of the area. When the implementation of the Car-free Zone started to introduce unconventional commercial establishments and rising land prices, the policy triggered concerns about lost urban identity, or what I call a narrative of loss. Paradoxically, attempts to provide a safer and more pleasant walking experience have been pointed out as contributing to negative changes in the urban environment.

However, the changing commercial ambience and rising land prices have formed part of larger processes in accordance with the urban redevelopment plan put forward in the late 1970s. Labelling the Car-free Zone as the sole cause of the urban transformation of Insadong fails to take various factors, such as the Gongpyong Redevelopment Plan, into consideration.

In addition, I argue that the narrative of loss, which places the blame on 'lowered cultural taste', takes a narrow interpretation of Insadong's 'urban identity', and poses the danger of using the word 'culture' as a means to conceal class divisions and underlying economic interests. The current disputes regarding the 'identity' of Insadong assume that it possesses a fixed identity, a normative image that privileges certain cultural forms while excluding others. These assumptions about fixed identity are in part based on the construction of a dichotomy between 'high culture' and 'mass culture'. Recent rediscoveries of tradition and discussions of a 'loss of authenticity' should be interpreted as aspects of the tension between different class and demographic interests. At the same time, such narratives of loss fail to acknowledge the various spatial practices that have the potential to constitute new identities for the place. Notwithstanding the stereotypical interpretation of 'kitsch' products in Insadong, this chapter shows that the heterogeneous urban aesthetics of Insadong is evidence of global connectedness, including wider political and human rights issues affecting the world at large. I argue that the current 'messy' appearance of Insadong does not represent a 'loss of identity' since it reflects the ongoing processes of local negotiations regarding what constitutes 'Culture Streets'. The recent urban transformation of Insadong has been a mixed blessing, in the sense that although the area experienced some level of gentrification, it was followed by the introduction of cultural diversity.

In order to analyze the recent urban transformation of Insadong, this chapter first examines the changes in the South Korean political economy that stimulated the conceptual and practical discussions of Culture Streets and of the right to walkable streets. Then, I move on to discuss the historical background and the recent urban transformation of Insadong that triggered the narrative of loss. The urban redevelopment of the area since the 1970s and Dosi-yŏndae's recent activities suggest that implementation of the Car-free Zone was an anomaly, rather than a continuation of the larger gentrification process. Finally, the booming interest in teahouses and Korean cuisine is discussed along with the heterogeneous urban aesthetics which contributed to Insadong's contemporary cultural milieu.

Insadong as a 'Culture Street' and 'Car-Free Zone'

The designation of Insadong as one of Seoul's Culture Streets is part of a wider government project to promote the concept of the 'soft city' and its characteristics which fit this description, such as tourist resources. The project was first proposed by the Korean Culture and Arts Foundation (KCAF, currently the Art Council Korea), a government-affiliated organization, in the 1992 study conducted to find ways to improve urban environments.[1] According to the definition given by KCAF, Culture Streets (figure 3.2.) are 'street territory which can utilize independent cultural resources and develop into a place with a distinct cultural identity, with its value perceived and shared by many people' (Korean Culture and Arts Foundation, 1992, p. 77). Cultural resources are defined broadly as potentially containing 'natural landscapes, built structures, monuments, histories, folk stories, folk cultures, historical incidents, historical places, continuous actions, events, well-known local products, and foods' (Ibid., p. 83). After describing several foreign examples, such as New York's Soho and Paris's Montmartre, as examples of neighbourhoods with 'Culture Streets', the

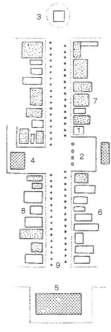

Figure 3.2. The conceptual map of a sample Culture Street, in *Dosi Munhwa Hwan-gyŏng Gaesŏn Bang-an Yŏngu*.

1 Information Kiosk	2 Plaza and Small Park	3 Monuments
4 Theater	5 Museum	6 Malls
7 Specialty stores	8 Accommodation	9 Gate

study mentions Insadong as possessing a distinct physical quality due to the presence of many *hanoks* (*Ibid.*) Just like The Shambles in the city of York in England, Insadong is considered an historic urban fabric, with its history going back to the Chosun Dynasty (1392–1897).

The effort to construct Culture Streets should be situated within the wider policy changes planned to usher in a transformation of the economy from industrial production to the information and service industries. The concept of Culture Streets originated shortly after the Seoul Olympic Games, which triggered various discussions of how to promote international tourism. Although the successful hosting of the 1988 Olympic Games resulted in an increased number of foreign tourists in South Korea, the lack of amenities and poor management of heritage sites have been pointed out by the media and policy-makers as major obstacles to the further growth of the global tourist industry (Cho, B.H., 1999). Another study observed that developing specialized tour programmes that include 'circulation courses which connect various cultural festivals by timing them flexibly' would greatly improve the current city package tours (Suh, 1987, p. 86). In such a context, the government embarked on different projects to sustain the increased tourism, including the designation of Culture Streets. In Insadong, residents and merchants formed an Association for the Preservation of

Insa Traditional Village in 1987 and started to hold yearly festivals in the middle of October (Song, J.I., 2000). With the passage of the Local Governance Act in 1995, local governments were encouraged to discover and develop various cultural districts in order to promote the local economy.

At the same time, the designation of Insadong as a Car-free Zone reflected South Koreans' increasing demands for improved standards of living as well as a growing interest in cultural folk items. Increasing political voices from civil society included demands for walkable streets, which had been suggested by NGOs such as the Green Traffic Movement. The successful lobbying of such organizations brought the issue of urban accessibility to the attention of policy-makers and political representatives, culminating in the establishment of ordinances designed to promote *boheng-gwon*, or 'the right to walk'.[2] Although the concept was new in South Korea, it has started lively discussions of the tendency to prioritize car traffic above pedestrian traffic. The concept also contributed to the establishment of Dosi-yŏndae in 1996. With the changes in political culture brought about by the democratic movement of the late 1980s, central and city governments exhibited a more open stance towards citizens' demands. In the 2000s, many policy discussions regarding the right to walkable streets were held among national assembly representatives and members of NGOs.

Given such changes in government policies and political dynamics, the annual festival held in Insadong changed to the weekly Car-free Zone on Sundays. Although Dosi-yŏndae expressed some criticism over the project of Culture Streets, the weekly car-free day was supported. For instance, Dosi-yŏndae criticized some aspects of Culture Street projects by pointing out examples of indistinguishable programmes/designs as well as destruction of physical environments (Dosi-yŏndae, 1999). However, Dosi-yŏndae supported the idea of the Car-free Zone when its feasibility study in 1997 concluded that small alleyways in Insadong are 'more appropriate for pedestrians rather than car traffic' and that to 'maintain the continuity of pedestrian space' is to be recommended (Citizen's Transportation Culture Center of Dosi-yondae, 1997, p. 37). The Jongro District Office and the city government responded to the Association's decision favourably, by announcing a plan to expand the implementation of the policy to Saturday afternoons in addition to Sundays (Choi, H.Y., 2003).

There are many reasons for the designation of Insadong as a Culture Street and Car-free Zone. According to Choi Hong-yol, a professor of Korean Studies, the historic quality of Insadong stems from the continuous production of older art forms such as calligraphy and *soo-mook-hwa* (ink-and-wash paintings) since the Chosun dynasty (Choi, J.S., 2009). Although forms of contemporary arts – both Korean and non-Korean – have become more prominent since the 1970s, older forms of handicrafts and ceramics have also become widespread. At the same time, restaurants specializing in *hanjŏngsik* (Korean traditional *table d'hôte*) and teahouses serving a variety of Korean teas have become popular ways of experiencing 'traditional Korean' cuisine. Some of these restaurants use the *hanok*'s form to advertise their Korean cuisine. Despite changes in trade structures and the introduction of modernization projects, the area, unlike the rest of Seoul, has retained its antiquated urban layout, reminding pedestrians of forgotten street patterns that were once a dominant feature of pre-industrial Seoul.

The Narrative of Loss: What was Lost?

Figure 3.3. The products sold in Insadong include a Hello Kitty doll wearing a Korean costume.

The combined effort of the local government and Dosi-yondae to promote Insadong's streets was met with criticism which argued that the plan to prohibit car traffic brought negative consequences. The measure to remove cars aimed to increase pedestrian safety but, while it led to an overall increase in the number of visitors to the area, there were mixed reactions to some of the unanticipated consequences. According to Ungkyu Bae, a professor of urban engineering at Chung-Ang University, one of the changes brought by the implementation of the Car-free Zone was the lowered average age of the visitors (Bae, U.K., 2008). Other changes included an increase in the percentage of foreigners among the visitors and a decrease in the number of older shops and galleries (*Ibid.*, 2008). As consumers, these visitors had limited purchasing power and, as a result, were unable to buy luxury items such as original artwork and antiques (Kim, S.Y., 1999). This led to an increase in cheaper souvenirs and products manufactured outside South Korea.

Many South Koreans expressed concern and fear about these changes in Insadong. Shop owners took issue with the excessively designed street markers used to separate pedestrian walkways from the street. An American shopper, who had been living in

South Korea for 20 years, repeated similar sentiments by noting that 'this place has become very crowded and commercialized'.[3] Many urban studies and environmental reports on Insadong observe that the streets are filled with vendors selling cheap souvenirs and eclectic products (figure 3.3). The fact that many of the products are not produced in South Korea – that they are of 'unknown nationality' – is another source of frequent concern (Yu, J.Y. *et al.*, 2000). A study conducted by the Korea Culture Policy Institute (which in 2002 became the Korea Culture and Tourism Institute) observed that the 'urban problems' in Insadong included the 'high pressure for redevelopment, conflicts between old forms of culture and new forms, a deepening crisis of traditional cultural identity, and recessions' (Lim, H.S., 1999, p. 52). Although the study acknowledged that 'changes in commercial ambience cannot be judged entirely as vulgar or bad', it nevertheless concluded that 'indigenous cultures cannot function properly in cultural chaos due to [the] absence of [an] autonomous mediator' (*Ibid.*, p. 49).

Such statements conveying a nostalgic feeling of loss were echoed in academic fields as well. Lee Song-wuk, a researcher at the Korean Research Institute of Human Settlements, criticized the deleterious effect of labelling Insadong as 'traditional streets' when 'rampant forms of pseudo-traditions fill up the streets of Insadong' (Lee, S.W., 1999). He concluded that so-called 'traditions' in Insadong are fake for two reasons – the dominance of cheap 'kitsch' products on the commercial scene and the disappearance of spontaneity as staging the area as a 'traditional street' took over (*Ibid.*, 78–79). Similarly, a scholarly article published in 2004 in the Journal of Architectural Institute of Korea noted that 'the quality of street landscapes is going down due to shops with a strong commercial character, most of them having opened after the implementation of the Car-free Zone' (Kim, Y.H., 2004, p. 153). Similarly, another scholarly article published in the journal of the Korean Institute of Landscape Architecture lamented the phenomenon of 'the decreasing number of traditional cultural elements such as *hwa-rang* art galleries/antique shops on the one hand and the increasing number of commercial establishments such as souvenir shops and bars on the other' (Cho, J.S. and Kim, 2002, p. 20). Such statements assume that some stores are more commercial than others although there is no indication that *hwa-rang* art galleries are less profit seeking than souvenir shops. At the same time, it also illustrates that the critique of modernization overlaps with the impulse to blame 'vulgar' or 'low-brow' forms of culture. It is unclear what exactly are the characteristics that distinguish 'real traditions' from 'pseudo-traditions'. While critique of the snowballing effect of government-led construction is valid, it is questionable whether constructing a dichotomy between different kinds of traditions and between 'staged' and 'spontaneous' activities is an appropriate way to address urban problems.

It is interesting that the main complaints against 'excessive commercialization' focus on the increase in cheaper (and assumed therefore to be of lower quality) goods. The growing tension between long-time shop owners and temporary street stall owners shows that 'urban identity' has some very murky terrain. The proliferation of street stalls and the sale of non-Korean-made products have generated concerns among professionals and members of various NGOs. For instance, a study conducted by the Dosi-yondae indicated that 41.3 per cent of merchants associated the introduction of the car-free policy with the sale of 'products Insadong stores did not carry before [the policy] that damage Insadong's image' (Citizen's Transportation Culture Center of Dosi Yondae , 1997, pp. 52–53). The proliferation of street stalls almost led to the abandonment of the car-free policy, though it resumed after the Jongro District Office promised to strictly regulate illegal commercial activities. The shift in ambience and the loss of cultural authenticity is often blamed on street vendors who started selling mass-produced products in the area.

In fact, criticism regarding changes in Insadong combines 'cultural' qualities with economic concerns. Just as there are many factors that determine the speed of continuous urban redevelopments, there are various desires implicit in the drive to preserve the 'authenticity' or 'identity' of a particular place. It is unclear whether it is the non-Korean origin or the cheap quality of these items that is to blame for the changed ambience of the area. Nor is it clear which kinds of products 'damage' the image of Insadong and which do not. The distinction between 'souvenirs' and 'antiques' itself is ambiguous when most 'antique shops' in Insadong sell cheap products in addition to their more valuable merchandise. In their defence against the city government's policy of driving them out, some street vendors observed that since 'there is no difference between the products they [antique shopkeepers] sell and those we sell', vendors should not be considered detrimental to the traditional ambience of the neighbourhood.[4]

The argument that the sales of mass-produced non-Korean-made products harm the image of Insadong assumes that the area has a fixed identity, one that is associated with 'Korean high culture'. Although the decreased sales of handcrafts and the changing commercial ambience in Insadong can be attributed to economic stagnation and changing consumption patterns, it is more often blamed on 'poor cultural tastes'. Labelling one form of culture as 'inferior' to another, however, poses the danger of concealing bigger structural problems such as the increased number of the homeless or recently unemployed, many of whom became street vendors following the Asian financial crisis. Arguably, misgivings about the changing ambience of Insadong stem from genuine concerns about the possibility of gentrification that often follow large-scale urban developments.

The Transformation of Insadong

During Japan's rule, Insadong prospered as a marketplace for antiques and ceramics as well as paintings and old manuscripts. Pressed by declining economic conditions,

Figure 3.4. Historical photos of Insadong in the period immediately before the Korean War.

descendants of the old *literati* class began to sell their heirlooms to antique dealers in Insadong who, in turn, sold the items to those who could afford them, either foreigners or Koreans. At this time, the Korean middle and upper class were contracting and, as a result, a significant number of these items ended up in the hands of the Japanese colonists or US military personnel following the Korean War. Cases of illegally smuggling cultural assets out of the country were rampant throughout the colonial period and in the period following the Korean War. In one case, a 48-pelt leopard skin rug, once used by the assassinated Queen Min, the last queen of the Chosun Dynasty, was reportedly purchased for $25 by a US soldier.[5] Even in the 2000s, attempts to trade stolen cultural properties in Insadong were mentioned in the pages of major newspapers (Lee, H.W. and Lee, S.W., 2011).

However, as art objects designated as national treasures became rarer and the trade regulations stricter, it became more difficult to purchase historical artworks in Insadong. Galleries and old bookshops changed their merchandise to include less valuable artefacts as well as reproductions of famous paintings. Contemporary gilt-framed oil paintings began to appear in Insadong alongside traditional ink and wash paintings. More spacious art galleries began to appear next to older *hwa-rang* where Korean-style scrolled ink and wash paintings were stored in relatively small areas. With the infusion of new art forms and the industries associated with them, Insadong continued to function as the centre of painting and other artists' activities throughout the 1980s (figure 3.5).

Despite the historic ambience of the pre-industrial period that Insadong retained, many redevelopment projects put forward by the Gongpyung Redevelopment Plan

Figure 3.5. A photo of the main street in Insadong, 1988. The placard reads 'June 18, the Day of Insadong's Traditional Cultural Festival'.

resulted in the introduction of large high-rises in the area. The Gongpyung Urban Environmental District was officially designated in 1978 in Notification No. 285 of the Ministry of Construction as a part of the wider metropolitan redevelopment plan (Jon, Y.G., 2008). Although the first urban redevelopment plan of Seoul was established in 1962, it was in the 1970s that the redevelopment projects began to be actively implemented (HAUD [Housing Architecture Urban Design], 2010). While the initial redevelopment plans in the early 1960s were targeted at illegal squatter settlements, the new plans increasingly focused on changing the urban image of Seoul by replacing smaller and low-rise buildings with high rises of 'at least twenty storeys, and preferably forty to fifty storeys high' (Son, J.M., 2003, p. 168). This change in the direction of urban planning reflected changing political dynamics and economic conditions. Combined with the ambitions of a modernization project, urban redevelopment became one of the major tasks for the South Korean government.

Although the policy changes of the central government encouraged urban redevelopment, most of the projects were carried out by large corporations which possessed the capital to construct such high rises. Local merchants and owners of buildings initially resisted urban redevelopment plans, but they had limited means to do so given the authoritarian political regime at the time. In addition, the city planning bureau employed various methods such as sending local land owners to an 'overseas urban redevelopment tour (including Philadephia's Penn Center and New York's Rockfeller Center)', which 'showed them that middle/small businesses do not take part

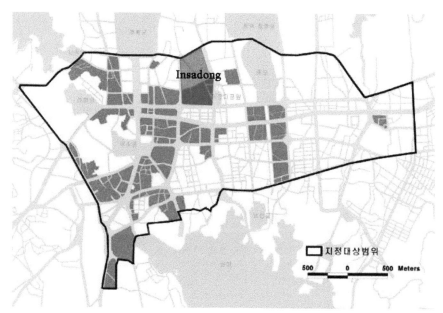

Figure 3.6. The redevelopment plan of 2004 shows the area designated for redevelopment in the urban centre of Seoul. The black line indicates the boundary of the redevelopment area.

in redevelopment projects' (*Ibid.*). In the early 1980s, the pressure to redevelop the urban centre only increased with the impending hosting of the Olympic Games. In Insadong, the urban redevelopment drive led to the construction of corporate-owned buildings such as the SK Construction office building in 1986. In another instance, the Taiwha and Hanaro Buildings were built by the Methodist Foundation. According to the study by Dosi-yondae, the Gongpyung Redevelopment Plan (figure 3.6) resulted in rising land prices and the subsequent relocation of older art galleries and antique shops to the Gangnam area (Citizen's Transportation Culture Center of Dosi-yondae, 1997).

The metropolitan redevelopment plan went through several phases of alteration in the 1990s and 2000s when the need to preserve and cultivate the historic character of Seoul was recognized by the government. The new policy, promulgated in 2000, recommended the conservation of historic buildings in some districts designated as redevelopment project sites (HAUD, 2010). However, despite increasing emphasis on preserving the historical ambience of Seoul, the tendency to encourage high-rise redevelopments persisted. In 2004, the Seoul metropolitan government put forward the plan to relax regulations on building heights for residential developments (Seoul Metropolitan City, 2004, p. 2). While calling for the preservation of historic ambience, urban planning policy reasserted the primacy of growth by allowing large-scale developments. This simultaneous pursuit of economic efficiency and historical preservation resulted in a juxtaposition of buildings of contrasting scales and ages. The

Figure 3.7. Samsung's Jongro Tower was built to celebrate the new millennium.

construction of skyscrapers such as Jongro Tower (figure 3.7) near Insadong and the increasing presence of corporate investment throughout the area in the 1990s brought changes within the commercial districts dominated by small shops. Also known as Samsung Millennium Tower, Jongro Tower – designed by Rafael Viñoly Architects and Samoo Architects & Engineers – rises to a height of 131 metres. Built to celebrate the approaching millennium, the project, completed in 1999, received a gold award from Seoul Metropolitan City in 2000. Similarly, the construction of Fraser Suites, the 24-storey serviced apartment complex owned by the Singaporean firm Frasers, began to reshape the skyline of the area. The construction of the complex was consistent with the Gongpyung Redevelopment Plan, which designated the area for office and residential uses (Bae, J., 2007, p. 64). Therefore, the gentrification process of Insadong should be traced back to the urban redevelopment policy, which consistently encouraged the construction of high-rise office towers and residential structures.

The government's urban redevelopment plans put forward in 2004 were criticized by civil society organizations such as the Citizen's Coalition for Economic Justice (CCEJ, or Gyŏng-sil-ryŏn). CCEJ announced a petition, signed by a hundred experts, which asked for the withdrawal of the plan at a press conference held on 25 May 2004

(Gyŏng-sil-ryŏn, 2004). Given that most commercial buildings in Insadong are only three to four storeys high, such large-scale development initiated debates regarding what kind of impact it would have on Insadong's distinct physical characteristics. For instance, Koo Youngmin, a professor of architecture, noted that the 'abnormal composition introduced by the skyscraper contributed to contextual disparity' (Koo, Y.M., 2003, p. 273). Other scholars echoed this opinion by commenting that construction of Jongro Tower at the former site of cultural heritages such as the Hwashin Department Store showed a lack of appreciation of historic architecture (Shin, J.J. *et al.*, 2004, p. 38).

When the Ssamzi Corporation purchased land in Insadong, the sense of crisis felt by storeowners started what became a community-wide movement to preserve the physical integrity of the neighbourhood and to limit outside commercializing forces. The success of the movement led to a series of ordinances that 'fundamentally prohibit[ed]' the construction of buildings higher than four storeys (Kim, Y.H., 2004, p. 160). It also initiated the construction of smaller-scale art galleries that showed more respect for the pedestrian-friendly urban contexts of Insadong. A recently constructed shopping mall consists of a series of small shops selling various objects. Ssamzigil, a commercial development in the heart of Insadong, became the testing ground to measure the prowess of the grassroots movement against the forces of gentrification.

The Saving Small Stores Campaign and Insadong's Ssamzigil

Figure 3.8. Insadong's Ssamzigil was constructed with the plan to incorporate the original twelve shops that were initially planned to be demolished.

One of the most prominent structures in Insadong is Ssamzigil (figure 3.8), a four-storey commercial structure in which all units are linked together by a multi-level ramp. The 2005 project sparked intense debates as the community raised questions about the twelve shops that occupied the planned site for the Ssamzigil building and that had been acquired by the Ssamzi Corporation. The sense of crisis felt not only by the owners of the twelve shops but by patrons of Insadong more generally led to a 'Saving Small Stores Campaign'. The main fear was that corporate plans for mega-structures would eliminate the area's small alleys and the existing 'mom-and-pop' businesses, and, as a result, would fundamentally damage Insadong's unique character. To support local merchants, members of Dosi-yŏndae worked to politicize the event, depicting it as an infiltration by big corporations designed to destroy Insadong's local identity. Unlike the struggles typically associated with urban renewal projects, this effort focused primarily 'on signature-seeking campaigns involving broad participation by city residents and renowned persons' (Song, J.I., 2000, pp. 71–72). A consensus was reached between the small shop camp and Ssamzi whereby the twelve shops would be able to continue their businesses in the newly constructed Ssamzigil structure.

In addition, the Ssamzigil building was designed to respect the existing urban context and to reflect the intimate scale of Insadong's streets. As a result, Ssamzigil stands in sharp contrast to more typical shopping centres. Although the building itself is a new construction, it avoids being overly conspicuous by maintaining the scale of the neighbouring alleys. Walking along the multi-level ramp is reminiscent of walking down nearby alleyways, especially given the fact that the structure is lined with small shops and features activities in its central courtyard. Less intent on making a prominent visual statement, the building was described by architects and critics as 'more than just eye-candy', and an example of how architecture can help fabricate 'pleasurable walking experiences' (Kim, J.A., nd). A representative of Janghak Construction Company, which undertook the project, noted that they used 'only three materials – brick, concrete, and wood – which accentuate the architect's intent to make the structure merely a backdrop' (*Ibid.*). The completion of the project won Mun-gyu Choi and Gabriel Kroiz, the architects, several awards including the 2005 Korean Architecture Award and the AIA Maryland Design Award in 2005.

Despite the successful negotiations between the company and the storeowners, the outcome of the campaign was a mixture of success and failure. Although the NGO's campaign defended merchants and their rights, it nevertheless could not prevent the demolition of the existing structures. At the same time, the NGOs inevitably rely on a cultural logic in which 'tradition' and 'modern' are conceived as binary opposites. A study conducted by Dosi-yondae observed that as 'older *hanoks*/antique shops/galleries and newer structures mingle together', the result is an 'encroachment on the existing urban characteristic' (Citizen's Transportation Culture Center of Dosi-yondae, 1997). As such, new developments were perceived as contributing to an incongruous image of the neighbourhood. The success of the NGOs' campaign was partly due to its emphasis on preserving 'traditional cultures' as a key factor in protecting small businesses. While this strategy proved to be beneficial in drawing in a wider support base that included

Figure 3.9. The streets of Insadong show dense and narrow alleyways dating from the late Chosun Dynasty.

upper-class patrons, it also contributed to the mixed reactions to the designation of Insadong as a Car-free Zone.

Yet the urban identity of Insadong does not simply consist of material things such as the products sold and displayed on the streets. More importantly, the independent cultural resources of Insadong include its history as a place for expressing political resistance through direct and indirect means. Maze-like alleyways in Insadong (figure 3.9) were called *Pimatgol*, literally meaning 'alley of avoiding horses', and they date back to the late Chosun dynasty when commoners and low officials were obligated to kowtow whenever high officials passed by on horseback or in carriages (Jeon, J.H., 2009). By frequenting alleyways, the commoners did not have to express respect and obedience to government officials. In addition, the marketplaces of Insadong provided a prime site to express more direct protest against the state's abuse of power. Historically, market places have functioned as the stage for the state to express its power as well as the place where the masses show their ability to resist and subvert such attempts (Foucault, 1995). The history of the different uses of the marketplace in Korea is filled with records of the monarchy ordering gruesome executions to showcase its ability to control and subdue possible threats to the regime (City History Compilation Committee of Seoul, 2007). However, marketplaces were not simply tools for conveying the disciplinary power of the monarchy since commoners also used them to criticize the corruption of local officials. For instance, one resident of Jeju Island posted an anonymous letter in the marketplace as early as 1323, complaining about the re-appointment of a corrupt and exploitative official (*Ibid.*, p. 46). During the Japanese colonial regime, political activists recruited supporters in the marketplace, where crowded streets functioned as protective cover.[6] Anti-colonial feelings also festered in the marketplace as a result of the frequent conflicts between Korean and Japanese merchants.

Insadong played a role similar to the earlier markets as the extremely exploitative economic structure of the colonial regime initiated a period of political turmoil. In addition to the presence of shops and galleries, Insadong was where anti-colonial sentiments were transformed into a political movement against the Japanese colonial regime. On 1 March 1919, the so-called March 1st Movement began as a popular uprising in Tapgol Park (also called Pagoda Park), located in the southeast corner of Insadong (figure 3.10). While the thirty-three representatives of the movement changed the meeting place to nearby Taehwagwan, those who congregated in the park were mostly students who had learned about the impending demonstration. Though the demonstration was peaceful, the Japanese police force responded with brutal violence. Shortly after the initial demonstration on 1 March, the movement quickly spread to other towns. In many places, demonstrations were launched at the local

Figure 3.10. A stone carving indicating the site of the March 1st Movement commemorates the historic event.

marketplace. These venues were naturally conducive to large congregations and they helped maximize the visibility of these events.[7] Insadong's strategic location between two palace complexes and the steady flow of pedestrians within this district were key factors in its role as the starting point of the independence movement.

Although the March 1st Movement did not lead to the overthrow of the Japanese colonial regime, it triggered a new campaign for independence and had a significant impact that was felt in many different spheres. The incident brought Japanese colonial policy under far greater international scrutiny. For instance, George W. Norris, a senator from Nebraska, denounced the colonial regime, describing a case of 'Japanese persecution' in which Christian Koreans were burned (Caprio, 2009, p. 113). The criticism by international powers put considerable pressure on Japanese officials although no further action was taken immediately. While the colonial administration continued its repressive policies, it also recognized that it needed to seriously reconsider its strategy in order to maintain its control over the Korean population. Introduced under the new Governor General Saito Makoto, a subsequent pacification policy known as 'culture rule' (*bunka seiji*) provided more educational opportunities as well as freedom of the press. The change in colonial policy, however, was nothing but a thinly veiled form of continued domination that actually tightened control over the Korean population through an expanded police force. Nevertheless, it enabled some Korean intellectuals and artists to engage in cultural activities relatively more freely than under the previous policy.

During this period, various Korean literary styles and artistic innovations began to flourish. The Joseon (Chosun) Theatre (figure 3.11), established in Insadong in 1922, was a popular venue where artists experimented with various forms of modern theatre. It was a place where many literary groups, such as Towŏlhoe and Kŭkyesulyŏnguhoe, performed regularly, introducing Western realist dramas such as works by Henrik Ibsen and Nikolai Gogol. Members of what was referred to as the New Drama Movement (*Singŭk Undong*) sought to incorporate Western realism into theatrical productions in colonial Korea. According to Suk-hyeon Ahn (1994), the popularity of several Russian plays – such as Tolstoy's – was due to the similarity between Russian peasants under the Tsar and Koreans under Japanese rule. Although the exact nature of the New Drama Movement's contribution to nationalist sentiments or the independence movement is unclear, it nevertheless helped to diversify the available range of artistic influences. Experiments with foreign movements and different ideologies, which were possible during the 1920s, were a vital component in the moderate branch of the nationalist movement called *Shilryŏk Baeyang Undong* (the Growing Capacity Movement).

Joseon Theatre was where many of the Western plays were performed and where many popular movies were screened. Located next to Insadong's busiest thoroughfare, the theatre occupied a very prominent position within the district. During the 1920s, entertainment businesses were very profitable thanks to a booming economy and

Figure 3.11. This poster advertisement for the Joseon Theater in the early 1930s shows portrait photos of silent-film narrators.

the changing lifestyle brought by Japan's emphasis on modernization. Along with a few other theatres such as Dansŏngsa in Myŏngdong, Joseon Theatre was where high- and middlebrow forms of entertainment mingled. This mixture produced a rich cultural *milieu*, which in turn contributed to the area's reputation as the home of *avant-garde* artists and self-fashioned 'modern boys' and 'modern girls'. As an amalgam of progressive politics and entertainment, Insadong was considered to be a dangerous influence for some portions of the population. According to the 'dual cities' structure of colonial segregation, Insadong, as a part of *Jongro*, was considered native Korean territory while other parts of Seoul – such as Myŏngdong and Chungmuroh – were where Japanese resided comfortably (Kim, B.K., 2005). With its history of political speeches, anti-colonial demonstrations, and commercial vibrancy, Insadong was correctly regarded as harbouring dangerous sentiments that could be unleashed at any moment.

Thus, the combination of overt demonstrations against the colonial regime and the more indirect strategies of the artistic movement are an integral part of Insadong's history. Calling Insadong a Culture Street without understanding the traditions of resistance in the marketplace, therefore misses an important ingredient of its 'cultural resources'. Although material conditions – such as the presence of *hanoks* and small winding alleys – contributed to the historical appearance of the area, they are not the only evidence of 'Korean tradition' present in Insadong. The history of Insadong during colonial times includes experiments with new media forms and artistic devices, often including Western art forms and ideas. The current discussions surrounding Insadong's physical transformation should be situated in such an historical context, as the area was not simply the container of Korean arts and crafts but also the central stage of political turmoil and experimental art movements aimed at social change.

The fixation on the authenticity of urban environments has served to overlook a deeper dimension of globalization and the diverse ways the processes of globalization are expressed. On one hand, the distinction between what are considered 'traditional cultural elements' and what is considered 'modern' has become harder to detect. Rituals or artefacts considered by many South Koreans as 'authentic' or 'timeless' forms of culture are often a by-product of cultural hybridization and recent social developments. On the other hand, it is notable that increasing signs of foreign cultural influence and increasing emphasis on Korean customs occur simultaneously. The next section discusses the development of 'tradition-related' industries in Insadong and how they were 'rediscovered' amidst an increasing need to reconfirm Korea's modernity. This phenomenon culminated in a proliferation of tea drinking and *hanjungsik* restaurants in Insadong. Contrary to the notion that such rituals represent 'timeless traditions', temporarily lost during the period of rapid economic development, these developments are better understood in the context of diversifying dining patterns and burgeoning connoisseurship among the middle-class population. In order to understand the continuous popularity of Insadong as a repository of 'Korean cultures', it is necessary to examine how rediscoveries of Korean cuisine fit into the urban environment.

The Construction of Traditions in Insadong: Teahouses and Korean Cuisine as Rediscoveries

While most of the products and services available in Insadong seem to be based on deep-seated cultural practices, enterprises such as teahouses and *hanjongsik* (traditional Korean restaurants) are very contemporary phenomena. For instance, many people believe that tea drinking is an integral part of Korean culture. However, despite the increasing popularity of teahouses in Insadong (figure 3.12) and Korean tea in general, scholars argue that there is a discrepancy between the historical evidence and what

Figure 3.12. An example of a tea house which uses decorative elements of the *hanok*'s post-and-beam structure.

people believe. According to a study by Ae-ryung Yu (1997), tea drinking did not occupy a significant position in Korean culture, unlike China and Japan. Instead, only a small portion of the educated *literati* class consumed it occasionally.[8] Similarly, the practice of *hanjongsik* was an exclusive feature of royal cuisine far removed from the everyday meal enjoyed by most Koreans. Tea drinking and consuming *hanjongsik*-style meals were also very private activities that took place at private residences instead of in public view.

Other scholars such as Sang-mi Park (2000) argue that tea drinking and consuming Korean-style cuisine should be considered elements of 'distinction' since they are often associated with the possession of cultural capital. In contrast to typical Korean barbecue restaurants, which focus on the consumption of a large amount of meat, *hanjongsik* emphasizes 'skills' and elaborate preparation involved in the cooking of each dish (*Ibid.*, p. 255). Thus, the consumption of *hanjongsik* implies a more distinguished lifestyle, an appreciation of sophisticated cuisine rather than the simple satiation of hunger. Whereas these rituals were once required as a standard part of court etiquette, they now indicate a conscious choice designed to signify one's socioeconomic status. As Insadong became known as the place to enjoy 'Korean cuisine', it witnessed a sharp increase in both *hanjongsik* and foreign restaurants. During this time Korean-style restaurants also diversified to include simpler *hanjongsik* and cheaper specialty food chains.

The simultaneous increase in Korean teahouses and foreign cuisine in Insadong illustrate that 'rediscovered traditions' are part of diversifying consumption patterns rather than a genuine return to 'tradition' for its own sake. Contrary to the concern of urban scholars that such diversification of shops and restaurants represents 'fake traditions' or 'staged authenticity', they should be regarded as the result of social revolutions that involve amalgamation of new and old practices (MacCannell, 1973). At the same time, they are the result of the vernacularization of 'highbrow' cultural practices that reflect the desire to be incorporated into a higher social status. Denying them the status of 'spontaneous tradition' or 'urban identity' just because of the government project to promote a Culture Street is to deny the agency of the larger population, including those who initiated the implementation of the Car-Free Zone policy. At the same time, disowning the current urban identities of Insadong inadvertently ossifies the concept of 'Korean tradition'.

The notion that there is a fixed category of Korean tradition is unfounded. As discussed, many activities considered 'traditional', such as tea drinking, also fulfil the desire to be modern. What is more important is how certain activities and built environments are incorporated into the category of tradition and how they simultaneously indicate new possibilities for the future. Although changing urban aesthetics and building styles have generated concerns, these changes do not amount to fundamental shifts in how streets are used. While the diminishing number of older art galleries and antique shops has been lamented by many, they have been replaced by other forms of cultural activitiy that have sprung up in their wake.

Despite the worries about Insadong's changing urban environment, there are signs of a continuation of spatial practices that can be traced back to the pre-industrial historical period. Demonstrations and political statements continue to be visible in the streets of Insadong despite complaints that the area has become too commercialized. In addition to reminding pedestrians of Seoul's pre-industrial past, Insadong is still able to accommodate public gatherings and political rallies. The rising number of visitors and pedestrians as well as the absence of car traffic on major thoroughfares has also attracted street performers, promoters of various political issues, and organizers of NGOs. Events sponsored by the city government, such as performances of Korean-style dance, take place in the designated plazas at the end of the main streets. Other, more informal, activities take place in the middle of main thoroughfares. Alongside the commercial bustle, there are political presentations on human rights issues in North Korea and China (figure 3.13). At other times, gay men join the global 'Free Hug Movement' in a bold political and personal statement. While the increased amount of pedestrian traffic has attracted street vendors selling cheap snacks and mementos, it has also provided ample opportunities for chance encounters with various activities.

Figure 3.13. At the weekends, the streets of Insadong become the place to promote different political causes and draw attention to social issues.

Human rights issues concerning North Korean defectors have had popular appeal, and a related exhibition held in Gana Art Centre in Insadong drew an unexpectedly large number of visitors. Yim-sook Ha, the curator of the art centre, noted that 'the reason why this exhibition is so successful [drawing more than a thousand people] was because of Insadong's Culture Streets' (Kim, H.Y., 2011). A sixty-three year old visitor expressed surprise at the fact that 'so many of the younger generation came to see the exhibition' (*Ibid.*) This phenomenon was regarded as surprising since, unlike older South Koreans, many in the younger generation are less interested in North Korea or the issue of unification. In other instances, Insadong's streets have become the prime site for hosting various demonstrations such as street speeches by the minority Democratic Labor Party which drew 'more than a thousand people in less than ten minutes' (Byon, nd). Similarly, demonstrations against the Korea–US free trade agreement in 2008 that started in front of the city hall continued into Insadong where the implementation of the Car-free Zone facilitated the gathering of people by preventing car traffic.

It is important to acknowledge that crowds bring diversity and the opportunity to disseminate different ideas. Similarly, an increasing number of generic 'made-in-China' products was followed by increased interest in global political issues. The processes of globalization involve the circulation not only of products, but ideas as well. At the same time, the processes of globalization are varied, some encouraging emphasis on one's own cultural practices while others trigger interests in foreign cultural elements. As the colonial history of Insadong illustrates, the process of globalization and cultural mixing stretches beyond the current era. Amalgamations of foreign and Korean cultures should be understood in terms of what they achieve, rather than in terms of what they look like. The peaceful co-existence of heterogeneous cultural practices and products should be accepted as a condition of contemporary Korean society rather than criticized as 'kitsch'. The question of place identity in Insadong remains open, just as the meaning of a 'Culture Street' remains unresolved.

Conclusion

So far this book has examined how the notion of tradition as rediscovery has shaped the *hanok* renaissance in Bukchon and the discussions of 'the loss of urban identity' in Insadong. Whereas the 'rediscovery' of remodelled *hanoks* became a sign of sophistication and cultural modernity, the absence of such 'rediscoveries' in Insadong has become a source of concern. Although the movement to implement a Car-Free Zone and save small stores was started as a means to prevent further large-scale developments, these efforts have ironically sparked a narrative of loss rooted in a rigid construction of Insadong's urban identity and a dichotomy between 'high' and 'low' culture. Increased numbers of pedestrians, many of them young adults in their twenties and thirties, have been associated with an increasing number of mass-produced products, perceived by scholars as a threat to Insadong's urban identity.

Admittedly, some of the concerns about the urban transformation of Insadong stem from the gentrification the government redevelopment plan introduced to the area. While the small storeowners in Ssamzigil were able to stay and continue their businesses, others left the area in search of cheaper rents. However, the current narrative of loss focuses on cultural representations as the principle source of urban problems rather than placing blame on the socioeconomic aspect of the area's development. At the same time, targeting the Car-free Zone as the main contributor to the 'loss of authenticity' endangers a hard-won right to walkable streets. Rather than concentrating on the question of whether something is 'traditional' or 'authentic', it is more important to raise questions as to what is being sacrificed in the name of tradition or culture. As the case of Bukchon shows, keeping faith with the representational form of 'high culture' does not guarantee retaining classical virtues or being somehow less commercial. Nor is it possible to preserve 'traditional form' without modifications to suit contemporary needs. In the cases of both Bukchon and Insadong, aestheticizing the South Korean past has worked to obscure the increasing socioeconomic divisions and discourage certain uses of urban space.

Contrary to the popular notion that the 'urban identity' of Insadong is threatened by the homogenizing forces of globalization, changes in Insadong are complemented by the diversification of cultural practices and street activities. This chapter has shown that the processes of globalization encourage interests not only in foreign things but also in local cultural practices, including those that have previously been considered exclusive. At the same time, the presence of 'kitsch' products should be regarded as the consequence of global connectedness which promotes not only consumption but also attention to larger political issues affecting the world. Rather than being unidirectional, the processes of globalization are multidirectional, encouraging the simultaneous presences of heterogenous cultural elements and practices.

Next the book turns to two other Global Cultural Zones – Dongdaemun and Itaewon – to examine how the processes of globalization are aligned in the government project to promote the status of Seoul. The cases of urban development in Dongdaemun and Itaewon illustrate different paths of urban transformation in the age of globalization. In contrast to Insadong's smaller-scale urban development, the design of Dongdaemun Market deliberately opts for the continuation of large developmental projects by redesigning and enlarging existing shopping malls in order to enhance its status as a design capital. In contrast to the urban discourse surrounding Insadong, cultural heterogeneity is celebrated as 'the urban identity' of Itaewon. Continuing with the theme of 'culture' and the changing role of political actors in South Korea, the next chapter moves on to the patterns of migration and the resulting different ethnic groups reflected in processes of urban transformation. At the same time, it shows how seemingly marginalized groups can generate a new urban aesthetic to counter Seoul's imagined status as a design capital.

Notes

1. The Korean Culture and Arts Foundation is a government organization established in 1973 in accordance with the Culture and Arts Promotion Act. Its name changed in 2005 to Art Council Korea.
2. According to Jangwon Jin, a professor of urban engineering in Cheongju University, the word *boheng-gwon* was first used by the NGO Green Traffic Movement in 1993 (Jin, 2001).
3. In an interview conducted on 14 October 2009 by the author.
4. Interview conducted on 21 October 2009 by the author.
5. This incident was reported in an article titled 'The Sergeant's Souvenir' in *Life* magazine on 20 August 1951, p. 48.
6. For instance, the Declaration of Independence was posted in the Jongro night marketplace to encourage public participation.
7. In Cheon-An, demonstrations began in Ah-Woo-Nae, in Byŏngchŏn Market (Sichang). In the Gang-Sŏh district of Pyŏng-An province, Hap-Chŏn Gangyang-Myŏn, Namwon, and Yik-San, demonstrations started in the marketplace as well.
8. Those who enjoyed drinking tea were limited to the royal family, a small portion of the *literati* class, and Buddhist monks, for whom tea-drinking was an important part of meditation.

Chapter 4

Rediscoveries and Redesigns: Dongdaemun History and Culture Park

The World Design Market will become a design business hub: where design related projects and transactions will be conducted, business partnership will be pursued, new designs will be introduced. Libraries and data will be available both on- and off-line. From 2010, the Design Market will be the key business sector of the Dongdaemun Design Plaza and Park that leads the design industry of Seoul.

Seoul Metropolitan Government, 2009

The ambition to promote design-related businesses through the construction of Dongdaemun (Eastern Gate) Design Plaza and Park (DDPP) (figure 4.1) is expressed quite clearly in the statements of the Seoul metropolitan government. The Seoul Metro Dongdaemun Stadium Station was renamed Dongdaemun History and Culture

Figure 4.1. A bird's eye view photo of DDPP in Fall 2013 prior to opening.

Park Station in December 2009, when the sports stadium, which first opened in 1926, was demolished to make way for DDPP. Designed by Zaha Hadid, the plaza and park complex was originally planned to be completed by July 2013, but it opened almost a year later in March 2014. The site is located on the eastern edge of historic Seoul, near the landmark of Dongdaemun and of Dongdaemun Market (a large commercial district in the area) (figure 4.2). Occupying a total area of 65,232 square metres, it is considered a new landmark not only for the Dongdaemun Market but also for the city of Seoul. DDPP is promoted not only as a public park which adds amenities to the existing fashion industry in the area but also as a potential world-famous landmark, like the Sydney Opera House and the Guggenheim Museum in Bilbao (Seoul Design Foundation, 2009). Although the overall cost of demolition and construction is 375,500 million KRW (about $313 million), the presence of DDPP in Dongdaemun Market is expected to generate an even bigger influence on tourist activities in Seoul to offset the

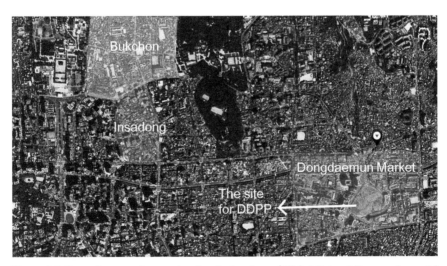

Figure 4.2. From the top, a diagram showing the locations of Global Cultural Zones and an aerial map of Dongdaemun Market showing the construction site of DDPP.

cost (Lee, S.Y., 2009). The construction of DDPP, which started in 2010 when Seoul was selected as the World Design Capital by the International Council of Societies of Industrial Design (ICSID), is part of the local government's Design Seoul campaign to elevate Seoul to the hub of the world design industry.

In addition to high-rise shopping malls with trendy shops, the construction of DDPP, funded by the Seoul city government, is expected to generate more profit by rebranding Seoul from an industrial city to a post-industrial 'culture city'. The construction of DDPP is an example of a series of new developments that have characterized the transformation of the urban landscapes of Dongdaemun Market. Since the late 1990s, the construction of high-rise shopping malls has started to add a new ambience to the marketplace, which contains many smaller retail shops and wholesale markets. Although sales of goods in general plummeted during the Asian financial crisis in 1998, sales in newly constructed mega-shopping malls such as Doota and Migliore have boasted a phenomenal growth, coining the phrase 'the myth of Dongdaemun'.

The idiom 'myth of Dongdaemun' was coined because the commercial success of retail shopping malls in the late 1990s looked miraculous in the context of the IMF crisis. The presence of many tourists and foreign buyers ordering products are reported as signs of the 'global fashion town', which maintained the momentum of the recent *Hallyu* phenomenon, also known as the Korean wave and meaning the popularity of Korean movies and dramas overseas. As the result of the continuous construction of high-rise shopping malls, the area exudes the youthful atmosphere of hip and fashionable lifestyles. This chapter investigates the impact of *segyehwa* policy and the transnational migration of labour on the functioning of Dongdaemun Market. Although it is one of the Global Zones, the Dongdaemun area is quite different from Insadong since it is located at the periphery of the historical fabric. The rise of light industry in the area has signalled an even faster rate of urbanization and growth. If Bukchon and Insadong make up the historical core of Seoul and are associated with practices of 'Korean tradition', Dongdaemun is the place going through constant transformation. Despite its long history as the gate to the capital (its name means 'the Eastern Gate'), the Dongdaemun area occupied a peripheral position in terms of political power in Korean history rather than being at the centre. Historical records focus on its history as a market, rather than its political and cultural aspects.

Instead of simply regarding Dongdaemun Market as an empty stage where market activities unfold, this chapter examines the area as an arena where complex processes of political and cultural views compete to be acknowledged. Continuing on the theme of 'tradition as rediscovery' discussed in previous chapters, this chapter illustrates how the integration of the rediscovered city walls dating back to the fourteenth century has become a part of the rationale for the city government to assess Hadid's metonymic architecture as 'respecting Korean tradition'.[1] The theme of preservation and development in Dongdaemun Market becomes even more complex as the construction of DDPP involves destruction of a structure which can be considered both as heritage and colonial legacy. There is another dimension to the project since it is a part of the Design Seoul campaign, the city government's project to brand Seoul as the 'new design capital', by constructing a series of monumental buildings. In the case of Dongdaemun, the focus is centred on the future, rather than the past.

The expectation of mobility and economic progress can be readily sensed in the descriptions of the ambitious project to elevate the area as the hub of a global fashion industry. The Soft City discourse, which emphasizes a change from industrial to post-industrial production, can also be seen in the government's use of terms such as 'world design capital'. The word 'design' is used as a catch-all phrase which justifies and facilitates the process of urban redevelopment. Urban planners and city officials view the Design Seoul project as benefiting residents by providing a space which shows consideration for the non-economic and emotional well-being of citizens. However, such a clientelist approach has been challenged by sports fans, student artists, and street vendors who have encouraged discussions of the role of design as well as what defines the status of a 'global city'. This chapter shows that the process of globalization involves an interpenetration of local concerns and global ambitions. Despite the trend of globalizing the production and consumption of architectural practice, the act of conferring meanings as well as making use of that physical space remains at the local level.

On the other hand, I trace the under-represented kind of mobility, the one which takes shape without much media attention or visible controversy. Following the project of building a 'multicultural society', the notion of cultural mobility as well as economic mobility has become widely accepted in the South Korean political scene. While most policy discussions of multicultural society revolve around the issue of foreign brides, the issue of social justice with respect to migrant workers has been less discussed in the South Korean political sphere. Even newspaper articles, policy documents, and academic works, which deal with the issue of non-marital immigrants, rarely link such increased mobility to past historical events. The link between the increasing number of foreign workers and colonial experiences is rarely discussed. This chapter pieces together some of the missing links between the mobilities of the present to those of the past. In particular, it focuses on how the movements of ethnic Koreans during the colonial era are reflected in the present immigration patterns. Although cases of non-marital immigration are from diverse countries, it should be noted that the majority of such migrant workers have some ancestral roots in Korea. In fact, *Chosun-jok* (Korean-Chinese), whose grandparents relocated to China under the Japanese colonial regime, make up the biggest ethnic group.[2] In Dongdaemun, returning Russian-Koreans played a big role in the emergence of Little Russia – a commercial district which caters for the central Asians – adjacent to Dongdaemum Market. Most Russian-Koreans have been in exile since the 1930s when the Koreans in Manchuria were forcibly relocated to Russia by Stalin. The return of Russian-Koreans in Dongdaemun is the result of a globalization policy enabling the migration of foreigners willing to open up businesses hiring a given number of Korean nationals.

This chapter first analyzes how the structural changes in the South Korean political economy since the 1980s have affected production networks and how these changes are reflected in the physical landscapes of Dongdaemun Market. In particular, the transformation of the market from cramped factory floors to the ultramodern shopping mall is the result of changing labour market conditions. The relocation of production elsewhere, including to other parts of Seoul and China, has ushered in an enlargement of shopping malls and a steadily increasing presence of conglomerates. The changing commercial ambience in Dongdaemun is promoted as a sign of endless adaptability, one of the factors necessary to become rich in the ever-changing economic conditions. I question the thesis that design-oriented spaces bring further economic growth, let alone produce 'global space'. The emphasis on constructing DDPP as an urban showpiece shows a lack of imagination with respect to the word 'global'. The rise of Dongdaemun as a new fashion town between the late 1990s and the present is partly due to the migrant workers who replaced the Korean factory workers of the 1960s and 1970s. Yet the experiences of those workers and the greater risks faced by small businesses are not adequately integrated within the urban discourse of building a 'global city'.

A History of Dongdaemun Market

A brief examination of the contested history of Dongdaemun Market reveals not only the complicated place-marketing practices but also how commercial activities have always been shaped by larger political forces. The predecessor of the current Dongdaemun Market was Yee Hyun Market (figure 4.3), which was one of the three biggest markets of the late Chosun Dynasty (City History Compilation Committee of Seoul, 2007). Dongdaemun Market was established in 1905 when Korean merchants formed Gwangjang Corporation to mitigate the financial loss caused by the Currency Readjustment Project. The currency readjustment replaced the Beckdonghua, the currency of the late Chosun state, with the Japanese one, bringing a change which was highly inflationary. At the same time, the expanding businesses of Japanese merchants began to threaten the economic status of Chosun merchants in areas such as Namdaemun Market and Yongsan. To counter increasing Japanese commercial influence, Chosun merchants with enough capital started Gwangjang Market near Dongdaemun.[3] The continued prosperity of Dongdaemun Market represented the remaining strength of Korean merchants against the colonizers.

After the brief cessation of commercial activities during the Korean War,

Figure 4.3. This historic photo of the Dongdaemun Market in the late nineteenth century shows crowded streets filled with pedestrians, horse carriages, and various goods including dried vegetables.

Dongdaemun Market expanded to incorporate refugees and rural migrants who opened unlicensed markets. The construction of Dongdaemun General Market (a commercial structure within Dongdaemun Market) on the garage sites of outdated streetcars in 1970 signalled the stabilization of commercial activities.[4] Under the developmental regime of President Park, industrialized manufacturing enabled faster production of goods, which was met by an explosive demand from war-deprived consumers in the late 1950s and 1960s. Before the 1970s, the state's economic policy emphasized the growth of light industries, such as the manufacture of clothes and shoes. In this context, proximity to the Pyunghwa (Peace) Market (figure 4.4), containing many sewing factories and labourers, was conducive to the further commercial success of Dongdaemun Market.[5] The rise of Dongdaemun was in large part due to the long hours of labour provided by young women who migrated to Seoul from the rural countryside. Most of them worked fifteen hours a day in a very cramped environment – often illegally subdivided into two floors with a height of about four feet each – getting minimal wages (American Friends Service Committee, 1970). By the late 1970s, Dongdaemun Market had become the biggest clothing market in Seoul. With the abolition of curfew, commercial activities continued during the night, making Dongdaemun Market a haven for night-time shopping.

Although individual shoppers could purchase items in Dongdaemun, most of the

Figure 4.4. Pyunghwa Market in the 1960s was the centre of manufacturing. The growth of light industries was possible due to urbanization and the increasing numbers in the labour force.

commercial activities were centred on wholesale products (Kim, Y.H. and Shin, Y.N., 2001). The clustering of manufacturing functions and economies of scale enabled the production of cheaper goods in Dongdaemun Market. Small business owners leased lots in a larger market structure called *sang-ga*; Dongdaemun market currently consists of about 30,000 shops and thirty sang-ga.[6] By 1970 when the Dongdaemun General Market was established, Dongdaemun Market was responsible for 70 per cent of the domestic production and distribution of clothing items (Shin, Y.N., 2005). Efforts to confer a more visually coherent appearance on the market followed the growth of light industry and accumulation of capital. As the group of smaller shops in nearby Jongro area was being redesigned by famous architects like Kim Soo Keun, Dongdaemun area was no exception. The architectural plan of Dongdaemun General Market in 1970 shows the modernist architectural aesthetic which reflects industrialized and centralized production networks (figure 4.5). Although some parts of the plan, such as the circular tower, were later discarded due to a high construction cost, the

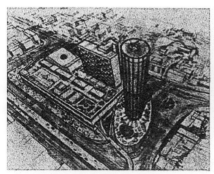

Figure 4.5. The model of Dongdaemun General Market in the 1970 proposal shows rectangular buildings and a high-rise tower. However, the plan was later modified to exclude the tower.

construction of Dongdaemun General Market signalled the epitome of the expansion of light industry.

However, the economic conditions that allowed the spectacular growth of light industry began to change in the mid-1980s. Labour organizations began to gain strength as a result of the democratic movement. When the military dictatorship ended in 1987, suppressed labour movements brought worker's rights to the forefront of the democratization process. For instance, the labour movement earned collective bargaining rights and increased the percentage of union membership from 13.6 per cent in 1987 to 18.6 per cent in 1989 (Cho, H.R., 2005). Although a series of negotiations led to an increase in the minimum wage and the formal recognition of collective bargaining, the labour movement had limited success since the negotiations simultaneously brought the liberalization of the labour market (Chang *et al.*, 2009). In return for recognizing collective bargaining, conglomerates now had increased labour flexibility. At the same time, the improvement of labour conditions was limited since enforcing standards for smaller businesses presented massive challenges for the state. According to Chung and Kirkby (2002, p. 83), South Korean workers in *chaebol* (conglomerate) companies experienced significant wage increases while the state was 'incapable of extending such improvements to small and medium firms'. When confronted with labour disputes and strikes, many small and medium-sized businesses simply took the option of temporarily closing down their businesses. As a result, those employed in small and medium-sized sewing factories in Dongdaemun experienced a high level of job insecurity.

In addition to institutional changes, the outbreak of the Asian financial crisis in the late 1990s resulted in disruption of the existing production and distribution networks of small businesses. The overall sales of small and medium businesses decreased rapidly due to the recession. Unlike big corporations, small and medium-sized businesses could expect much less monetary support from financial institutions. At the same time, the governmental policies during the IMF crisis were focused on restoring foreign exchange liquidity and financial restructuring rather than seeking a comprehensive plan to solve the problems faced by small and medium-sized businesses (Song, U.G., 1999). Thus, the most adversely affected by the changed labour conditions were small business owners and manufacturing industries.

Yet the economic recession of the late 1990s did not stop the building of mega shopping malls in the area. Large retail shopping malls built in the late 1990s, such as Doota and Migliore, generated huge profit, giving rise to the phrase 'the myth of Dongdaemun'. In the context of financial difficulty and the downsizing trend prevalent in the aftermath of the IMF crisis, the success of the new retail shopping mall named Migliore in the late 1990s seemed miraculous. Economists and urban scholars have attributed the success of this mall to the entrepreneurial ability to detect the emergence of increasing consumption by teenagers (Yu, J.Y., 2002). Merchants at Migliore

Figure 4.6. This picture of the Doota Fashion Mall shows a tall building with the advertisement 'Fashion is war'.

undertook the novel marketing strategy of targeting teenagers who had limited budgets. The success of retail shopping malls in Dongdaemun led to the construction of department store-like shopping malls in Dongdaemun Market. Doota (figure 4.6), Hello APM, and Good Morning City are examples of the retail shopping malls built in the 2000s following the strategy of catering for the casual fashion interests of the young. Notwithstanding the continuation of wholesale trade, retail trade became the more prominent commercial activity of Dongdaemun Market.

The construction of such large commercial structures became the standard in Dongdaemun Market because of two conditions. First, production sites diversified. The traditional clustered pattern of production networks still persists in Dongdaemun Market, but some businesses started to rely on the globalized production sites. At the same time, foreign workers introduced as industrial trainees under Kim Young Sam's administration in 1992 were alleviating the labour shortage in small businesses. As a result of unstable employment in small businesses many South Koreans left the shop floor. However, although skilled workers were still in short supply, a continuous flow of both unskilled and skilled workers from overseas helped to maintain the level of production.

In addition, a series of urban redevelopment projects, which focused on the experiential aspects rather than efficiency, were promoted at the level of local and national government. In 2004, the introduction of the five-day working week in large companies and public institutions in South Korea meant that regular workers had more free time during weekends.[7] This policy did not guarantee shorter work hours since it did not apply to smaller businesses and temporary workers in big businesses. However, it had the effect of bringing more people onto the streets during weekends, making them potential consumers. According to research by the LG Economy Institute, household leisure expenditure increased 3.4 per cent between 2003 and 2005 (Yu, S.H., 2011). Leisure-related businesses, such as tourist companies, restaurants, and concert venues expected increased sales due to the implementation of the policy. Local governments began to embark on various projects to redesign the cityscape to suit the new production and consumption patterns. A study by the Seoul Local City Officials Training Institute (2003) recommended that the city government implement various programmes, such as centres for the study of the natural environment and cultural exploration courses, to 'make good use of the leisure time' created by the five-day working week law.

The urban development plan for Seoul in 2004 included a plan to realign and rearrange existing shopping malls (figure 4.7). For instance, the city government and the Jongro district office invested 1.3 billion KRW (about US$11 million) in remodelling

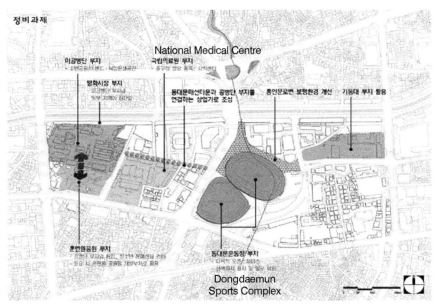

Figure 4.7. The 2004 Urban Development Plan of Dongdaemun Market mentions that Dongdaemun Sports Complex is slated as a multi-purpose open space while the area surrounding the stadium needs sidewalk improvement. The area of the National Medical Center is scheduled to relocate as the result of the development plan.

Dongdaemun General Market in 2003 as a way to 'improve shopping environments in association with the river restoration' (Seoul Metropolitan City, 2006b). Such governmental policies assured individual investors that increased sales would guarantee the profit necessary to recover the cost of construction. Ironically, the very success of Dongdaemun Market during the colonial period and the Asian financial crisis led many to believe that the combination of entrepreneurial instincts and business skills alone would result in individual prosperity. In a sense, the expansion of Dongdaemun Market represented the continuation of the developmentalist framework, which was based on a belief in the possibility of continuous material growth. This belief resulted in the peculiar practice of leasing out the lots to tenant merchants before purchasing the land and before getting a construction permit in Dongdaemun Market (Kim, H., 2003). While it is customary in South Korea to sell or lease individual apartment units to prospective residents before construction is finished, it is extremely rare to parcel out commercial units given the high risk associated with managing individual shops.

Preservation vs. Development

It was in such a political and institutional context that Seoul was selected as the World Design Capital (WDC) by the International Council of Societies of Industrial Design (ICSID) in 2007. Immediately after the selection of Seoul as the WDC, Seoul city government embarked on the Design Seoul project, which included construction of the Dongdaemun Design Plaza and Park (DDPP), redesigning the national landscape of Nam Mountain, and hosting the Seoul Design Olympics. Seoul city government established an organization called Design Seoul Directing Headquarters in order to

Figure 4.8. Dongdaemun Stadium Memorial, on the left, located on the eastern edge of the park contains cultural artefacts such as baseballs bat and other related objects.

implement various projects. As part of the renovation efforts, Seoul Sports Stadium (also known as Dongdaemun Stadium), considered obsolete by some urban planners, was scheduled for demolition to make way for the park. While Dongdaemun Stadium hosted many historically important sports activities in Seoul, its presence was no longer considered essential because of traffic issues, low level of use, and weakening competitive edge (Dongdaemun Forum, 2001). Supporters of the construction of the park argued that Dongdaemun Market desperately needed a public space where pedestrians could take a rest.

Notwithstanding the warm reception and favourable portrayal of DDPP in official sources, voices of dissension and criticism toward the project came from various camps. Sports fans who associated the Dongdaemun Stadium with cherished memories of urban sports activities and historically significant events opposed the demolition. Although simply called Dongdaemun Stadium, it used to be a multi-sports complex including baseball and soccer stadia, and a swimming pool. Before independence from the Japanese in 1945, important sports events such as Chosun Women's Tennis Tournament in 1926 and Chosun Soccer Games in 1927 were held at the complex. After independence, many high school baseball games were held there, and before professional baseball leagues were formed in South Korea, high school baseball matches were very popular among Seoul residents. Many residents still remember the place with ardent support for different teams. Other types of sports event, such as professional boxing and soccer matches were held in an ancillary facility of the complex. Before the Olympic Stadium was constructed, Dongdaemun complex was the home ground of the national soccer team. Sports fans opposed the demolition by arguing that the stadium was the Mecca of amateur baseball games and the cradle of many sports stars (Choi, Y.J., 2007). Others noted that the decision to demolish the eighty-year-old sports structure reflects that 'more attention is given to development and profit rather than everyday memories associated with urban space' (Kil, Y.H., 2007, p. 36).

Another challenge to the image of Dongdaemun Market as a seamless collection of sleek shopping malls came from the street vendors. While the baseball stadium was in use as late as 2007, the soccer stadium, which closed in 2003, functioned as a parking lot. The demolition of the sports complex became a big issue since the soccer stadium had been designated as the Pungmul Market, occupied by relocated street vendors who came from the Cheonggyecheon area. Since the vendors had already been relocated due to Cheonggyecheon Restoration, another urban redevelopment project in the early 2000s, the decision to demolish the stadium became a source of resentment (Park, S.R. and Kim, 2008). In addition, street vendors in Dongdaemun also lost their space as significant portions of the sidewalks were closed off during the construction. In response to the protests by vendors, the initial position of city government was that it was not necessary to provide an alternative since their businesses were illegal from the start. Although it later sought a more conciliatory approach by proposing an alternative site in Sinseoldong, street vendors remained indignant over the series of forced relocations.

Despite the protests of sports fans and street vendors, the entire complex, including the baseball and soccer stadia, was demolished in 2008. As a token gesture, the newly opened DDPP now contains a small memorial dedicated to the memory of the sports events held in the complex (figure 4.8). The former glory of the sporting events can only be glimpsed through the artefacts/graphic panels exhibited in the memorial, and the two light towers, the only remains of the original structure, located in the far eastern edge of the park.

Heritage vs Colonial Legacy

Conflicts between preservation and development of Dongdaemun Market had another layer of complication, as some urban heritage was considered less important, or even undesirable, given its origin during colonial times. In Design Seoul, adding a 'sense of history' to the city involved the resurrection of certain artefacts at the expense of others. For instance, the brochure promoting DDPP emphasized the fact that the old sports stadium was first constructed during the Japanese colonial period to commemorate the marriage of the Japanese crown prince (Seoul Metropolitan City, 2010). Supporters of new construction at Dongdaemun Market argued that the rationale for demolishing the sports stadium was not only based on practical issues – that the stadium was not used frequently – but also on the historical fact that it was built to celebrate the marriage of the Japanese crown prince during colonial times. Such facts have made the stadium appear as an obsolete artefact of colonialism rather than the centre of recreational activities in the recent past. Older artefacts such as part of the old city wall and *Hadogam*, a military training base during the Chosun Dynasty, were discovered in the area. While acknowledging the role of Dongdaemun Stadium in modern Korean sports culture, the government brochure emphasizes the fact that older castle walls were destroyed in the construction of the stadium (Seoul Design Foundation, 2009). Compared to the older historical forms associated with the Chosun Dynasty, the stadium is relatively new, with the stigma of colonial history. Furthermore, the discovery of the old city walls during the demolition process and the architect's decision to integrate them into DDPP added a sense of urgency to removing the colonial relic and 'rescuing' the older cultural heritage.

The fact that many valuable historical artefacts were demolished to make way for 'modern' urban infrastructure during the Japanese colonial times cannot be denied. The most blatant example is that of Changgyeong Park, an urban park which contained a zoo converted from one of the royal palace complexes. In cases involving important government buildings, structures with past political affiliations were deliberately hidden from view so as to give prominence to the Japanese colonial regime, as is the case with the Gyeongbok Palace behind the Japanese Governor-General building. Structures of a lesser scale and political prestige were regarded as a cumbersome obstacle to urban redevelopment in the eyes of colonizers. In Korea as well as in other countries colonized by Japan, historic city walls were destroyed in the process of carrying out so-called urban 'improvement' plans (Fu, 2014).

Yet the discovery of the old city wall was accidental as this came after the demolition of the sports stadium. While preservation of the city wall and other historic relics are important, this was an unanticipated event rather than a premeditated project. In such a context, the need to eradicate colonialism becomes convenient justification for urban redevelopment. The decision regarding what to keep and what to discard becomes subjected to a highly selective process of defining what 'heritage' is. This process may not necessarily reflect public opinion about the given heritage. Contrary to the assertion that the demolition of the stadium was necessary to eliminate the remnants of colonialism, sports authorities argued that the stadium has accumulated different meanings as layers of positive memories replaced faded histories of the colonial period. Compared to colonial buildings with strong connotations of subjugation, such as the Japanese Governor-General Building (see above), the sports stadium is a much weaker political symbol since most Koreans were unaware of the original rationale for its construction. In particular, sports fans claimed the structure as their own, despite the fact that it was built by the Japanese. This shows that spatial practice has become more important than the original rationale behind the construction of a given structure.

Even after the completion of the project, most of the artefacts such as porcelain discovered on the site were removed and relocated elsewhere. Although a small portion of the park was designated for an exhibition of the excavation site, it is dwarfed by the huge mass of the adjacent DDPP. Because the relics were moved while the excavation site between the contemporary structures was retained, most visitors cannot easily

Figure 4.9. On the left, the architectural rendering of Zaha Hadid's design in 2009 shows the historic city wall occupying a significant portion of the park. On the right is actual site after the construction in 2014.

recognize the significance of the site. Tellingly, at an event called *Picatsu* (one of the characters of the famous Japanese animation *Pokemon*) *Showtime* held on 15 November 2014, many visitors were seen stepping onto the excavation site in order to see moving figures wearing Picatsu costumes (Han, Y.H., 2014). While the media lamented the lack of civic respect among visitors, the location of the excavation site and the manner in which it was presented to the public prevented visitors from understanding its importance. Similarly, part of the old city wall and the Yigansumun (Yigan Flood Gates) were preserved, yet their presence is diminished by the way the contemporary structures envelop them. In contrast to the initial rendering by Hadid, the city wall is much lower, and only a small portion is visible above the ground (figure 4.9).

Iconic Design and Branding

Amid the controversy surrounding the demolition of the stadium, design competitions for a new park began in 2007. Among many contestants, Hadid's design was selected as the winning project. The selection of her design reflected the desire not only to provide appropriate urban amenities but also to promote Seoul as the centre of the fashion industry by using the brand power of a star architect.

Using iconic architecture by famous architects to facilitate urban development is fairly common. While branding is conventionally associated with everyday commodities such as clothes and shoes, it can also be applied to urban environments. For instance, the construction of Guggenheim Museum in Bilbao by Frank Gehry in 1997 was expected to generate an architectural tourism in the area. In the case of Dongdaemun Market, having an urban icon which epitomizes the future envisioned for the area as a global fashion town became imperative in the minds of policy-makers. The official DDPP brochure created by Seoul city government explicitly states the case of Bilbao as a successful example of using architectural design to promote local economy (Seoul Metropolitan City, 2010). Yet it is not clear whether using such an iconic design will actually generate a unique urban identity in the area in question. Architectural scholar Anna Klingmann (2007, p. 3) has argued that more often than not, uses of urban branding 'have resulted in a culture of the copy, imitating one another in their offerings and aesthetics'. While using architectural design to respect 'heterogeneity of places' and 'inclusive objectives of urban development' is possible, she warns that brandscape can also flatten urban experience by using 'short-lived images of dazzling signature projects' (*Ibid.*).

The construction of DDPP in Dongdaemun Market is part of the larger rubric of encouraging the use of urban design to facilitate the transformation of Seoul. The Design Seoul campaign, which started in 2008, is an effort to resituate South Korea within the global economic structure by transforming it from a 'hard city' to a 'soft city'. While Seoul represented an industrial 'hard city' emphasizing speed and efficiency, the concept of a soft city emphasizes 'soft' aspects of a city such as appreciation of 'traditional cultures'. In this urban discourse, contemporary South Korean society is imagined as having 'lost touch' with emotional wellbeing and other values because of the emphasis on rapid economic growth. Planners have argued that it is time to reverse this tendency by 'rediscovering' the cultural heritage of South Korea (Yang, G.Y., 1995). Consequently, cultural heritage and historic relics need to be actively incorporated as elements of the new urban landscape. By doing so, it is hoped that pedestrians' appreciation of 'Korean culture' will improve.

In an interview, Jin-bae Park, a representative of Seoul Design Foundation, mentioned that the design development stalled several times due to the discovery of many artefacts beside the historic wall.[8] Although the basic concept of Hadid's design remained unchanged, the part containing the event hall went through significant changes. According to Park, Hadid's project management team did not have the will to accommodate the various functional requirements which Seoul Design Foundation requested. This led to an increase in conflicts, and eventually, a design supervisory committee made up of architectural scholars and lawyers specializing in international contracts was established. Some members took issue with empty spaces within DDPP while others questioned whether Hadid's design reflected any part of Korean culture. Despite the mounting conflicts, Hadid's team and the supervisory committee reached a consensus when the project manager apologized for the seeming lack of concern for its functional capacities while asking for respect for the fact that the city chose Hadid's design in the first place. Park acknowledges that the reason Hadid's design was selected was because of the regenerative capacity of her design rather than functional competitiveness. In other words, the role of the building as a landmark and a tool for economic revitalization played a greater part than that of service provision. In fact, Seoul Design Foundation has yet to decide how to make use of some interior spaces such as Design Dul Rae Gil, meaning 'Design Round Path'.

'Caring for Citizens' and the Changing Notion of Citizens

The official rhetoric of the Design Seoul campaign regarded residents as the clients and beneficiaries of the design campaign. The mission statement of Design Seoul includes five *considerations* – rather than policies – for the economy, the environment, everyday life, culture, and empathy.[9] These five considerations are designed to fulfil the ultimate objective of caring for citizens. Compared to government-led projects under the previous authoritarian regime, the language describing the project is much softer, emphasizing friendliness and sensibility rather than a top-down dominance. The main objective of caring for citizens is to be carried out by improving the quality of public space through design. As such, improving the appearance of public spaces such as sidewalks and streets is considered to contribute to the pleasant experience of

Figure 4.10. Posters advertising the Design Seoul Campaign became ubiquitous in Seoul in 2009. On the left, a poster placed on the roof of a subway train car reads 'It is worth living thanks to (good) design'. On the right, a poster shows a businessman smiling with a bubble reading 'Seoul is great!'.

everyday life. To promote the concept of Design Seoul, the city government has used friendly images in its posters and signs emphasizing the new aspect of the project of transforming Seoul's urban landscape (figure 4.10). These images convey the message that in contrast to previous development projects, contemporary urban projects are designed to satisfy individual needs and comforts rather than fulfilling abstract national goals.

In the posters, people in Seoul are imagined as optimistic individuals who carry out their daily duties with faith in progress and technology. Although Seoul residents are mainly the beneficiaries of services, they can also become participants in the campaign by making suggestions thanks to a variety of advanced communication technologies. For instance, citizens' congratulatory messages sent from smartphones for the opening ceremony of the Seoul Design Festival in 2010 were displayed in real time on a big screen. Also, the websites of the Seoul Design Committee and the Seoul city government offer an online bulletin board for people's opinions and suggestions regarding the specifics of the campaign, while the city government established the opportunity to engage in on-site conversations with the mayor that included the issue of Seoul's design policy. However, most recorded messages and conversations, while addressing the direction or the scope of the policy, stopped short of discussing the specifics of the programmes.[10]

Urban planners imagine that it is possible to elicit a certain kind of emotion by engineering physical environments. The official statement of the Design Seoul Committee notes that 'the twenty-first century is changing from a city selling functions to a city selling feelings/senses'.[11] In the book *Designing Seoul*, the director of the Design Seoul campaign observed that Seoul needs to be in tune with global trend of using design to demonstrate competitiveness (Kwon, 2010). Such a fashion- and design-oriented view of urban development is in line with the city government's policy of cultivating various programmes and themed streets in order to 'make good use of leisure time' in changed economic conditions.

Others who criticized the project viewed it primarily as the expression of the mayor's personal political ambition. During the Citizen's Open Forum Regarding Design Seoul in September 2010, many voiced dissent against using urban projects as a political means to generate public support. For instance, during the discussion, a member of Congress from the opposition party suggested that current urban projects in Seoul put excessive emphasis on visible accomplishments (Yoon, H.S., 2010). Another participant, a design critic, argued that Seoul's design policy had been used as the political propaganda of the mayor (Lee, D.Y., 2010). Interestingly, the controversy surrounding DDPP failed to discuss the political and socioeconomic dimensions of the project as the word 'politics' carried primarily negative connotations. Instead, the discussions revolved around historical aspects of the site and the architectural aesthetics of the proposal.

A more successful attack on the Design Seoul campaign came from those who politicized the urban projects to their advantage by drawing attention to socioeconomic issues. Young artists started to use guerrilla design tactics to question the legitimacy of the project by using humour directed at the preaching tone of the government campaign. The local government's strategy of manufacturing consent through 'selling feelings' backfired when exaggerated portrayals of residents as progressive and satisfied people were met by counter-images of disgruntled individuals. A significant proportion of Seoul residents did not share the rosy view of the Design Seoul campaign and did not hesitate to express their opposition. Some said that an excessive campaign which bombards the public space with posters and stickers is irritating, sometimes inducing 'design nausea' (Park, W.J., 2010). More adventurous individuals took to guerrilla design strategies by designing parodies of the government posters and displaying them in strategic places.

For instance, an organization called FF Group, made up of freelance artists, engaged in an 'I Like Seoul' campaign by placing a sticker over the official Design Seoul posters that twists the original message (figure 4.11). While the original word bubble said 'I like to design', and 'Seoul is great!', the new bubbles in the stickers said 'children skip meals because [the city government focuses on] design' and 'only Gangnam (South of the Han River) is great'. Such acts pointed out that the portrayal of citizens as passive city dwellers benefiting from the Design Seoul campaign did not always match their actual lived experiences. One member of the FF Group explained that the group's interest in Design Seoul began when the city started to use the phrase 'Seoul is the design capital

Figure 4.11. 'I Like Seoul' projects included placing stickers over the word bubbles of official posters to change the meanings.

of the world' in the advertisements of Design Seoul projects. He explained that group members questioned whether such a thing as a design capital could be defined. When asked what the group thought about the role of design in current urban developments, another member noted:

It is something like this... Imagine that your neighbour has an ugly tree which protrudes into your garden. You want to get rid of it. You use the word 'design' as a pretext to cut down the neighbour's tree. The word 'design' is like a master key that can be used for anything.[12]

The group was initially formed by four college students 'concerned about the possibility of having to work on something they did not want to do in the future'.[13] However, the group's involvement in media arts soon grew to include social issues, such as displacement and socioeconomic polarization. After graduating from college, members of FF Group questioned the way the Seoul city government used the term *design* to promote urban redevelopment. In another project, they decided to test whether the rule of law is respected in public spaces by displaying provocative political messages while not breaking any laws.[14]

The contrast between smiling faces and dissatisfied comments in the bubble comes across as a comical spin on the original poster. However, it does not stop at being a simple prank commenting on the official campaign. With relatively little investment, such tactics successfully subverted the image of contented citizens happily carrying out their routines in the city by delivering counter-narratives, for example on the regional inequality between Gangbuk (North of the Han River) and Gangnam (South of the Han River). The 'Like Seoul' campaign also questioned the current city government's emphasis on design-oriented developments, arguing that public funds spent on the Design Seoul campaign could have been spent on more pressing issues such as the provision of free school meals for all children. In another instance, young artists have taken a more ambitious stance by actively imagining the future of a current project.

In an art exhibition titled *There Is No Gold Medal in the Design Olympics*, one artwork depicted an image of DDPP being demolished in the year 2040. Aptly titled 'Alzheimer City', it raised the question whether the current project can be sustainable when the very impetus for its construction requires constant renewal.

Although the FF Group's 'Like Seoul' campaign was meant as a general criticism of government projects by citizens, they were viewed suspiciously as the deliberate sabotage against the current mayor by the opposing political party. The main organizer of the campaign was asked to report to the police station where he was asked who the mastermind political power behind the campaign was.[15] Although he was not convicted after revealing his identity as a student and explained the purpose of the campaign, such an episode highlights the heightened ambiguity about the role of NGOs in the political context of a newly democratized society. According to Kim Ha-young, a Korean political scientist, many leaders and chairs of NGOs 'have not refused to take governmental seats with excuses of more effectively reflecting political opinions of civil society in government policies' (Kim, H.Y., 2009, p. 98). Some NGOs have become a quasi-governmental organization by receiving financial support from the government. Hee-yon Cho (2001, p. 237), a professor of sociology at Sungkonghoe University, argues that South Korean democratic transition through 'a [political] improvement of the regime', rather than its destruction, has led to 'the preservation of previous political initiatives, which contributed to the birth of anti-*minjung* or non-*minjung* NGOs'. At the same time, many scholars observe that South Korea's NGO protest movements are led by a small number of professional experts rather than the general public (Kim, T.H., 2008). In such a context, the general increase in the number of NGOs does not necessarily mean the presence of consensus regarding the scope of NGOs' activities.

Such counter-narratives demonstrate that the depiction of Seoul's residents as contented beneficiaries of the urban park project is far from the whole truth. Many protesters and artists refused to accept the claim that urban projects are designed to 'care for citizens'. Rather, they awakened policy-makers and planners to the fact that citizens are not mere followers, but recalcitrant political constituents who might not give their consent to the project in the first place. At the same time, they redefined the geographical boundary of this socio-political issue from a global scale to a local one, by implicitly arguing that local problems – such as inequality between the southern and northern parts of Seoul – should be addressed before taking on the task of making Seoul a global design capital. The FF Group's strategy is more effective than accusing urban projects of being 'too political', since their strategy avoids constructing a self-imposed obstacle to political participation.

Despite the strength of the guerrilla design tactics, the protesters did not question the underlying economic structure that made the promotion of the Design Seoul projects possible. Although many critics remain sceptical of the feasibility of the city government-led campaign to elevate Seoul to the position of 'design capital', larger institutional and policy changes which provided the necessary conditions to initiate such projects have not been closely associated with recent urban transformations. The government's vision of 'keeping up' with other cities by aggressively marketing newly designed urban environments is not only based on structural inequalities but also threatens to intensify the negative externalities associated with liberalizing labour conditions. Despite the reported successes of small business owners in Dongdaemun Market in the late 1990s, the 'myth of Dongdaemun' did not hold against the changing economic conditions and policy initiatives encouraging self-employment.

Yet against the milieu of the clientelist approach city government has taken towards residents, different types of citizens also emerged as the result of the Korean globalization process. This involved the emergence of a hybrid cultural landscape. Around the time that mega shopping malls providing a more comfortable shopping environment were built, changing political and economic structures contributed to the emergence of 'Little Russia' (figure 4.12) in Dongdaemun. This is due to a set of complex factors, including the presence of Dongdaemun Market, changing immigration and labour laws, and colonial legacies. The rise of Little Russia shows that the process of globalization can be a double-edged sword, since it contains both positive and negative externalities. The convoluted history of Korean-Russians (*Koryo-in*) in Dondaemun is the most illustrative of the complex patterns of globalization.

After the period of Perestroika and the increase in trade between South Korea and the then-Soviet Union, accommodation and restaurants catering to Russian and Central Asian traders appeared in Gwanhee-dong area in Dongdaemun. The owners of these restaurants and shops such as Край родной (*Krai Roud-noi*), are Korean-Russians.[16] Most of them are the descendants of Koreans who moved to Russia for various reasons. Some moved to avoid economic hardship while others chose to relocate for political reasons. Some were forced to work in the mines of Sakhalin under the Japanese regime. According to Victor Nam (2011), a professor at Toshkent Davlat Pedagogical University, there were three waves of ethnic-Korean (by then subjects of Chosun dynasty) immigration to Russia. First, famine caused by a flood followed by a frost in the northern regions of Korea in 1869, led some 6,000 ethnic-Koreans to migrate to the Maritime Province of Siberia. The second wave of migration started after 1910 when Korea was incorporated into imperial Japan. The migrants included patriotic participants in the independence movement. By 1917, ethnic-Koreans who migrated to Russia reached 100,000. By the 1930s, the ethnic-Korean community occupied a significant part of the Far Eastern Republic, a semi-independent state which operated as 'a buffer state' between the Soviet Union and Japan (Norton, 1923, p. 129).

However, the rising tension between Japan and the Soviet Union initiated the forcible relocation of ethnic-Koreans to the Central Asian region. Although many joined the Soviet Union in the armed struggle against the Japanese during the 1920s, the growing population of ethnic-Koreans near the border was perceived by the Soviet leaders as a political threat and a possible source for the breach of national security. The rationale for the forcible relocation was to prevent espionage by the Japanese spies among the ethnic-Korean community (Lee, B.K., 2011). There was no room for the tolerance of a minority population whose facial phenotype closely resembled that of the Japanese enemies. The forced relocation meant weeks of riding on makeshift trains converted from livestock carriages – not even pregnant women and invalids could escape the trip (Yun, B.S., 2005, p. 589). Due to insanitary conditions and the reckless rate at which they travelled, many infants and the weak perished. Even those who survived the trip had to resettle in a foreign environment populated by other ethnic groups who did not always welcome the sudden presence of ethnic-Koreans.

After a brief period of independence, following the Korean War, and the division of Korea, coming back to South Korea became virtually impossible for Korean-Russians. It was only in the 1990s that some descendants of the Korean-Russians returned, when the opening of the Russian economy and South Korea's *segyehwa* policy contributed to favourable conditions for them to settle and find businesses. Larisa Kim, a third generation Korean-Russian, was able to open a Central Asian restaurant in Dongdaemun after the passing of the Foreign Investment Promotion Act in 1998 which allows permanent residence status for those who satisfy investment requirements (Lee, N.H., 2005). At the same time, frequent trips by Russian wholesale buyers to Dongdaemun Market generated a demand for Russian and Central Asian businesses.

Although the number of Russian traders has decreased significantly due to Russia's recession in the new millennium, Little Russia continues to function as the social nucleus for migrant workers from Central Asia. The introduction of the Industrial Trainee System under President Kim Young Sam in 1993 encouraged the movement

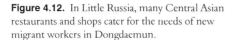

Figure 4.12. In Little Russia, many Central Asian restaurants and shops cater for the needs of new migrant workers in Dongdaemun.

of unskilled labour from Third World countries. Although most manufacturing industries in Dongdaemun moved abroad to look for cheaper labour, small sewing shops continued to suffer from a labour shortage (Ministry of Industry and Resources, 2005). An increasing number of foreign migrants started to work in smaller garment workshops where South Korean workers are unwilling to work due to job instability and harsh working conditions. In the Changsin-dong and Gwanghee-dong areas adjacent to Dongdaemun Market, many migrant workers from Nepal have found employment in small garment shops. Although the establishment of Little Russia (figure 4.12) was due to Russian buyers who came in large numbers in the mid-1990s, the current patrons are those working in shop factories (Park, J.J., 2006). While the number of Russian patrons decreased significantly, migrant workers from Mongolia and Uzbekistan have increased steadily (*Ibid.*). Social gatherings for Uzbek immigrants are often held in the Dongdaemun area in order to provide networking opportunities for Uzbeks and South Koreans. In an interview with *Hanguk Ilbo*, one migrant worker from Uzbekistan noted that he visits Little Russia once or twice a week when he is tired of company dormitory food or when there is a farewell party for another worker going back to his country (Lee, W.G., 2004).

Thus, the *segyehwa* drive and related economic policies have been a mixed blessing with respect to the community development of Dongdaemun Market. While the liberalizing economic conditions have adversely affected small and medium-sized businesses, they have contributed to the formation of a new ethnic community. The flow of capital and the relocation of manufacturing industries overseas have contributed to the simultaneous phenomena of job instability and a shortage of labour. However, foreign direct investment has also proved to be a channel for historically marginalized Korean-Russians to come back to their home country and function as the cultural bridge between Central Asian immigrants and South Korean society. Although the aim of the economic policies was to recover from the foreign exchange crisis in 1997, they also had the unanticipated effect of diversifying the ethnic makeup of Dongdaemun Market.

Globalization as Global Models for Successful Development: The Hidden Cost of the Design Capital

Not everyone who put faith in the possibility of continuous material growth was rewarded with entrepreneurial success. In 2003, the embezzlement of the lot distribution fund (paid by the prospective tenants) by a representative of a shopping mall named Good Morning City generated a crisis among 3,400 prospective tenants who invested capital for the right to manage a lot in the shopping mall. Since the costs of constructing the shopping mall had not been paid yet, it was declared bankrupt. Tenants formed a contractors' council and borrowed money from banks to recover

Figure 4.13. There are many empty lots in newly constructed high-rise shopping malls such as Good Morning City.

the construction costs. The shopping mall finally opened for business in November 2008. Located adjacent to DDPP, the building stands twenty storeys high, and contains about 4,500 lots for shops. This case of embezzlement brought national attention to the problematic real estate transactions in Dongdaemun Market.

The high risk of doing business in Dongdaemun is not only a question of the methods of real estate transactions. Another risk shop owners face originates from the fact that the number of small business owners increased sharply due to changing economic conditions and policy directions. Starting in the mid-1990s, the South Korean government started to emphasize the need for investment in technological development and inventions with the upcoming opening of markets. The Small and Medium Business Administration (SMBA) was set up in 1996 to encourage the independent development of smaller yet more competitive businesses. Local business associations and local governments started to provide financial support for small businesses qualified as 'venture businesses' which satisfy one of the four criteria established by the 1997 Special Measures for the Promotion of Venture Businesses Act. The initial policy was written with the model of Silicon Valley venture companies in mind. However, according to SMBA, the South Korean definition of 'venture businesses' is different from the US case since venture businesses in Korea are 'the targets of support which let businesses grow to [become] world class companies through governmental policies' rather than 'the result of [independent] success' (SMBA, 2000, p. 4).

Although the policy initiatives contributed to promoting technology-driven businesses, they also ushered in a flood of other small businesses when the aftermath of the structural adjustment in the late 1990s left many people jobless. It is estimated that the number of street vendors alone more than doubled after the IMF crisis (SDI, 2001b). With the increased number of self-employed came the proliferation of books, magazines, and websites giving advice to starting small businesses, ranging from opening a café to online shopping malls. Many success stories and testimonials could be seen in various mass media. As the unemployment rate went up, local governments began to encourage start-ups by setting up job centres to provide resources. For instance, the Seoul city government proudly announced that its Iljari (Job) Plus Centre, established in 2009, was helping the increasing cases of Chang Op [Startups] (Seoul Metropolitan City, 2011). Although many new small businesses were not technologically innovative, increasing the rate of the self-employed did contribute to lowering the unemployment rate. Many of those who started fashion-related businesses, such as online shopping malls, began to compete with shopping malls in Dongdaemun.

In contrast to the late 1990s, many shop lots in big shopping malls currently remain empty due to oversupply. According to Yil-san Kim, the representative of the Korean International Trade Association in Dongdaemun, there is a joke that 'there are a greater number of shops than merchants' and that 'agents [who sell lots] leave with big money while merchants have to engage in a repechage' (Kim, I.S., 2002, p. 74). Jung, a small business consultant, explained that there are many shopping malls that closed down due to the oversupply of lots (Jung, S.I., 2000). After 3 years, the shopping mall still contained many empty lots (figure 4.13). Most of the newly self-employed were expected to demonstrate ingenious entrepreneurship and business skills in order to survive in the increasingly competitive market. Yet, it was becoming extremely difficult for new business owners to achieve the same level of financial success previous owners enjoyed until the late 1990s. Jaehee Choi (2004), the head of United Chang-Op Support Center, noted that 'while there were many success stories thanks to explosive demand, such cases are becoming harder to find in the current era of rapid information exchange'.

Despite the tragic case of the Good Morning City shopping mall, many tenants invested capital, believing in the Dongdaemun myth of the late 1990s. In May 2007, a merchant in Dongdaemun remarked that although sales in every shopping mall in Dongdaemun had decreased, merchants were holding out because of the expectation of further profit after the urban redevelopment project in Dongdaemun Stadium (Kim, K.M., 2007). Despite the fragmented ownership of Good Morning City, the Lotte Corporation declared a plan to rent the entire building and introduce department-style stores (Kim, T.S., 2011). In fact, notwithstanding the reported surplus of shops, new shopping malls continued to be built near DDPP such as Hello APM and Maxtyle. The Maxtyle Management Company advertised its proximity to DDPP, which is expected to generate a floating population of 750,000, which will make business in the building profitable for many merchants (Kim, S.H., 2010).

In the meantime, long-term business prospects look bleak for most sewing businesses due to the shortage of labour. While sewing companies specializing in higher-end products or possessing special skills continue to thrive, the economic condition of the sewing industry in general is in decline. According to Byong-tae Rah (2008) the president of Dongdaemun Garment Sewing Association, skilled South

Korean workers in the sewing industry were decreasing at a rate of 10 per cent a year. Since young people no longer aspire to learn sewing skills, most of the trained workers in the sewing industry are in their fifties (Rah, 2008). Although migrant workers have replaced the Korean workers since the implementation of the industrial trainee system, their working conditions have not improved much since the 1970s. According to Sunhee Park, the director of Seoul Foreign Laborers' Center, most workers in garment shops make 1.2 million to 1.5 million Korean Won (US$1100–1400) per month while working 12 hours a day including Saturdays (Park, S.H. *et al.*, 2010). Furthermore, migrant workers' visas expire when they are about to master the skills necessary to produce higher-end products.

Although migrant workers play a vital part in the continually weakening sewing industry, they are frequently subjected to unannounced and often illegal arrests. During the New Year's holiday in 2010, the police force from Gyonggi Province surrounded the Nepalese restaurant in Dongdaemun and arrested Nepalese immigrants without the consent of the restaurant owner. Although the police representative explained that the incident was a response to 'tips that Nepalese workers engage in illegal gambling', those without proper registration or a visa were promptly transferred to the immigration office for deportation, making the validity of such a claim questionable (Kim, M.G., 2010). The precarious legal status of many migrant workers, in turn, makes migrants unwilling to participate in the labour movement. Although the new Employment Permit System, implemented in 2004, guaranteed migrant workers a minimum wage and collective bargaining rights *in principle*, it 'failed to make businesses assume legal liability in the case of non-adherence' (National Human Rights Commission of the Republic of Korea , 2010, p. 47). While the textile workers in the 1970s and 1980s engaged in lengthy labour negotiations, many migrant workers are hesitant to participate in any attempts to redress their labour conditions as joining a labour union might negatively affect the possibility of contract renewal.

The trend of increasing numbers of shopping malls and the construction of visual landmarks such as the DDPP have ushered in rising real estate values and an increasing separation between production and distribution. This latter trend is worrisome to many shop owners since one of the advantages of Dongdaemun Market was the organic connection between the production and marketing processes. The success of retail shopping malls in the late 1990s was not simply due to cheap prices. Unlike department stores and boutiques, there is a much greater selection of new products in the malls, which enables young adults to stand out as persons with a unique style (Korean Publication Ethics Commission, 2000). The clustering of production and distribution has contributed to the rapid appearance of new fashion styles in Dongdaemun. In fact, it is not uncommon to see clothes displayed in one of the shopping malls in Dongdaemun which look surprisingly similar to those worn by a celebrity on a TV drama a few days ago. In other words, the competitiveness of the Dongdaemun

Market stemmed from the intertwining of the production and distribution networks as much as from the improved shopping environment. However, this characteristic is threatened by impending demolition even as the Design Seoul campaign promotes Dongdaemun as a global fashion district.

On the other hand, the invocation of anti-colonialism in the urban design campaign to demolish the old sports stadium has not been followed by the public arousal of attention to the plight of Korean-Russians and Central Asian migrant workers who are victims of colonial history. While those with enough capital to qualify as foreign investors enjoy relative socioeconomic stability, others who work in factories and on shop floors continue to suffer from discrimination and legal vulnerability. In July 2005, Nina Lee, a third-generation Korean-Russian migrant worker, committed suicide when she was unable to claim overdue wages before her visa expired (Yun, P.H., 2005). Although the government rhetoric regarding Design Seoul involves a political discourse of improving the competitiveness of Seoul, it says little about the unequal effects of changed labour conditions. Despite the improvement of streets and other public amenities, they are not accessible to the economically marginalized who do not enjoy the same level of benefits as corporate workers. The 'competitiveness' generated by the appearance of crowds strolling through fashionable urban environments has become possible thanks to invisible economic toil and the long working hours and job insecurity of temporary workers.

Conclusion

This chapter has examined how the strong association of Dongdaemun Market with entrepreneurial success has been appropriated to suit an agenda of urban redevelopment that privileges certain uses of public space over others. Associating the construction of DDPP with the preservation of 'tradition' was based on the rediscovery of pre-colonial artefacts as a valid heritage and the abandonment of colonial traces. As the city government selectively removed older physical structures, the urban scenes of Dongdaemun Market lost the dynamic quality generated by the coexistence of diverse – old and new – constituents. While the provision of amenities and the preservation of history have been used as justification for selecting iconic architecture, such factors become secondary to the possible economic impacts generated by the building's presence. In the meantime, the imagined distinction between Seoul's recent past and present – as a 'hard' or 'soft' city – functions as the new developmental paradigm which enables the implementation of constant urban re-design in many areas, including Global Cultural Zones. However, the rhetoric of 'caring for citizens' did not guarantee the acceptance of the new development projects in everyday practice. Defining the appropriate cultural representations of Dongdaemun became a hotly controversial issue as sports fans, young artists, and street vendors actively participated in the renegotiations. Resistance to official urban design strategies by guerrilla design groups as well as street vendors demonstrates that an emphasis on constructing visual landmarks can be subverted by the production of counter-narratives and counter-aesthetics. The artist group's questioning of the Seoul city government's urban policies demonstrated that citizens are not simply beneficiaries of construction projects but also political agents capable of judging the legitimacy of the projects.

Within the process of using newly designed urban space as the engine of development, existing structural conditions that contribute to socioeconomic polarization become less noticeable under the phrase of 'design capital'. The reorganization of economic policy has deepened the gap between big businesses and small business owners as well as the gap between official employees and temporary workers. Foreign migrant workers have provided labour in the rapidly declining sewing industries. However, poor working conditions and the absence of job security continue to threaten the long-term viability of the design capital. Despite the continuity of unequal labour conditions and hasty construction transactions increasing the risk involved in running a private business, many choose to believe in the 'myth of Dongdaemun' in the face of economic recession. Yet the case study of embezzlement in one of the shopping malls and intensifying competition among the tenants make it difficult to predict that design-oriented development will bring expected economic growth for all.

It is difficult to predict what kind of economic benefits or misfortunes the construction of Dongdaemun Design Park and Plaza will bring to Dongdaemun Market. However, the challenges to the government's vision of urban environments suggest that urban politics will never follow a meta-narrative of globalization theory. Despite the trend of globalizing production and consumption of architectural practices, the act of conferring meanings on a given structure as well as making use of the physical environments remains at the local level. In the next chapter, I continue with the theme of migration by discussing Itaewon's 'multicultural streets' and the emergence of ethnic and sexual minorities. A continuous flow of migrant workers has been incorporated into the urban environment of Itaewon, considered as the most exotic district in Seoul. In the chapter I question whether the government-led effort to build a 'multicultural society' in South Korea provides an adequate basis for housing policies by examining the political and economic contexts in which the discussion of a 'multicultural society' emerged.

Notes

1. Oh Se-hoon, the Mayor of Seoul, has commented that DDPP is a gesture towards respecting Korean tradition. See Soyoung Lee, 'Dongdaemun Design Plaza & Park Siwon hage Chotsap Ttutdda'.
2. As of 2011, there are about 1.41 million foreigners living in South Korea. Approximately 700,000, or 50 per cent of which are Chinese citizens. Among those 700,000, about 470,000 are Korean-Chinese. *Source*: Korean Statistical Information Service (http://kosis.kr/learning/learning_002007.jsp).

3.   Among the merchants was Park Seung-jik, the founder of Seungjik Store in Dongdaemun, which later became the Doosan Group.

4.   While Dongdaemun Market refers to a collection of all the retail buildings in Dongdaemun, Dongdaemun General Market refers to a specific building in the Dongdaemun Market.

5.   Pyunghwa Market not only contained wholesale stores but many sewing factories, which produced domestic products as well as textile goods for export.

6.   Official website of the Special Tourist District in Dongdaemun Fashion Town, http://www.dft. co.kr/ko/index.htm.

7.   The five-day, or 40 hour, working week policy was first introduced in large companies and governmental offices. It was applicable to businesses with 50 to 100 workers from 1 July 2007. One year later, it was applicable to businesses with more than 20 workers. On 1 July 2011, it was extended to businesses with less than 20 workers as well.

8.   An interview held on 13 May 2013 in Dongdaemun Design Park and Plaza, Seoul.

9.   Official website of Design Seoul, http://design.seoul.go.kr.

10.   Although the official website of Design Seoul contains the online 'Design Seoul Discussion Forum' open to everyone, all postings were confined to the topic of 'the Appropriate Function and Program of DDPP'.

11.   Official Website of DesignSeoul http://design.seoul.go.kr/.

12.   In an interview held on 4 June 2011.

13.   In an interview held on 4 June 2011.

14.   The group placed a large-scale helium balloon with messages criticizing the government project near the statue of Sejong the Great (a king during the Chosun Dynasty) on a busy Seoul thoroughfare. This created the comical impression of the historical king scolding the current government. Their exhibition was met with a hasty warning from the police to remove it.

15.   In an interview held on 4 June 2011.

16.   The owner of **Край родной**, meaning 'hometown' in Russian, is Larisa Kim, a third-generation Korean-Russian.

Chapter 5

A Foreign Country in Seoul: Itaewon's Multicultural Streets

[Itaewon] is a liberating district where the boundaries between sexes, races, and classes become mixed up.

Hankyoreh 21, 25 December 2007

During the night, the area transforms into a leading entertainment district of Seoul, filled with drinks, dance, and food. There are many commercial venues equipped with new facilities and services in kind, as well as a seductive ambience generated by attractive people.

Culture and Tourism Department, 1999

Itaewon (figure 5.1) was designated as a Special Tourist Zone by the Seoul Metropolitan government in 1997 due to the development of diverse patterns of commercial establishments. The reputation of Itaewon as the centre of the entertainment industry as well as of foreign cuisine has become a selling point in local and international tourism. A concentration of trendy nightclubs, bars, ethnic restaurants, and shops led to the portrayal of the place as the 'gateway to the world' as well as 'a foreign country in Seoul' (Moon, G.R., 2009). Media descriptions of the area as being a centre of entertainment culture as well as a shopping paradise have encouraged the city government to promote Itaewon as the centre of tourism and cultural exchange. The presence of diverse ethnic populations and different customs has led to the designation of Itaewon as one of the Global Cultural Zones in Seoul. Although it first emerged in the urban landscape of Seoul as the site of a US military base, Itaewon began to transform as the US presence in the area dwindled when the decision was made to relocate the military installation elsewhere.[1] At the same time, as the number of immigrants from non-Western countries (outside Europe and the US) increased, the town became a hip and cosmopolitan entertainment district where a visitor could enjoy various ethnic foods as well as night-time activities. While vestiges of the Cold War still remain, the area has become imbued with multiple layers of cultural representations as increasing numbers

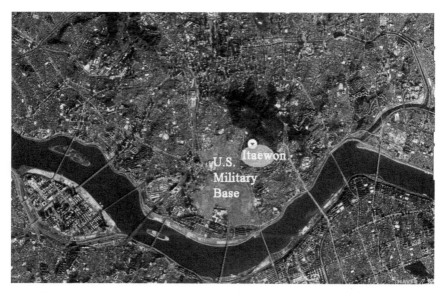

Figure 5.1. Aerial photo of Itaewon and environs (English text added by the Author).

of foreigners from Southeast Asia and Africa have begun to produce visual markers in a landscape previously dominated by the American influence.

Examining the urban development of Itaewon is relevant in studying how the cultural city discourse is applied in a place characterized by a conspicuous mix of different cultural representations. In Itaewon, the processes of globalization produced intricate layers of cultural representation that reveal divergence as well as continuity in the construction of foreign and Korean identities. Itaewon is a place where the mix of different cultural identities through consumption is highly visible. Although the initial rise of Itaewon as an entertainment sector was due to the military base, it has unexpectedly become the repository of cultural change and experimentation. The Design Seoul Street plan and Han-nam New Town Project in Itaewon exemplify the government's attempt to categorize various cultural representations into manageable compartments. In the context of celebrating difference, the presence of multicultural representations in Itaewon is welcomed as material evidence of Seoul's 'global' status.

This chapter examines the historical development of Itaewon, including its beginning as a US army town, the rise of the entertainment district, and its current designation as a 'global zone' with a proliferation of ethnic restaurants and shops. I argue that the emergence of cultural diversity in Itaewon is the result of coincidental historical events rather than consistent implementation of government policies. In contrast, the contemporary political rhetoric of building a 'multicultural society' is not accompanied by concrete and consistent plans to provide material conditions for cultural diversity in Itaewon. The urban redevelopment plans, including the Design

Seoul Street schemes and Global Pavilion Park in the Han-nam New Town plan – designed with the expectation of the impending relocation of the US Army base elsewhere – fail to consider the negative effect of gentrification on cultural diversity. At the same time, they diminish the diverse cultural experiences, including those of gay activism and Muslim immigrants, and become a means to divert attention from the economic problems residents of low-income neighbourhoods face in the era of globalization.

In order to situate historically and geographically the current multicultural campaign by the South Korean government, it is necessary to analyze the historical urban development of Itaewon from the time of its rise as a US Army base town to its current unpredictable urban exuberance. The plan to redevelop the Yongsan area, including Itaewon, can only be understood when its urban history as an army base town is analyzed.[2] While the presence of the US military had various effects, it inadvertently contributed to the reputation of the area as a 'free zone', relatively unfettered by the censorship of the previous authoritarian government. This chapter analyzes the construction of Itaewon as 'multicultural streets' in accordance with the South Korean government's 'multicultural policies'. After examination of the specificity of Korean 'multicultural' policies/campaigns, the last part of this chapter discusses the gentrifying effect of the impending redevelopment plan and Han-nam New Town projects, and how such design schemes threaten to disperse the multicultural community.

A Recent History of Itaewon

Many historical accounts of Seoul explain the beginning of Itaewon as the area providing accommodation for governmental officials and travellers in the early Chosun dynasty (at the end of the fourteenth century) (City History Compilation Committee of Seoul, 2007). It was originally to the north of its current location; the centre of Itaewon changing as a result of the construction of a tunnel through the Nam Mountain. While originally a large area of open fields with many pear trees, Itaewon began to develop when the Japanese colonial administration established its military headquarters in the Yongsan area nearby. After the Second World War, US military forces replaced the Japanese bases with the Yongsan Garrison, which now has nearly 17,000 US military personnel and civilians.[3] The initial use of the area as a military base was related to its proximity to the river dock, and the subsequent military presence continued, reusing existing infrastructure. Thus, for South Koreans, who experienced the oppression of the colonial period and subsequent Korean War, Yongsan became strongly associated with foreign military presence and unequal international power relations. Although the administration of the military base changed from Japanese to American, the area was stigmatized as a symbol of Korea's prolonged dependence on foreign power.

The continuous military presence from 1910 to the present has also resulted in the development of commercial interests and trade industries associated with military personnel. The illegal circulation of army supplies as well as American radio broadcasts generated a new economic structure in a country devastated by war. The existence of a US military post generated a new base town in Itaewon, populated by increasing numbers of migrants who settled in the area to benefit from trading with US soldiers. Korean souvenir shops with multiple English signs, groceries, and other convenience stores burgeoned in order to cater for the needs of the soldiers. The rising popularity of Korean singers performing at the base evidenced the quick spread of American pop culture in South Korean society (Choi, J.I., 2003). Aid from the US combined with state-led industrialization focusing on exports meant that goods were relatively abundant in Itaewon, even in the war-deprived economy of the country at the time. A severe food shortage in Korea and the abundance of American commercial goods contrasted sharply and created a sense of yearning for American culture in general. Scholars argue that the existence of US military bases resulted in 'South Korea's Americanization through the generation of desire to consume US goods as well as various forms of American pop culture' (Choi, J.I., 2003, p. 26).

Another effect of the base town was the arrival of an increasing number of jobless female migrants from rural areas who found employment in bars, nightclubs, and other adult entertainment venues for US soldiers. Contrary to the popular notion that the prostitutes in base towns were 'loose' women with expensive habits, most were driven to prostitution by dire poverty. Katherine H.S. Moon noted that most of the prostitutes were migrant women who moved from job to job, such as bus clippie and kitchen maid for well-to-do families, before ending up in the area called 'Hooker Hill' (Moon, K.H.S., 1997). While the South Korean government's attitude in past decades ranged from turning a blind eye to active management, sex workers in Hooker Hill were socially stigmatized and earned the derogatory nickname of 'Western princess [yang-gongju]'. The image of Itaewon thus became a symbol of US military superiority as well as of the adverse side effects in the form of commercial sex patronized by the American GIs.

Ironically, the presence of a foreign army base and the association of Itaewon with morally loose characters have contributed to the reputation of the place as a territory that could liberate South Korea from conventional social norms. Due to the proximity to the base and the presence of GIs, there was less presence of Korean law enforcement (Moon, K.H.S., 1997). This tendency was even stronger in the entertainment district, where the government consciously refrained from pursuing prosecution of certain forms of adult industries. The reduced presence of state control made room for new kinds of social experimentation. Many disgruntled Korean youths oppressed by the authoritarian regime of the 1960s and 1970s frequented bars and cafés in Itaewon where they could free themselves from the oppressiveness of their everyday experiences elsewhere (Kim, E.S., 2004). While men with long hair were prosecuted mercilessly by the military regime as signs of 'Western vice', they were relatively safer in Itaewon. Labelled as 'hippies' and 'a sign of threat to traditional customs' by the military dictatorship, young South Koreans became increasingly subjected to cultural censorship. However, the authoritarian regime's prohibition of certain folk songs and an intensive crackdown on rock cafés for narcotics served to underscore the transformative potential of the foreign culture. Although having a certain hairstyle or listening to a certain type of music does not necessarily indicate political dissent, furious reactions by the government were enough to mark participants as political resistors. Conceivably, the strong association of the so-called 'hippie culture' with the American civil rights movement in the 1960s was part of the reason behind the prohibitory measures. As the South Korean military regime often put a strict limit on social norms and acceptable behaviour, including enjoyment of American culture such as rock music, this signified a thirst for political freedom for many young adults.

The image of Itaewon as a liberating territory or 'free zone' gradually began to change beginning in the 1990s when the end of the Cold War was followed by a souring of the relationship between South Korea and the US. While the US remained a military ally of South Korea, it stopped playing the role of economic supporter when the South Korean economy began growing rapidly. The existing negative reputation of Itaewon became even stronger in the post-Cold War era when the economic benefits of the American army base began to be offset by detrimental elements. Criminal activities by American GIs, which were less discussed in previous regimes, became a hotly debated social issue as the result of democratization and the subsequent desire to address the negative externalities associated with the military dictatorship. Meanwhile, the economy generated by the Hooker Hill prostitution began to decline as prostitution to American GIs was not as lucrative as that catering for wealthy South Korean men (Moon, K.H.S., 1997). As many South Korean women stopped working in Hooker Hill, many establishments closed or substituted Korean sex workers with migrants from China and Southeast Asia (Gillem, 2007). The popular media's portrayal of Itaewon in the late 1990s focused on an area supposedly filled with 'binge parties with secret sex clubs and backstreet drug dealings' (Jung, J.O., 1999). Objections to the unequal nature of the SOFA (Status of Forces Agreement) coincided with the heightened media attention to misconduct of US soldiers. The tense relationship between the US military and the South Korean public meant that American cultural forms no longer presented a liberating potential. The portrayal of Itaewon as a 'Special Sex Zone' – a satirical twist on its official designation as a Special Tourist Zone – in an article accusing GIs of indecent behaviour, illustrates the souring relationship between Korea and the US (Shinyun, D.W., 2007). Reflecting the decreasing popularity of US military involvement in Korea both inside and outside the US, the Yongsan US army base near Itaewon is scheduled for relocation.

Emergence of Ethnic and Cultural Diversity in Itaewon

From the 1970s Itaewon began its transformation as the centre of a minority religion in South Korea. Construction of the first mosque in Korea (figure 5.2) in the southern part of Itaewon Street, established in 1976 with the aid of Muslim countries including Saudi Arabia, was one of the catalysts for development of the new religious community. In the 1970s, many South Korean workers started going abroad to Middle Eastern countries to work on construction projects. The importance of building amicable diplomatic relations with oil-producing countries was acknowledged when the South Korean regime donated the land in the 1970s for the construction of a mosque. In an interview, Hong, the imam of the Korean Muslim Federation, noted that although there was only a small Muslim population in Korea before the opening of the mosque, many joined the religion when 'people about to go to the Middle East came [here] to get cultural training about the Muslim way of life or even change their religion [to Islam]' (Hong, S.P., 2008, p. 111). In South Korea, the dominant religion is Buddhism, comprising about 48 per cent of those affiliated with a religious group, with Christians comprising about 20 per cent (Ministry of Culture, Sports, and Tourism, 2008).

Figure 5.2. Central Masjid in Itaewon, constructed in 1976, became a magnet that drew many Muslim immigrants to the area.

Although many workers who returned to South Korea changed back to their original religious beliefs, the construction of the mosque would have a lasting effect in Itaewon when Muslim immigrants came in increasing numbers.

After the Middle East oil boom, numbers of new immigrants from Southeast Asia and Africa increased steadily. There is no official data about the exact size of the Muslim population. However, Ahn Jong-guk, a professor of Middle Eastern Studies, estimates that there are about 137,000 Muslims living in Korea (Ahn, S.C., 2011). Due to the presence of a mosque and associated businesses, many decided to settle in Itaewon. The presence of the mosque led to the opening of many related businesses such as Muslim bookstores and halal grocery stores.[4] On Friday afternoons many Muslim residents in Itaewon as well as those who live elsewhere gather to participate in religious worship. In addition to the religious reason, relatively cheaper rents have enabled ethnic minorities and new migrants to settle in the area. Besides Southeast Asian immigrants, migrant workers from African countries, such as Nigeria and Ghana, became a significant minority population, comprising 16 per cent of foreign residents of the total population living in Itaewon 1 dong and 2 dong (Yongsan Gu Office, 2010).

The Muslim and African communities in the South Itaewon Street area have played a significant role in ameliorating the transition of migrants into South Korean society. For instance, in an interview with *Yonhap News*, one Nigerian male noted that it is much more convenient to buy goods in Itaewon, while the supermarkets in other cities 'often says [it is] not available' (Hwang, J.H., 2010). The presence of many shops, churches, and religious institutions provide African migrants with opportunities for networking. Similarly, Friday services provide Muslim migrants with the opportunity to meet and communicate with other members of their religion. According to Hong, Itaewon's Muslim community functions as a 'cultural refuge' in a foreign country, where the sharing of religious services and prohibitions becomes a way of 'reinforcing their cultural identity and emotional well being' (Hong, S.P., 2008, p. 52). In fact, one South Korean female who joined the religion after marrying a man from the Middle East noted that it is 'easier to discuss subjects like Ramadan and other religious taboos here than in other places since most South Koreans do not know about [them]'.[5]

On the other hand, the rise of 'Gay Hill' adjacent to what used to be Hooker Hill has become associated with the image of Itaewon as a free zone. The presence of Gay Hill appears to celebrate gay rights, while dingy and run-down Hooker Hill represents South Korea's embarrassing past. In the progressive South Korean media, gay bars are introduced together with other trendy bars and exotic restaurants, linking gay bars with the cosmopolitan tolerance of different lifestyles. While streets signs such as 'Transgender Club' (figure 5.3) proudly advertise the sexual orientation of their business clientele, older bars and clubs in Hooker Hill appealing to heterosexual males exude a less glamorous presence.

The rise of Gay Hill, however, does not represent the triumph of the gay rights

Figure 5.3. Nightclubs in Itaewon include 'Transgender Club' as well as a more conventional night club called 'Manhattan'.

movement, as many government policies fail to consider gay rights. Although South Korean society went through a democratization process in the late 1980s that significantly improved individual political rights, discussion of gay rights was excluded. What is more, the rising awareness of HIV in the late 1980s led the South Korean media and government to designate the gay population as potential 'disease carriers', which stigmatized the sexual minority. One *Hanguk Ilbo* article written in August of 1994 noted that 'homosexuality, unhygienic sex, and sexual promiscuity are the most apparent channels of distributing sexually transmitted diseases such as AIDS and amoebiasis' (Yu, J.S., 1994). Despite changes in the media and government documents' portrayal of the gay population influenced by the international and domestic gay rights movements, subtler forms of stigmatization persist. For instance, one study concluded that the routine distribution of free condoms by ISHAP (Ivan Stop HIV/AIDS Project), financially supported by the Ministry of Health and Welfare, constitutes 'reconfirmation of abnormality by the state' rather than a gesture to promote the health of the gay population (Kwak, S.Y., 2009, p. 98). In other cases, gay activists have observed that conditions in the Korean military, seemingly more tolerant with no cases of expulsion for revealing gay sexual identity, present bigger challenges. Unlike highly reported debates surrounding military policies in countries like UK and US, there is almost 'no public discussion', since 'there is no acknowledgement of the presence of the gay population in the military' (Solidarity for LGBT Human Rights of Korea and Chingusai, 2008, p. 63). Some South Koreans observe that Gay Hill in Itaewon is often associated with the social stereotypes of 'gays as excessive pleasure-seekers' in the minds of the heterosexual population (*Ibid.*, p. 85).

Given that public policy or discussion regarding gay rights is virtually non-existent, some degree of representation of gay culture in Itaewon is remarkable. Responding to negative portrayals of gays, many Korean gay rights and support groups, such as Chodonghoe and Kirikiri, were formed around university campuses in the early 1990s. Gay activists at Chingusai, a gay support group, are aware that places like Itaewon and

Jongro, where gay bars are visible, are among the only social spaces for gays although 'their official activities require keeping a certain distance from bars to promote "wholesome gay culture"' (Choi, S.U., 1996, p. 21). However, such self-policing practices ironically become another form of discrimination since heterosexual human rights activists do not feel the need to apply the same level of self-scrutiny as gay activists. At the same time, events like the Stonewall incident in New York showed that bars and other social places can become the birthplace for a gay liberation movement. In fact, despite the media portrayal of 'unwholesome activities' in Itaewon, many gays regard Itaewon as a 'safe haven' where their sexual identities are better protected than in other places. According to Eun-sil Kim (2004), a Professor of Women's Studies, the proliferation of gay bars and nightclubs in Itaewon was partly due to the area's reputation as the place where 'anything goes'. Despite the presence of a few gay bars in the Jongro area, many young gay men who disliked the exclusive and old-fashioned ambience of the old bars began to go to Itaewon instead (Cho, S.P., 2003). Thus, Itaewon became the symbol of a liberating place not just for heterosexual South Koreans but also for the gay community.

To summarize, the rise of sexual, ethnic, and religious minority cultures in Itaewon was the unexpected side effect of the absence of government policies regarding ethnic and sexual minorities rather than presence of policies. Although the case of the Muslim community may be regarded as an example of active efforts on the government's part, the state was primarily interested in its construction insofar as it functioned as a friendly gesture towards oil producing Middle Eastern countries. The subsequent formation of a Muslim immigrant community was the result of various factors, including cheap rents, ease of transportation, and the presence of a mosque. In the case of the gay bars in Itaewon, the government did not attempt crackdowns because of its proximity to the US army base and the culture of silence that surrounds the discussion of gay rights. Inadvertently, the unwillingness of the South Korea government to cause friction over the US army's presence and over the issues of gay rights contributed to the formation of the gay entertainment district.

Han-nam New Town Plan and 'Cultural Streets' in Itaewon

The decision to relocate the US army base (figure 5.4) was the result of prolonged discussion going back to 1987 when Korea's growing economic strength and military prowess rendered the presence of the US army in the capital less desirable. The location of the army base and amount of land it occupies (about 632 acres or 256 ha) have been noted in the South Korean media as 'the roadblock to urban development' (Yu, Y.W., 2001, p. 29). This is exacerbated by the low-density development of the base, including 'their own 18-hole golf course', compared to the rest of the over-crowded city (Moon, K.H.S., 1997, p. 31). According to Mark L. Gillem, while the defensive

Figure 5.4. The wall of Yongsan Garrison appears formidable with its 'Trespassing Prohibited' sign and barbed wire.

periphery of the base can be attributed to fundamental security concerns, the layout of residential and recreational space shows a desire to replicate lifestyles at home (Gillem, 2007). Not surprisingly, recent discussions of the relocation of the US army presented an opportunity for the city government to envision what could be done with such a vast empty piece of land. For instance, an article in *Chosun Ilbo* noted that different government departments 'came up with different suggestions according to their agenda, such as an international technology centre and a cultural/art centre' (Choi, W.S., 2002, p. 3). In addition to building new city offices there, the Seoul city government planned to construct Yongsan Minjok Park (Seoul Metropolitan City, 2006a). However as the relocation has been rescheduled from the original date of 2015, it is unclear exactly when it will now happen. In spite of this, there have been real estate speculations and heated talks about investing in urban infrastructure in Itaewon and Yongsan. However, as of 2015 the larger Yongsan Redevelopment Plan is stalled because of lack of funds. Yet there are expectations that the project may resume given that Park Guen Hye, the current President, has urged the Korail, one of the main supporters in the plan, to reconsider and negotiate further on the plan.

Itaewon-dong, where the vibrant multiethnic community is located, has been designated as the site of the New Town plan, put forward by the Seoul city government in 2003. The New Town is an urban redevelopment project with a focus on promoting

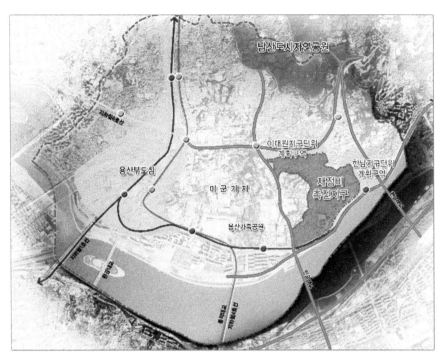

Figure 5.5. The Han-nam Redevelopment Plan shows areas designated as project sites. The dark area to the right, South Itaewon, is the primary target for redevelopment.

balanced growth among the different regions of Seoul. According to a policy document published by the Ministry of Construction and Transportation, it is a comprehensive plan that includes not only residential quarters, but also infrastructure such as parks, schools, roads, and other urban amenities. Initially, the project included three model districts, and later it encompassed twelve more districts, such as Yongsan Han-nam district, which includes Itaewon (figure 5.5). To imbue the area with a physically distinctive quality, the city of Seoul plans to build Green Hill, which includes Global Pavilion Park (figure 5.6), with thematic spaces dedicated to the representation of different foreign cultures. In addition, another schematic design called Ground 2.0 shows a plan to construct streets with low-rise commercial buildings punctuated by high-rise residential towers.

The appearance of diverse ethnic cuisine and stores did not go unnoticed in the popular media. In the case of Itaewon, a relatively high concentration of foreign residents and the presence of exotic cuisines have led many South Koreans to call the area 'multicultural'. For instance, the weekly newspaper *Jugan Hanguk* has observed that Itaewon presents a 'multicultural laboratory' (Park, W.J., 2009). In *Meeting the World in Itaewon*, a photojournalist book introducing various commercial venues and social organizations, Itaewon is portrayed as 'the Mecca of the world cuisines' (Moon, G.R., 2009, p. 197). Jang-gyu Chang, the former head of the Yongsan district office, has

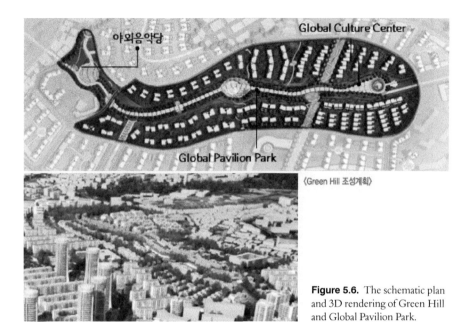

Figure 5.6. The schematic plan and 3D rendering of Green Hill and Global Pavilion Park.

mentioned Itaewon as the example of what multicultural policy is aiming for (Jon, G.W., 2010). Many multicultural festivals have been held in Itaewon, including the Itaewon World Village Festival in 2008. The media was quick to make the flippant observation that the place is the 'address number one of multicultural [representations]' (Lee, W.J., 2011, p. A16). Media discussions of Itaewon recognized its history of embedded meanings and changing cultural significance through consumption. However, such discussions did not question the construction of Itaewon primarily as a popular entertainment destination. Despite the largely benign descriptions of the Muslim community, most descriptions of the minority population stop short of complimenting the stylistic elegance of the mosque in contrast to the banal rows of seedy bars and other ubiquitous urban venues.

Urban planners have acknowledged the reputation of Itaewon for its 'multicultural streets' in various street design schemes related to the Han-nam New Town plan. With the designation of the Itaewon area as both a Special Tourist Zone and a Global Cultural Zone, administrative attention has centred on how to realign the eclectic development of various cultural elements. Many policy-makers regard existing commercial establishments catering for the foreign population as cultural assets. For instance, Keum Ki-yong, a researcher at the Seoul Development Institute, observed that 'Itaewon has the potential to become the most attractive tourist destination since there are diverse cultural forms introduced by foreigners' (Moon, G.R., 2009, p. 312). However, the remnants of entertainment industries developed in the Cold War era were identified as possible targets for elimination. According to a study conducted by

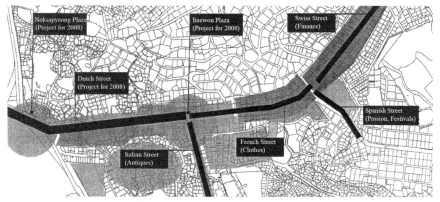

Figure 5.7. *Above*: Itaewon Redevelopment Plan; *below*: plan for Itaewon Street, showing a bus stop in the Design Seoul Streets plan.

the Seoul Development Institute, the weaknesses of the Special Tourist Zone include not only the concentration of 'unwholesome' activities but also 'chaotic and sometimes insanitary commercial structures as well as the lack of a well-organized shopping environment' (Seoul Development Institute, 2005). Responses from architects and city planners to such perceived weaknesses included schemes to group sections of streets into themes, thus giving them a more coherent and unified appearance. One such scheme called for the construction of multinational streets such as French Street and Italian Street on Itaewon Street (figure 5.7). In another project called Design Seoul Street Plan, a part of the Design Seoul campaign, Itaewon Street is depicted as a place with rows of brick buildings reminiscent of houses in Amsterdam (figure 5.7). The design schemes also include plans to expand roads as well as construct new roads penetrating into the existing urban fabric to alleviate traffic congestion.

Both the Han-nam New Town Plan and the Design Seoul Street Plan illustrate the theme of providing and caring for the residents, the principle of 'soft city' discourse. Phrases such as 'welfare' and 'well being' are used in project descriptions to emphasize the value of the emotional aspects of design. For instance, the official objective of the New Town Plan is described as ultimately constructing 'high-quality welfare residential environments fit for the twenty-first century' (Kim, B.I., 2003, pp. 65–66). Although the term 'welfare' is a misnomer in the sense that the project does not involve free provision of housing, the term is used in its literal meaning to indicate a general sense of wellbeing. Reflecting the changes in urban policy rhetoric, the four strategies of Design Seoul Street are described by the Seoul city government as 'emptying, integration, participation, and sustainability'.[6] The use of the word 'emptying' instead of 'demolition' comes across as poetic rather than forceful. Instead of constructing complicated structures characteristic of chaotic urban life, the project seeks to impress residents in an attempt to restore a sense of visual order.

At the same time, the media descriptions of 'multicultural streets' and design schemes to create themed streets were influenced by the 'multicultural policies' put forward by the central government. South Korea's demographic changes are partly a result of government policies taking place since the late 1990s, such as promoting the increasing flexibility of the labour market and relaxing regulations on marriage immigrations. With the start of the industrial trainee system implemented during Kim Young Sam's administration, an increasing number of unskilled workers from foreign countries were allowed into Korean workplaces (Seok, 2009). International marriages between Southeast Asian women and Korean men became common in the mid-2000s. Many scholars, including Kim Hyun-mi, have noted that the current 'multicultural' policies are highly selective, focusing on 'multicultural families', which reproduces a patriarchal system since the majority of international marriages are between foreign brides and South Korean men (Kim, H.M., 2008). At the same time, situating 'multicultural' policies only in terms of ethnicity poses a danger of dismissing diversity among ethnic Koreans.

Many policies supporting 'multicultural families' were designed and implemented in the 2000s. Following the policy recommendation, local governments began developing language programmes designed to facilitate foreign brides' acculturation and learning the Korean language. The Ga-pyong and Yang-pyong local governments put forward plans to provide financial aid of up to 10,000,000 won (US$10,000) for marriages between South Korean men and foreign brides (Kim, G.E., 2009, p. A27). At the same time, the Ministry of Law started recommending education programmes

Figure 5.8. Government multicultural campaign posters advertise the importance of diversity. The poster on the left reads 'everyone's different and precious'. The one on the right reads 'our little minds come together to make Korea warm'.

for South Korean men seeking to marry foreign brides in order to ameliorate the high divorce rate (Son, J.S., 2010, p. A10).

Many multicultural streets and festivals were designated, such as Ansan's Multicultural Street and Sorae Village. In Itaewon, Itaewon Global Village Festival was held in 2010. Although policy initiatives concentrated on education and training, the presence of many urban neighbourhoods with a high concentration of foreigners motivated studies of spatial strategies to help migrants integrate into Korean society. For instance, a series of studies titled *Reinventing Urban Policy in Response to Ethnic Diversity* were conducted by the Korean Research Institute for Human Settlement in 2009 and 2010 (Park, S.H. *et al.*, 2010).

However, celebratory remarks regarding 'multicultural Itaewon' have not been followed by concrete urban plans to prevent the deterioration in South Itaewon. The Han-nam New Town Project, scheduled to be constructed in South Itaewon, threatens the long-term viability of Itaewon's cultural and ethnic diversity by facilitating the gentrification process. It has already attracted many real estate investments, including one by the Samsung group (Choi, B.Y. and Song, H., 2010, p. B5). The design schemes for Itaewon's streets mentioned above stop short of treating the presence of diverse ethnic cuisines and shops as mere façades to attract tourists, rather than as vital social networking places for the community and as a sign of Itaewon's cultural diversity. The current discussions of Itaewon as a multicultural space overlook the past and present political and cultural struggles that sexual and religious minority groups face even in the era of a 'multicultural society'.

Han-nam New Town and Gentrification

The southern part of Itaewon represents one of the last remaining neighbourhoods not affected by the numerous urban redevelopment projects of Seoul from the 1980s onwards. As such, it retains earlier subdivisions and old buildings that contribute to the run-down appearance of the district. The homes in the southern part of the street are run-down row houses with steep and narrow stairways (figure 5.9). The availability of smaller apartments was another factor which contributed to the settlement of immigrants with little money. In a TV interview, Kim Jaeyong, an immigrant from Bangladesh living in Itaewon, noted that the Korean system of *jeon-se* is too expensive for people with no significant savings.[7] In addition to the already dilapidated conditions, the announcement of the New Town plan halted repairs or renovation of the existing houses in the expectation of demolition. The designation of the area as a New Town Plan site has generated speculative investments that have driven many local businesses and landowners to move out of the area. At the same time, the rapid flow of migrant workers in search of cheaper rents initiated the transformation of the area's demographic. With the proportion of rental housing in the project area as high

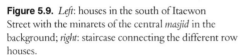

Figure 5.9. *Left*: houses in the south of Itaewon Street with the minarets of the central *masjid* in the background; *right*: staircase connecting the different row houses.

as 67 per cent, many new immigrants easily found rental housing in this area while older South Korean residents moved out (Kang, J.J., 2004, p. 29). What is notable is that this demographic change was not initiated by racial or ethnic prejudices but by the anticipated government-led urban redevelopment project, which was first announced in 2004.

Ironically, the very condition that enabled the formation of the minority community is also threatening to drive that community out of the area. The unwillingness of Korean residents to open business provided opportunities for migrant businesses but impending demolition makes their presence fragile and temporal. The proposed project does not include a plan to incorporate existing low-income residents or retain the small businesses that make the streets of Itaewon 'multicultural'. Insuk Yoon, a committee chair of the NGO Dosi Yondae, pointed out that the current New Town Project is focused on the place rather than the residents, and that it seeks to 'replace the current residential area with middle-class residences' (Yoon, I.S., 2004, p. 130). Despite the political rhetoric of 'multiculturalism' and the need to develop 'cultural streets', urban redevelopment projects contradict the principle of building a multicultural society. The most pervasive and problematic aspect remains the token multi-cultural slogans that call for inclusive cultural attitudes while neglecting the practical needs of immigrants, such as the need for adequate housing and education. The implementation of the Han-nam New Town Redevelopment Plan would displace a vibrant multiethnic community while providing an artificial 'global park'. It is contradictory to pursue the place-marketing strategy with a 'selling point' of cultural diversity while on the other hand the preconditions for the presence of such diversity are being destroyed.

Even for South Korean shop tenants who possess some capital to pay a security deposit and other fees, redevelopment projects have devastating effects. Although the foreign residents in Itaewon account for more than 10 per cent of the population, South Korean nationals remain the majority.[8] According to Lee, a branch director of Sharing and Future, a social business group focusing on low-income housing, the compensation given to shop tenants in another site in Yongsan District 4 was not enough for them to open new businesses elsewhere in Seoul although the redevelopment is predicted to bring much profit overall (Lee, J.W., 2009, pp. 22–28). The compensation given to tenants cannot cover the premium fee (*gwon-ri-gum*) customarily required for 'good business spots' but not formally acknowledged in legal documents. Although the compensation given by the city government includes the security deposit, the premium (which can be much more than the deposit) is not included. Cases of conflicts between soon-to-be evicted shop tenants and the local city government have been widely covered by the South Korean media in incidents like the Yongsan Catastrophe. The scuffle between the demolition force and the residents of the building scheduled for bulldozing became intense and resulted in several deaths.[9] The incident highlighted the adverse effects arising from the city's fast-track redevelopment process and the excessive use of police force.

Given the unlikelihood of recovering costs, the number of Korean tenants decreased sharply in the South Itaewon area designated for the Han-nam New Town project. However, foreign migrants continued to open businesses in Itaewon after leaseholders temporarily stopped requiring payment of the premium to foreigners in less-than-prime locations (Hong, S.P., 2008, p. 114). Although such measures help migrant businesses settle in Itaewon without worries about recovery of the cost, they also pose the danger of driving them out more easily since the government can simply pay them compensation. Alternative locations that the new immigrant businesses would be able to afford are very limited, since the occupation of 'good business spots' required the payment of a premium which can be very steep, sometimes as much as three to four times the deposit. At the same time, residents living in substandard rental units are required either to pay market rate or move out. In the current New Town scheme, there is no mention of preserving the current ethnic and cultural diversity, which unexpectedly burgeoned during the decades of urban development. Another news article dealing with redevelopment observed that the huge scale of the current redevelopment plan – which involves the relocation of thousands of residents – makes it structurally impossible to reach an agreement or consensus (Hong, W.S., 2009). In the impending demolition of a viable community, the design schemes to construct themed streets are viewed by residents and shop owners as typical 'armchair arguments' without consideration of real life conditions.[10]

The inequality that existed between American GIs and South Korean migrant women in the 1960s has disappeared with rapid urbanization and modernization. However, another set of inequalities continues to shape the contemporary experiences of migrant workers living in Itaewon. Despite celebratory media remarks about

Muslim communities in Itaewon, the lack of a consistent urban policy directed at a 'multicultural society' threatens to destroy the existing neighbourhood. Given the absence of discussions regarding housing problems on the south side of Itaewon, the urban landscapes of Itaewon have become akin to what Mike Davis has called 'fortress landscape' in the case of Los Angeles (Davis, 1990). Massive walls of houses on the north side of Itaewon Street are reminiscent of the defensive design of the Yongsan Garrison nearby. With extremely high walls and security posts, the neighbourhood has become an island of the rich separated from the south side by the rows of shops on Itaewon Street. The redevelopment of existing commercial streets poses the danger of facilitating the gentrification process already underway. Various 'multicultural' festivals and street events become one-off, random shows of benevolence rather than generating a significant re-examination of structural inequalities.

Conclusion

This chapter has examined how urban policies have shaped the development of communities of ethnic and sexual minorities in Itaewon. Although past government policies were not directed at promoting cultural diversity, they inadvertently contributed to the formation of an immigrant community and a gay entertainment district. On the other hand, the current policy promoting a 'multicultural society' fit for the global era fails to make an impact at the spatial level when urban redevelopment projects threaten to demolish low-income neighbourhoods. Despite the celebration of 'globalization' and 'multicultural' street events, such efforts stop short at tokenism when bigger economic issues such as housing conditions are not addressed. In this process of remaking Itaewon's streets, less well-off residents are silently eliminated from the larger picture. Although the process of gentrification is driven by economic forces, the end result follows the ethnic line since only migrant workers are settling in the area set out to be redeveloped. Ironically, the establishment of an ethnic minority community was predicated upon its eventual destruction. The case of Itaewon demonstrates the complex process where the conventional definition of 'the other' is being remade in the economic logic of globalization.

So far this book has examined four urban redevelopment sites in Seoul. In the first two chapters, the theme of rediscovering the Korean 'tradition' was analyzed in relation to the city government's efforts to transform Seoul from an industrial city to a post-industrial 'soft city'. Continuing with the larger theme of Korea's globalization drive and the reactions to policy changes, the second two chapters focused on the heterogeneity and changing demography in urban environments. Whether by emphasizing the rediscovery of Korean heritage or newly formed multiethnic towns, all the sites designated as global zones reflect the urban transformations of the capital city in the era characterized by the successful democratic movement and the slowing rate of economic growth. These chapters have illustrated how the concept of constructing a 'soft city' through urban design has been received and challenged by residents and NGOs. In the concluding chapter, I reflect on the implications of urban projects in the previously analyzed sites and how they cast light on the future studies of Asian cities aspiring to achieve the status of a 'global city'.

Notes

1. Attempts to relocate the US army base in Yongsan elsewhere have been made several times. Relocation was first suggested by President Roh in an election campaign in 1987 and later became the official policy. The project was re-initiated in 2002 and an agreement was signed by the Korean and US governments in October 2004.
2. The plan to redevelop the larger Yongsan area, including Yongsan International Business District, fell through in March 2013 when the Korail and Lotte Tour Development, the two main companies behind the project, reported lack of funds. Currently negotiations are underway, with a possibility of the project resuming.
3. From the official website of US Army Garrison-Yongsan, http://yongsan.korea.army.mil.
4. From the official website of the Korean Muslim Federation, http://www.koreaislam.org.
5. Interview, 19 May 2009.
6. From the Official Blog of the Seoul City Government, http://blog.seoul.go.kr/.
7. KBS2TV *Gamsong DaKyu Mijisu* [*Documentary of the Unknown*], broadcast 27 February 2010. Jeon-se is a kind of lease system unique in South Korea. Instead of monthly rents, a tenant pays a lump sum deposit for a year or two. After the end of the lease, the tenant receives the full deposit back. The landlord, in turn, can re-invest the money and recover the cost thanks to a high interest rate. The amount of the deposit varies from place to place. It can range from 20–30 per cent of the market value of the property to 80 per cent, depending on the availability of housing.
8. According to the Korean Statistical Information Service, of the 18,777 resident population in Itaewon 1 and Itaewon 2 dong, about 1,800 are foreigners.
9. The Yongsan Catastrophe was the violent clash on 20 January 2009 between the tenants of a building in Yongsan and the police and agents of the demolition company.
10. In *Itaewon ehsoh Segyerul Mannada* [*Itaewon: Gateway to the World*], Sukcheon Hong, a bar owner and well-known gay celebrity in South Korea, noted that the approach of the city government is cursory at best (see Moon, G.R., 2009).

Conclusion:
Going Beyond the Cultural City

Seoul is a global city, whose political economy is closely linked to the global economic system. To be sure, one could argue that almost all cities today are global. However, the continuous evocation of the global status of cities like Seoul, seen in terms of the rhetoric of urban development, reveals that being global is a relative concept, as some cities are more global than others. New Yorkers tend not to be concerned about the global status of their city since they can take it for granted. In the case of Seoul, the city has begun to shift from being a global production site, as it aspires to becoming a global site of consumption.

In Bukchon and Insadong, the prevailing rationale behind the recent physical changes in the sites was their perceived crisis of cultural identity owing to past development practices. Proponents of current urban projects considered proposals that were carried out under the developmental regime as underestimating non-economic values such as emotional ties to place and environmental protection. The implementation of village-scale remodelling in Bukchon (North Village) was largely due to the sense of an identity crisis caused by the disappearance of the traditional Korean houses known as *hanoks*. As many urban *hanoks* were demolished to make way for new construction, villagers and city officials felt the need to preserve those remaining, and promoted the construction of new *hanoks* in the neighbourhood in the hope of preserving the traditional architectural and cultural context of the site. While the success of the Bukchon Regeneration Project had the effect of shedding new light on, and renewing interest in, traditional house forms, it also brought about the gentrification of the area and a significant change in neighbourhood character from that of a quiet residential setting to a popular tourist site. The construction of new *hanoks* and maintenance of those remodelled is expensive, and requires investment of time and effort. Living in a *hanok* has become a status symbol among middle-aged and older Koreans. What started out as an effort to rediscover Korean cultural tradition has become a way to display social capital, and to accumulate wealth through new means of investment. While *hanoks* come in a wide range of styles, most of those remodelled in

Bukchon and elsewhere in South Korea are tiled-roof, literati-style, which have elitist connotations. These *hanoks* have become symbols of authority, power, and wealth. While the term '*hanok*' invokes a vernacular tradition in the minds of many Koreans, most of the remodelled *hanoks* in Bukchon are far from vernacular, as they are designed and built by professionals, which drives up their construction costs.

Similarly, streets in Insadong have become a target for change due to the sense of crisis which involves the cultural identity of the place. Many have said that Insadong has lost its urban character since its designation as a Car-Free Zone. Experts consider the physical changes that came with the Car-Free Zone harmful to Korean cultural tradition. With younger crowds, and more recently with an influx of international tourists, in the streets, many worry that the area has lost its 'traditional' ambience since many shops and vendors cater for the cultural tastes of the younger generation and foreigners. The Car-Free Zone was designed to promote pedestrian use of the city, and this change alone did not bring about a loss of place-based identity. However, the narrow definition of tradition employed by critics hindered the area's traditional spontaneous use of space. Challenging the criticisms of the Car-Free Zone, this book has shown that changes to Insadong's urban landscape started much earlier, when an encroachment of corporate office buildings resulted from the redevelopment plan established in the 1970s.

While some of Seoul's global zones were redeveloped with the intention of promoting a leisurely appreciation of Korea's cultural traditions, others, where there was less sense of pre-industrial heritage, were redesigned to fit the fast-paced metropolitan culture, with development interventions on a much larger scale. For instance, Dongdaemun Market, another global zone, is being turned from a national garment production centre into a 'global fashion centre', to borrow the rhetoric of the Seoul Development Institute. The success of a few entrepreneurs in the Dongdaemun Market in the late 1990s, widely discussed in the mass media during the period of structural adjustment, has led to the construction of many high-rise fashion malls whose lots are rented by individual shop owners. With the increasing number of international tourists in the area, many attracted by *Hallyu*, the Korean Wave, there is an expectation amongst many people that more economic growth will follow. The construction of Dongdaemun Design Plaza (DDP), designed by Zaha Hadid on the site of the former Dongdaemun Stadium, represents the culmination of expectations shared by local merchants and city government officials. Yet, as this book has illustrated, such expectations are not always met, and many lots remain empty years after the completion of these shopping malls. The visual spectacle created by monumental buildings and mega shopping malls thus disguises the possible risks faced by those who strive to become successful entrepreneurs.

Other global zones, including Itaewon, also represent the promotion of a fast-paced metropolitan culture. In Itaewon, a mix of foreign and Korean cultural traditions is portrayed as the most attractive characteristic of the area. For instance, the presence of different exotic cuisines and ethnic groups has been hailed as evidence of its 'global' status. As many ethnic restaurants and bistros have opened in the area, Itaewon is considered a chic and hip party place among the younger generations. The plans to establish 'foreign themed streets' build on these perceptions. This urban image is largely due to particular conditions such as the US/South Korea military alliance, which has prevented strict state surveillance of civic activities. Yet, various urban schemes to promote foreign streets do not take into consideration the structural inequality that exists in the Itaewon area. On the one hand, certain parts of Itaewon have become a posh upper-class residential area, as foreign consuls and diplomats settled there, enjoying the sense of security provided by the presence of the US army base. On the other hand, the relative lack of government surveillance facilitated the rise of an entertainment district and compact inner-city dwellings. More recently, immigrants from Southeast Asia and Africa have started to live near Itaewon, where Seoul's first mosque is located. The living conditions of the lower-income groups have been deteriorating, while the wealthy have built fortress-like houses. Although the Yongsan Redevelopment Plan has been temporarily halted, the area is going through a phase of gentrification, which can only be furthered by the implementation of plans to establish artificial themed streets.

The case studies discussed thus far represent an effort to reposition Seoul and adjust its global status from that of a global production centre to a consumption-oriented metropole. Transforming Seoul into a 'global city' involves simultaneous processes of rediscovering the traditional and redesigning the modern. On the one hand, rediscoveries of lost aesthetics, such as Bukchon's *hanoks*, have become a sign of sophistication and cultural maturity. Despite a seemingly powerful notion of tradition, not all forms of tradition have lent themselves to projects of preservation and protection. Rather, the process of defining 'Korean tradition' is a highly selective and political one. In Bukchon, and other currently ongoing *hanok* village projects, a majority of buildings now are literati-style tiled-roof *hanoks*; other types of vernacular house have not been preserved or reconstructed. This selective process of preservation and rediscovery stems partly from Korea's colonial history. For instance, the 'rediscovery' of the old city wall in Dongdaemun Market illustrates that suppressing colonial traces and restoring a form of cultural heritage dating from before the colonial period has become very important. Similarly, the recent discovery of (and uproar against) Insadong's colonization by international coffee chains and made-in-China souvenirs cannot be understood outside the convoluted colonial history of the area, including illegal sales of national artefacts and political demonstrations against the Japanese colonial administration.

Yet the selective process of preservation cannot be explained solely by anti-colonial sentiments, since traces of 'modern history' after the colonial era have also become targets of demolition and redesign. The redesign of the modern involves the abandonment of heritage and more recently built structures. Considering that many residents of Seoul regard the Dondaemun Sports Stadium as an important cultural heritage, the fact that it was originally built by the Japanese colonial administration seemed less important to sports fans. Yet, the more modern associations of the stadium were under-estimated by policy-makers. Similarly, the history of the alternative cultural movement has been ignored in Itaewon, while the emergence of hip commercial establishments is celebrated as one of the advantages of having foreign-themed streets. In these sites, urban cultural forms are subsumed in the theme of a continuous project of economic growth and development.

Throughout the case studies discussed here, redesigning urban environments has been included under the rubric of creating 'cultural spaces'. In cultural city discourse, what are thought to be forms of tradition become essential aspects of urban culture. The spectacular commercial success of shopping malls in the Dongdaemun Market during the Asian financial crisis contributed to the belief that continuous material growth is possible, but only if urban developments take account of factors other than efficiency, such as 'culture', into consideration. Urban projects that promote Itaewon as a Special Tourism Zone involve redesigning the character of the space from a national to a global one by tapping into the presence of the ethnic shops and restaurants that sprang up as a result of the increased transnational movements of labour. In Dongdaemun and Itaewon, urban planners and policy-makers emphasized the need to build urban amenities that offered comfort and space for emotional relaxation. In addition to promoting sales of commercial items, they argue that the provision of 'cultural spaces' such as museums and exhibition spaces is important for urban dwellers. Policy-makers and planners argue that currently barren and harsh urban environments, focused on maximum returns on investment with a minimal allocation of space, can only be reformed through the supply of more open urban space.

Interestingly, the government's appropriation of cultural practices to promote economic accumulation has inadvertently invited political discussions regarding what constitutes urban culture and 'cultural space'. In the case of Dongdaemun and Insadong, appropriations of the government's project by independent artists and the grassroots community have given rise to new interpretations, showing that the state's clientelist approach will be questioned and challenged when more pressing local concerns are not addressed. As the humorous twists of the Design Seoul posters by the FF Group show, not all South Koreans agree with the definition of 'cultural space' articulated in urban renaissance projects. Whereas urban planners and policy-makers applaud the construction of Dongdaemun Culture and History Park as evidence of balanced growth, artists have depicted the structure as just another boring monument that will soon be demolished. Street vendors selling souvenirs in Insadong have questioned the rigid division between 'authentic stores' and 'vendors selling fake souvenirs' by noting that even the established antique stores sell products with made-in-China labels.

The architectural projects carried out in global zones and other areas in Seoul suggest that the city has indeed undergone considerable cultural change. Many transformations in the urban fabric of the city since the 1980s reflect a changing urban culture, including the emphasis on a pedestrian-friendly environment and the emotional satisfaction of inhabitants and visitors. At the same time, the celebration of differences in certain global zones like Itaewon is a sign that people in Seoul are more open to lesser-known foreign cultural traditions than before. This shows that Seoul's urban culture has diversified significantly since political democratization, and that the city has gone through another phase of globalization. Some of the ruptures in its urban culture include increasing divisions within groups that shared more or less common objectives under the developmentalist regime. The division within the group of historical experts in Bukchon regarding what deserves to be preserved shows that there is no consensus even among those who participate in urban renaissance projects. At the same time, members of NGOs seemingly promoting the preservation of cultural traditions also take part in flexible accumulation by reaping profits through land sales. The proliferation of quasi-governmental NGOs in South Korea raises questions regarding the distinction between the state and civil society. The intersections between the cultural and economic aspects of development projects have made it extremely difficult to pinpoint precisely the motives and desires behind the actions of a given group. Alternative forms of expression of political dissent continue, albeit generating much controversy. Rather than taking the overly simplistic view of globalization as either a top-down or a from-below process, I conclude that the reciprocal relationship between the state's global ambitions and the concerns of local inhabitants has done much to shape South Korean urban and suburban environments.

Yet there are continuities alongside the ruptures. The more recent urban redevelopment projects carried out in global zones under the theme of making a 'Culture City' share a commonality with past projects carried out under the developmentalist regime of the 1970s. The objective of both is the manipulation of the physical environment – whether they are traditional houses or foreign-themed streets – to promote regional economic growth. Whether Seoul was envisioned as a centre of production or of consumption, the urban development projects all treated the physical environment as a generator of economic growth rather than challenging the actual model of growth. In terms of spatial practices, less conspicuous yet meaningful articulations of Seoul's cultural streets have come from those who continued the understated spatial traditions by using public space as a stage for various political and social issues. Despite the narrative of loss prevalent in the discussions of Insadong's chaotic urban development, the presence of political activism on the main street suggests the existence of an historical commonality despite the appearance of disorder and cacophony. By drawing a parallel between the street activities of the present and past forms of civic movement, this study has illustrated how the less prominent forms of tradition continue to shape urban experiences. Where there is no causal relationship between the historical anti-colonial movements and the current political movement, both spatial practices are examples of resistance against the generalizing tendency of the dominant urban discourse of the time.

Continuous negotiations regarding what constitutes 'cultural spaces' in contemporary South Korea show that the battle over who defines culture is far from over. Although political strategies of achieving accumulation have diversified, grassroots resistance has emerged as a result of ever-changing socio-economic structures associated with globalization. Which cultural representations are appropriate for urban spaces in general remains an open question. As indicated by former President Lee's campaign speech, quoted in the introduction to this book, the processes of globalization have indeed brought threats as well as opportunities for South Koreans, partly in terms of the role that they should play in redevelopment projects. However, what are considered threats for some are considered opportunities for others. Disagreements about whether a given change in an urban environment is desirable or not are expressed in very different ways, depending on whether the change is perceived as a threat or not. At the same time, unexpected outcomes may result in an overly competitive and efficiency-seeking urban condition hostile to the development of a deep sense of community. Korean-Russian businesses in Dongdaemun and Muslim and gay communities in Itaewon have sprung up due to increasingly rapid movements of labour and capital. The elusive nature of the processes of globalization can make a certain group of people feel simultaneously vulnerable and empowered.

In June 2011, Park Won Soon, a new mayor of Seoul was elected, and he was re-elected in 2014, defeating the candidate from the ruling Saenuri Party. Since the President of South Korea was then from the ruling Saenuri Party, election of Park signalled a possible division between the policy direction at the national level and the city government level. Discussing large-scale urban redevelopments, Park has drawn a line between himself and former Mayor Oh by criticizing the construction of Dongdaemun Design Plaza and Park (DDPP) as a typical case of focusing on 'display', and an example of budgetary waste at the hands of the city government. During his administration, Seoul city government has embarked on various welfare projects, including the provision of free school lunches for every student. His election pledges included making Seoul pedestrian-friendly, and the construction of vegetable gardens in schools. Tellingly, the reuse of modern and contemporary monuments, instead of demolition and reconstruction, has become one of his policy objectives. Some scholars, like Myungrae Cho (2014), a professor at Dankook University, have noted that this represents a fundamental shift in Seoul city government's approach to urban development. According to Cho, the urban projects planned during Mayor

Park's administration are centred on community welfare and safety, rather than economic growth. The hope is that Seoul will become simultaneously global and vernacular. Instead of large-scale urban renewals that require large-scale relocations, his regeneration projects will be focused on small areas of the city, with residents' prior approval. Also, instead of reckless urban renewal, efforts will be made to reuse existing structures. For instance, the establishment of the 2030 Seoul Plan included the preservation of older heritages such as Seoul's historic city walls, and modern monuments such as the Saewoon Arcade, constructed in the 1960s.

Many residents who support Mayor Park's policies are hopeful that Seoul will become more liveable as a result. In one project, the Jangsu Village Project, creating a global vernacular city is imagined as a participatory project involving various civic organizations. Jangsu Village is located in the Seongbuk district of Seoul, near the historic city wall. The project is aimed at continuing to provide existing residents in the area with housing, while also providing them comfortable living environments. The project includes repairing deteriorated buildings, installing better street lights, and replacing of old sewer pipes. A notable change from previous urban projects is that while the project goal includes the preservation and re-use of the historical wall, it aims to do so while maintaining the current village community. The labour force needed for the project is expected to be provided from residents of the village, making it self-sufficient and participatory. The cost of the project, about 3,211 million won (about US$2.9 million), is supported entirely by Seoul city government.

It is too early to conclude that the urban projects carried out during Mayor Park's term will fulfil their promises. The progressive projects planned by him and his advisors may not bring about what they were meant to accomplish, due to pre-existing economic conditions and unanticipated side effects. The differences in the policy directions of the city government and central government may result in confusions or contradictory practices. It is uncertain whether the urban redevelopment of Seoul will affect the ways residents and visitors experience the city. Despite efforts to sustain vernacular heritage and everyday practices, many such attempts also prove to be short-lived, or appropriated by others with different aims in mind. For instance, Hong Kal (2011) has raised the interesting question whether the critical activities of grassroots arts communities, like the use of urban agriculture, may become just another form of spectacle in a neoliberal context. In other words, the ambiguities inherent in the urban development process can bring unexpected outcomes. Just as spectacles of neoliberalism can be appropriated by artist groups like the FF Group, the art projects that provide a social critique of mega-scale urban developments may become another tool of domination.

The objective of the urban projects discussed in this book, that of remaking Seoul's physical landscape to suit the image of Seoul as a global city, has been only partially fulfiled. For instance, the project of rediscovering a traditional ambience through remodelling traditional houses and streets has succeeded in renewing interest in traditional urban forms, but it has not resulted in a thoughtful re-examination of the way traditional built forms are produced. Similarly, the redesign of the modern has succeeded in introducing interesting architectural elements to certain parts of Seoul, but it could not challenge the modernist idea of technical rationality and the faith in economic growth generated by manipulation of the built environment.

This book has examined various spatial practices in Seoul that have either resisted or contributed to the city's globalization. While it has explored only certain sites in Seoul, many of the conditions that have contributed to the city's urban transformation have also affected the efforts of other Asian cities to take the title of 'global city'. It is my hope that this work will lead to further academic discussions on global spatial manifestations and the experiences of other cities in this regard. There is no such thing as a complete success or a complete failure. Ironically, ambitious undertakings – of the state, the city government, or the residents themselves – towards achieving recognition as a 'global city' can be taken as the evidence that they are still not yet considered as such. Cities like Seoul are sites of diverse manifestations of the project of being global. It is the unpredictable course of urban transformation that makes a city simultaneously different from and similar to the rest of the world.

References

Ahn, C.M. (2010) Yeouido's isolation and development in the process of urbanization of Seoul. *Hankukdoshiseoulgye Hakhoeji*, **11**(5), pp. 53–68.

Ahn, S.C. (2011) Hanguk ui Muslim ulmana duina? [How many Muslims are there in Korea?]. *Hankyoreh Newspaper*, 16 May.

Ahn, S.H. (1994) Hanguk Gungaeguk eh Michin Rusia Munhak gwa Yonguk ui Yonghyang eh Gwanhan Yongu [A Study of Korean Modern Drama influenced by Russian Literature and Drama]. MS thesis, Dankook University.

Alcoff, L. (1991/1992) The problem of speaking for others. *Cultural Critique*, **20**, pp. 5–32.

AlSayyad, N. (ed.) (2001) *Consuming Tradition, Manufacturing Heritage: Global Norms and Urban Forms in the Age of Tourism*. London: Routledge.

AlSayyad, N. (ed.) (2004) *The End of Tradition?* London: Routledge.

American Friends Service Committee (1970) *The Peace Market*. Philadelphia, PA: American Friends Service Committee.

Atkins, E.T. (2010) *Primitive Selves: Koreana in the Japanese Colonial Gaze, 1910–1945*. Berkeley, CA: University of California Press [Kindle DX Version].

Bae, J. (2007) Seoul Gongpyong Guyok Dosim Jaegaebal Daehyong Gonchukmul ui Ttuksong eh Gwanhan Yongu [A Study of Large-Scale Commercial Buildings in Gongpyong Urban Redevelopment in Downtown Seoul]. MS thesis, University of Seoul.

Bae, U.K. (2008) Cha Upnun Gori Sa-up Yihu Insadong Gyongwan Byonghwa [The Change in Urban Scenes of Insadong after the Implementation of the Car-free Zone] *Insadong 10 Nyon (1998–2007): Pyongga wa Jongmang* [*Ten Years of Insadong (1998–2007): Evaluation and Prospects*]. Paper presented at the Hanguk Gyonggwan Hyopuihoe Symposium, Seoul, 13 May.

Baek, S. (2007) *Bukchon Jiyuk e Jokhaphan Munhwa Gwangwang* [*A Culture and Tourism Programme Suitable for Bukchon*]. Seoul: Seoul Development Institute.

Broward, J. (2009) Korea at the tipping point of a multicultural society. *Korea Times*, 12 November.

Byon, G.H. (nd) Min-no, Insadong gŏriyŏnsŏl 1-chŏn-myŏng mol-ryŏh [A thousand people gathered for the DLP's Insadong street speech]. Available at: http://www. redian.org/news/articleView.html?idxno=10798.

Castells, M. (2000) *The Rise of the Network Society*. Oxford: Blackwell.

Caprio, Mark (2009) *Japanese Assimilation Policies in Colonial Korea: 1910–1945*. Seattle, WA: University of Washington Press.

Chang, P.U. (1996) *Han'guk Minga ŭi Chiyŏkjŏk Chŏn'gae [A Regional Study of Folk Houses in Korea]*. Seŏul Tŭkpyŏlsi: Pojinjae.

Chang, Y., Seok, H.H. and Baker, D.L. (eds.) (2009) *Korea Confronts Globalization*. London: Routledge.

Chatterjee, P. (2004) *The Politics of the Governed: Reflections on Popular Politics in Most of the World*. New York: Columbia University Press.

Cho, B.H. (1999) *88 Seoul Olympic ui gwangwang-e daehan yonghyang yongu [A Study of the Influence of the 88 Seoul Olympics on Tourism]*. Seoul: Korea Tourism Development Institute.

Cho, H.R. (2005) The Change of Labor Regime after 1987 in South Korea. Visiting Fellow Working Papers 19, Cornell University ILR School, 2005. Available at: http://digitalcommons.ilr.cornell.edu/intlvf/19.

Cho, H.S. (2007) The most beautiful house in the world, in Sanghae Lee *et al.* (eds.) *Hanok e Saroriratta [Let's Live in Hanoks]*. Seoul: Dolbaegae.

Cho, H.Y. (2001) Jonghapjok simin-undong ui gujojok song-gyok gwa byonhwa jonmang eh daehan yongu: chamyoh yondaerul jongsim uro [A Study of the structural characteristics of general civil movements and prospect of improvement: with a focus on *chamyoh yondae*] in Yu, P.M. and Kim, J.H. (eds.) *Simin Sahoe wa Simin Undong 2: Saero-un Jipyong ui Ttamsek [The Civil Society and Civil Movement 2: The Search for New Horizon]*. Seoul: Hanwul.

Cho, I.S. (2008) Current State of North Village's Preservation – Bukchon 2001–2008 Hanok Residence and Beautification. Paper presented at Monthly Seminar of the Korean Association of Architectural History, Seoul, October.

Cho, J.B. (2003) The Transformation of Urban Architectural Regulatory System and Urban Tissue in Bukchon Area, Seoul. PhD Dissertation, University of Seoul.

Cho, J.S. and Kim, N.J. (2002) Insadong ui mulijok simlijok image ui pyongga. [An evaluation on the physical and psychological image of Insadong]. *Hanguk Jokyung Hakhoeji [Journal of the Korean Institute of Landscape Architecture]*, **91**, pp. 12–22.

Cho, M.R. (2004) Shinsangryuchŭng ŭi bangju rosŏh ŭi Gangnam [Gangnam as an ark of the new power elite]. *Hwanghae Munhwa*, **42**, pp. 25–40.

Cho, S. (2005) Jontong ui munhwa gonggan Bukchon: Seoul ui uhje wa ohnul gurigo hanguk ui miga yigot eh [The cultural space of tradition: 'Bukchon' of Seoul yesterday and today, the beauty of Korea is all here…], *Weekly Hankook*, **2077**, pp. 6–25.

Cho, S.G. (2006) *Hanguk ŭi Minga [The Folk Houses of Korea]*. Paju: Hanul Akademi.

Cho, S.P. (2003) The Body Politics of Korean Gay Men in Gay Consumer Places. Master's Thesis, Yonsei University.

Choi, B.Y. and Song, H. (2010) Samsung dokbuneh ttunun Itaewon Comme des Garconsgil. [Itaewon's Comme des Garcons Street becomes popular thanks to Samsung]. *Chosun Ilbo*, 1 September.

Choi, H.Y. (2003) Insadong cha upnun gori toyo-yil oh-hu kaji hwak-dae [Expanding the Car-free Zone to Saturday afternoons]. *Chosun Ilbo*, 12 June, A12.

Choi, J.H. (2004) Chang Up-ja ui Anmok Gaebal [Developing a taste for small business starters]. *Mk Chang Up*. Available at: http://changup.mk.co.kr/.

Choi, J.I. (2003) A Study of Americanization in the Space of Itaewon. MS thesis, Seoul National University.

Choi, J.S. (2009) *Seoul Moonhwa Sulrae. [A Pilgrimage to Seoul's Cultural Sites]*. Seoul: Sonamoo.

Choi, S.U. (1996) Analysis of the Discourse of a Korean Gay Movement. MS thesis, Seoul National University.

Choi, W.S. (2002) Yongsan migungji om-gin jari-en daegyumo minjok-gongwon josong 5 manpyong en sichungsa dulohsoh. [A large scale *minjok* park to be constructed on the site, city offices will occupy 50,000 pyong area]. *Chosun Ilbo*, 21 January, p. 3.

Choi, Y.J. (2007) Pungmul sangin, yagoo fan koom ul hohmulda. [Torn down, the dream of baseball fans and pungmul merchants]. *NyouSu Meyiker [Newsmaker]*, 3 April.

Chung, J.Y. and Kirkby, R.J.R. (2002) *The Political Economy of Development and Environment in Korea*. New York: Routledge.

Citizen's Transportation Culture Center of Dosi-yondae (1997) *Insadong Guri Hwalsonghwa Banghyang gwa Gwaje e daehan Josa Yongu [The Research Regarding the Direction to Vitalize Insadong's Streets and Future Assignments]*. Seoul: Citizen's Transportation Culture Center of Dosi-yondae.

City History Compilation Committee of Seoul (2007) *Seoul ui Sichang. [Seoul's Markets.]* Seoul: The City History Compilation Committee.

Cohen, R. (1978) Ethnicity: problem and focus in anthropology. *Annual Review of Anthropology*, **7**, pp. 379–403.

Culture and Tourism Department (1999) *Seoul in the World*. Seoul: Seoul Metropolitan Government.

Cumings, B. (1999) *Parallax Visions: Making Sense of American-East Asian Relations at the End of the Century*. Durham, NC: Duke University Press.

Cumings, B. (2005) *Korea's Place in the Sun: A Modern History*. New York: London: W.W. Norton.

Davis, M. (1990) *City of Quartz: Excavating the Future in Los Angeles*. New York: Verso.

Diamond, L.J. and Kim, B. (eds.) (2000) *Consolidating Democracy in South Korea*. Boulder, CO: Lynne Rienner Publishers.

Dongdaemun Forum (2001) *Dongdaemun – Wigi ui Jaerae Sichang e Soh Fashion Moonhwa*

Myungsoro Dongdaemun [From Old Market in Crisis to Fashion and Cultural Attractions]. Seoul: Dongdaemun Forum.

Dosi-yŏndae (1999) *Munhwa ŭi Gŏri Josŏng ŭi Munjejŏm gwa Baljŏnbanghyang eh Daehayŏh [Regarding the Issue of the Problems and Future Direction of Culture Street Projects]*. Seoul: Dosi-yŏndae.

Eun, J.-H. (2010) Korea ready to embrace a multicultural society. *Korea Times*, 19 May.

Foucault, M. (1995) *Discipline and Punish: The Birth of the Prison*. New York: Vintage.

Fu, C.C. (2014) From political governance and spatial restructure to urban transformation and architectural achievements: discourse on architecture in the Japanese colonial period, 1895–1945, in Kuroishi, E. (ed.) *Constructing the Colonized Land: Entwined Perspectives of East Asia Around WWII*. Farnham: Ashgate.

Gale, J.S. (1901) Han-Yang (Seoul) *Transactions of the Korea Branch of the Royal Asiatic Society*, **2**(2), pp. 1–43.

Gelezeau, V. (2007) *Apatŭ Gonghwaguk [Apartment Republic]*. Seoul: Humanitas.

Gillem, M.L. (2007) *America Town: Building the Outposts of Empire*. Minneapolis, MN: University of Minnesota Press.

Gills, B.K. and Gills, D.S. (2000) Globalization and strategic choice in South Korea: economic reform and labour, in Kim, S.S. (ed.) *Korea's Globalization*. Cambridge: Cambridge University Press.

Gonggansa (1970) Dongdaemun Gujonchachagojigu Jaegaebal Gaehoek. *Gonggan*, **5**(8), pp. 32–43.

Gyŏng-sil-ryŏn (2004) *Seoulsi Dosim Jaebaebal Gibon Gyehoek Byon-gyong Cholhoe Chokgu rul Wihan Jonmunga 100-yin Sonon mit Gija Hoegyon Jin-heng [The Declaration and Press Conference by 100 Experts for the Withdrawal of the Seoul Metropolitan Basic Urban Plan]*. Seoul: Gyŏng-sil-ryŏn.

Han, G. and Han, G. (2007) Hangook jok Damoonhwajooui ui Yisang gwa Hyunshil [The ideal and reality of Korean multiculturalism], in Korean Sociology Association (ed.) *Hangook jok Damoonhwa Jooui: Choijong Bogoseoh. [Korean Multiculturalism: Final Report]*. Seoul: Northeast Asian Committee.

Han, Y.H. (2014) Dongdaemun eh Dengjang han Picatsu, Manun Yinpa Molryeoh… Yil bu Simin un Yugu Jonsijang Balgido [Picatsu appears in Dongdaemun, crowds gathered… Some stepped on the relic site]. *Online JoongAng Ilbo*, 15 November. Available at: http://article.joins.com/news/article/article.asp?total_id=16431914&ctg=1502.

Harvey, D. (2001) Globalization and 'spatial fix'. *Geographische Revue*, **2**, pp. 23–30.

HAUD (Housing Architecture Urban Design) (2010) *Paradigm Change for an Old Section of an Urban Improvement*. Seoul: HAUD.

Hong, K. (2011) *Aesthetic Constructions of Korean Nationalism: Spectacle, Politics, and History*. London: Routledge.

Hong, S.P. (2008) Jong-gyorul Maegaero Hyungsung doen Hannamdong Islam

Goriwa Woegukin Muslim Community ui Munhwajok Pinanchoh Yokhal [Religion-based Hannam-dong Islamic Street and the Muslim Community as cultural refugees]. *Jirihaknonchong*, **52**, pp. 99–128.

Hong, S.T. (2004) *Seoul eh Sŏh Seoul ŭl Chatnŭnda [Finding Seoul in Seoul]*. Seoul: KungRee.

Hong, W.S. (2009) Joomin yigwon Datume Seoul Jaegaebal Golbyung. [Residents' battle over interests causing Seoul's redevelopment serious health problems]. *Chosun Ilbo*, 29 June.

Hoogvelt, A. (1997) The politics of exclusion, in *Globalization and the Postcolonial World. The New Political Economy of Development*. Baltimore, MD: Johns Hopkins University Press.

Huppauf, B. and Umbach, M. (eds.) (2005) *Vernacular Modernism: Heimat, Globalization, and the Built Environment*. Stanford, CA: Stanford University Press.

Hwang, D.J. (2006) *Hanok i Dora Watta [Hanoks Have Returned]*. Seoul: Gongansa.

Hwang, J.H. (2010) Migun Ppajinun Itaewon eh Africa-town Senggyotta [Africa town replaces American camp]. *Yonhap News*, 13 April.

Ivy, M. (1995) *Discourses of the Vanishing: Modernity, Phantasm, Japan*. Chicago, IL: University of Chicago Press.

Jacobs, J.M. (2004) Tradition is (Not) Modern: Deterritorializing Globalization in AlSayyad, N. (ed.) *The End of Tradition?* London: Routledge, pp. 29–44.

Jang, R.J and Park, J.H. (2009) *Daehanminguk Apatu Balgulsa – Jongam esoh Hilltop Kaji, 1 Saedae Apatu Tamsek ui Girok [Excavational History of Korea's Apartments – From Jongam to Hilltop, the Records of the First Generation Apartments]* Paju: Hyohyung.

Jang, Y.J. (2013) Changjo Gyongjeron ui Songjang Peradaim Gujo wa Jongchek Bowan Gwaje [The structure of the creative economy's growth paradigm and the policy supplement task]. *KIET Sanup Gyonje*, April, pp. 8–18.

Jeon, J.H. (2009) Dosi Twitgolmok ŭi 'Jangso Giŏk': Jongno Pimatgol ŭi Sarye [Place memories of urban back lanes: the case of the *Pimat-gol* of Jongno, Seoul]. *Daehan Jirihakhoeji [Journal of the Korean Geographical Society]*, **135**, pp. 779–796.

Jeon, N.M., Son, S.W., Yang, S.H. and Hong, H.O. (2008) *Hanguk Jugeoh ui Sahoesa [A Social History of Korean Housing]*. Paju: Dolbegae.

Jeong, S. (2000) *Maul Danwi Dosi Gaehoek Silhyun Gibon Banghyang II: Bukchon Gakugi Saryeh Yongu [Basic Directions for the Village-Level City Plan II: A Case Study of Bukchon]*. Seoul: Seoul Development Institute.

Jin, J.W. (2001) Bohenggwon Hwakbo wa Yi-myon-doro Jongbi Bang-an [The procurement of the right to walk and the methods to modify side streets]. *Dosi Munje*, **397**, pp. 45–62.

Jon, G.W. (2010) Daehanminguk ui Sumun Jungsim Itaewon [Itaewon, the hidden centre of Korea]. *Nyusu Dayilri [News Daily]*, 27 August.

Jon, S.I. (2009) *Apatŭ e Michida: Hyŏnde Hanguk ŭi Jugŏ Sahoehak* [*Crazy for Apartments: The Sociology of Contemporary Residences*]. Seoul: Esoope.

Jon, Y.G. (2008) Yigosi Dosihwangyung Jongbi Sayop Ida [These are the urban redevelopment projects]. *Urban Development Press*, 16 January.

Jung, B.H. (2010) Apatŭ Nŭn Gara, Hanok eh Sarŏrirata [Get rid of Apartments, I want to live in a hanok]. *Economic Review*, 10 August.

Jung, J.O. (1999) Bam ui Itaewon un Sexu Mayak Ttukgu? [Is Itaewon at night a special sex and drug zone?] *Newspeople*, **369**, pp. 34–35.

Jung, M.J. (2003) *Arumjigi's Story of Building Hanok*. Seoul: JoongAng M&B.

Jung, S.I. (2000) *Fashion Valley: Nam, Dongdaemun Sichang* [*Fashion Valley: Nam/Dongdaemun Market*]. Seoul: Gyungchoonsa.

Jung, W.S. (2009) Bukchon Hanok Maul 'Ilguroh-jin' Bojon [North Village's distorted preservation]. *Weekly Kyunghyang*, 24 November.

Kang, J.J. (2004) A Study of the New Town Project of the Seoul Metropolitan Government with a Focus on Yongsan Gu Han-nam New Town. Master's thesis, Kwangwoon University.

Kang, J.M. (2002) *Hanguk Hyondaesa Sanchek: 1970s–1* [*The Journey through Modern History of South Korea, 1970s, book 1*] Seoul: Inmul kwa Sasangsa.

Kang, J.M. (2006) *Gangnam, Natsŏn Deahanmingook ŭi Jahwasang* [*Gangnam, the Unfamiliar Portrait of South Korea*]. Seoul: Inmul kwa Sasangsa.

Kang, S.M. *et al.* (2003) *Seoul Senghwal ŭi Balgyŏn* [*Discovery of Life in Seoul*]. Seoul: Hyonshil Munhwa Yongu.

Kang, Y.H. (1989) Han'guk Jŏntongminga Yŏngu ŭi Donghyang gwa Gwaje [The direction and task of the Korean traditional minga study]. *Gonchuk*, **147**, pp. 31–35.

Kang, Y.H. (1992) Han'guk ŭi Minga wa Hŭk ŭi ŭimi [Korean traditional houses and the meaning of earth]. *Gonchuk*, **166**, pp. 56–61.

Kendall, L. (2011) *Consuming Korean Tradition in Early and Late Modernity: Commodification, Tourism, and Performance.* Honolulu: University of Hawaii Press.

Kil, Y.H. (2007) 2007nyun 9wol, Seoul Ui KiukSangshiljung [September, 2007: Seoul's amnesia]. *Hankyoreh 21*, 8 September.

Kim, B.I. (2003) *Newtown Sa-op Mit Gyunhyongbaljon Chokjin-jigu Saop ui Chujinbanghyang.* [*The Direction of the New Town Project and Balanced Growth Area Projects*]. Seoul: Ministry of Construction and Transportation.

Kim, B.K. (2005) Politics of Urban Space in Colonial Seoul, 1904–1945. PhD dissertation, Seoul National University.

Kim, B.R. (1999a) *Rediscovery of Korean Architecture 1: A Container of an Epoch*. Seoul: Ideal Architecture.

Kim, B.R. (1999b) *Kim Bongryŏl ui Han'guk Gŏnchuk Yiyagi* [*Bongryol Kim's Story of Korean Architecture*], 3 vols. Seoul: Ideal Architecture.

Kim, D.W. (2011) *A History of Korean Architecture*. Seoul: Kimoondang.

Kim, E.H. (1995) Dosihyong Hanok ui Jung-gaechuk eh Gwanhan Yongu: Seoul-si Gahoedong, Yongdudong, Jegidong ul Jungsim Uro [A Study on the Extension and Renovation of Urban Traditional Housing in Seoul – The Case of Gahoe-dong, Yongdu-dong, Jeagi-dong]. Master's Thesis, Jung Ang University.

Kim, E.S. (ed.) (2004) *Byonghwa hanun Yosong Munhwa Umjick Yinun Jiguchon.* [*Changing Women's Culture, Mobilizing Global Village*]. Seoul: Purun Sasangsa.

Kim, G.C. and Jo, K. (2004) *Myongmuk ui gunchuk* [*The Architecture of Light and Calm*]. Seoul: Ahn-Graphics.

Kim, G.E. (2009) Gapyong/Yangpyong Gukje Gyol-hon Jiwon. [Support for International marriages in cities of Gapyong and Yangpyong]. *Chosun Ilbo*, 12 June.

Kim, H. (2003) Dongdaemun E Hwangkum Al Eun Upda [There is no golden egg in Dongdaemun]. *Hankyoreh 21*, **469**, pp. 34–36.

Kim, H.H. (2007) Munhwa Sobi Gonggan Urosoh Samchungdong ui Busang [The rise of Samcheongdong as a cultural consumption space: critical reflections on the art gallery boom and urban regeneration strategy of Seoul]. *Hanguk Doshi Jirihakhoeji*, **10**(2), pp.127–144.

Kim, H.M. (2008) 'Gongjonghan Tonghap?': Gyolhon Yiju Yohsong gwa Hanguksik Damunhwa Ju-ui. ['The Fair Integration?': The Marriage Immigrant Women and Korean Multiculturalism]. Seoul: Korea Institute for Future Strategies.

Kim, H.S. (2004) Pokryŏkjŏk Sengsanbangsik Bŏtgo Nŭrigo Dayanghage: Hyŭndae Han'guk Gŏnchuk ŭi Banghyang gwa Gwaje [Getting rid of violent production methods and going slowly with diversity: the direction and task of contemporary Korean architecture]. *Munhwa Yesŭl*, **302**, pp. 89–92.

Kim, H.Y. (2009) *Hanguk NGO ui Sasang gwa Silchon: Marukusu Ju-ui-jok Bunsok.* [*The Philosophy and Reality of Korean NGOs: A Marxist Analysis.*] Seoul: Chekgalpi.

Kim, H.Y. (2011) Bukhan Jongchibum Suyongso Jonsihoe Song-hwang [The successful exhibition of North Korea's political dissident prison camp]. *Voice of America*, 4 February. Available at: http://www.voanews.com/korean/news/nk-camp-115281189.html.

Kim, I.S. (2002) *Dongdaemun Sichang Ul Bomyun Don Yi Boinda.* [*If you see Dongdaemun Market, You Can See (the Ways to Make) Money*]. Seoul: Dunam.

Kim, J.A. (nd) *Saram, Gonggan, and Jeongchi* [*People, Space, and Politics*]. Available at: http://jkspace.net/21.

Kim, J.I. (2008) Constructing a 'Miracle', Architecture, National Identity, and Development of Han River. A Critical Exploration of Architecture and Urbanism: Seoul, 1961–1988. PhD Dissertation, University of California, Berkeley.

Kim, J.M. (2009) CoverStory: Madangjip Joah Ahyiga Utnunda [Cover Story: 'I like Madang, Children Smile']. *Dongah Ilbo*, 3 July.

Kim, J.S. (1999) *Formation of Modernity: Allow Dancehalls in Seoul*. Seoul: Reality Culture Studies.

Kim, K.M. (2007) Reportage: Good Morning City Ga Boo Hwal Shicho Duilka? [Will Good Morning City be the beginning of resurrection?]. *Maekyung Economy*, 23 May.

Kim, K.Y. (2003) Hyondae Doshi esoh Hanok ui Ui-mi: Seoul Bukchon ui Saryeh Yongu [The Meaning of Traditional House Hanok in Urban Korea: A Case Study of Bukchon in Seoul]. MS Thesis, Seoul National University.

Kim, M.G. (2010) Sol-ehdo Butjaphyogan Midungrok Yijumindul [Unregistered migrants arrested on New Year's Day]. *Hankyoreh Newspaper*, 16 February.

Kim, O.G. (1882) *Chido-yakron* 治道略論.

Kim, S.H. (2010) Dongdaemun Noryun Ja Wi Suh Jangsa Hashil Boon [Anyone interested in keeping a shop in the best spot of Dongdaemun?]. *Focus Newspaper*, 15 September.

Kim, S.J. (2009) Kim Sunjoo Column: Hanok eh Yisa Waboni… [Kim Sonjoo's column: after moving to a hanok…]. *Hankyoreh Newspaper*, 14 December.

Kim, S.Y. (1999) The changes resulting from Car Free Zone – a case of Insa-dong, Seoul. *Daejin Ronjip*.

Kim, T.H. (2008) A Study about the Limits of South Korean NGOs and Suggestions for Improvement. MS Thesis, Daejin University.

Kim, T.S. (2011) Lotte, Dongdaemun Good Morning City Yipjom [Lotte comes into Dongdaemun's Good Morning City]. *Seoul Economics*, 7 February.

Kim, Y.H. and Shin, Y.N. (2001) The resurrection of the old market and its implications, in Dongdaemun Forum (ed.) *Dongdaemun: Wigi ui Jaerae Sichang esoh Fashion Munhwa Myongsoro* [*Dongdaemun: From the Old Market in Crisis to Fashionable Cultural Space*]. Seoul: Dongdaemun Forum.

Kim, Y.H. (2004) Yŏksamunhwa Tambangro Josŏngsayŏp Yihu ŭi Garogyŏnggwan Bunsŏk Yŏngu: Insadong ŭl Jungsim ŭro [A study of street landscapes after the construction of history and culture routes: with a focus on Insadong]. *Tehangonchukhakhoe Nonmunjip: Gyehoekgye*, **184**, pp. 153–160.

Kim, Y.S., Hwang, J.M. and Lee, J. (2007) *Daminjok Da-munhwa Sahoe ro-ui Yihengul Wihan Jongchek Paradigm Guchuk 1: Hanguk Sahoe Suyong Hyonsil gwa Jongchek Gwaje.* [*Construction of Policy Paradigm for the Transformation to a Multiethnic and Multicultural Society 1: The Reality of Acceptance in Korea and the Policy Implications*]. Seoul: Korean Women's Development Institute.

Klingmann, A. (2007) *Brandscapes: Architecture in the Experience Economy*. Cambridge, MA: MIT Press.

Koo, Y.M. (2003) Dosi ui Tum, Tum-sok ui Dosi [The gaps of cities, cities in gaps]. *Dangdaebipyong*, **22**, pp. 265–276.

Korean Culture and Arts Foundation (1992) *Dosi Munhwa Hwan-gyŏng Gaesŏn Bang-an Yŏngu* [A Study of Methods to Improve the Urban Cultural Environment]. Seoul: The Korean Culture and Arts Foundation.

Korean Publication Ethics Commission (2000) *Chong Sonyon Onduh Munhwa Hyonjang Yongu: Munhwa Sengbija Rohsoh Chong Sonyon* [*Study of Adolescents' Underground Cultural Scenes: Adolescents as Cultural Consumers*]. Seoul: Korean Publication Ethics Commission.

Kwak, S.Y. (2009) Hanguk AIDS Toechiwundong gwa Gay Sexuality [A Crusade against HIV/AIDS in Korea and Gay Sexuality, Focused on a Distribution of Free Condoms]. MS thesis, Seoul National University.

Kwon, Y.G. (2010) *Seoul ŭl Design Handa* [*Designing Seoul: The 22 Principles*]. Seoul: Design House.

Lee, B.K. (2011) Jungang Asia Goryoin ui Gangje Yiju eh Daehayoh [On the forced relocation of Goryo people in Central Asia]. *Hanminjok Munhwa Yongu*, **38**, pp. 451–581.

Lee, D.H. (1988) Hanguk Hyondae Gunchuk ui Ttalgundaejok Jakpum Gyonghyang eh Gwanhan Yongu [A Study of 'Post-Modern' Trends in Contemporary Korean Architectural Works]. MS thesis, Sungkyunkwan University.

Lee, D.Y. (2010) Seoul Si Design Jung Chek 'Design San Up Hwa' 'Jung Chi Jok Sun Jun Yong' [Seoul's design policy 'industrialization of design' 'political propaganda']. *Dong-ah Newspaper*, 3 September.

Lee, H. (1966) *Seoul ŭn Manwon Ida* [*Seoul Is Full*]. Seoul: Moonwoo Publishing Company.

Lee, H.W. and Lee, S.W. (2011) Bok-jang Yumul Yi Mwŏ-gi-eh, Munhwajae Jŏldobŏm Dŭlyi… [What are the hidden treasures (inside the stomach of Buddha's statue) that the thieves stole?]. *Chosun Ilbo*, 24 March, A13.

Lee, J.J. (2008) Bojongwa Gaebal Sayi Hundulrinun Bukchon: Bujadul ui Second House? [Bukchon shakes between preservation and development, the rich's second house?]. *Maal*, **266**, pp. 82–85.

Lee, J.W. (2009) Yongsan Chamsa, Sokdoga Burun Jukum ui Janchi. [Yongsan catastrophe, the Party of Death brought by speeding]. *Bokji Donghyang*, March, pp. 22–28.

Lee, N.H. (2005) Woegukin Jachiguyok: Hanguk sok Jakun Yigukdul [The territory of foreigners: little foreign nations in Korea]. *Shin Dongah*, **544**, pp. 350–361.

Lee, N.H. (2007) *The Making of Minjung: Democracy and the Politics of Representation in South Korea*, Ithaca, NY: Cornell University Press.

Lee, S.W. (1999) Insadong un Jontong ui Guri Inga [Is Insadong a street of tradition?]. *Gukto*, **207**, pp. 77–81.

Lee, S.Y. (2006) Maul Mandulgi ehso Simindanche ui Yokhal [The role of the civil society organization in the place-making: case study of Bukchon in Seoul]. *Gonggan gwa Sahui* [*Space and Society*], **25**, pp. 99–130.

Lee, S.Y. (2009) Dongdaemun Design Plaza & Park Siwon hage Chotsap Ttutdda [The Groundbreaking Ceremony for the Dongdaemun Design Plaza and Park]. *Seoul Culture Today*, 28 April.

Lee, W.G. (2004) Gwanghee-dong JungAng Asia-chon Golmok, [The Central Asian Alley in Gwanghee-dong]. *Hanguk Ilbo*, 2 December.

Lee, W.J. (2011) Seoul sok Wheguk' Itaewon Beksuh: Migun Guri suh Dagukjuk Guri ro… Damunhwa Il Bunji. [A foreign country in Seoul Itaewon's White Paper: from the streets of American GIs to multinational streets… The first street of multicultures]. *Chosun Ilbo*, 22 February.

Lee, Y.I. (1987) Gaebal Dokjaeui Jong-un. [The end of the developmental dictatorship]. *Minjok Jisong*, **21**, pp. 126–133.

Lim, H.S. (1999) *Munhwa Jigu Josung Model Gaebal mit Jongchek Banghyang e gwanhan Yongu*. [*Developing the Cultural District Model to Vitalize City by Cultural Resources: The Case of Insadong District in Seoul Metropolitan City*]. Seoul: Korea Culture Policy Institute.

Lim, S.J. (2005) *Gunchuk, Wuri ui Jahwasang* [*Architecture, Our Self-Portrait*]. Seoul: Inmul kwa Sasangsa.

MacCannell, D. (1973) Staged authenticity: arrangements of social space in tourist settings. *American Journal of Sociology*, **79**(3), pp. 589–603.

MacCannell, D. (1999) *The Tourist: A New Theory of the Leisure Class*. Berkeley, CA: University of California Press.

McMichael, P. (1996) *Development and Social Change: A Global Perspective*. Thousand Oaks, CA: Pine Forge Press.

Ministry of Culture, Sports, and Tourism (2005) *Culture Policy for the Multicultural Society: Prelude to Migrants' Arirang*. Ansan: Ministry of Culture, Sports, and Tourism.

Ministry of Culture, Sports, and Tourism (2008) *Hanguk ui Jong-gyo Hyonhwang* [*The Present Status of Religions in Korea, 2008*]. Seoul: Ministry of Culture, Sports, and Tourism.

Ministry of Industry and Resources (2005) *Yongse Bongjeup Jiwon Daechek*. [*The Policies for Supporting Small Sewing Businesses*]. Seoul: Ministry of Industry and Resources.

Moon, G.R. (2009) *Itaewon ehsoh Segyerul Mannada*. [*Itaewon: Gateway to the World*]. Seoul: Joongang Ilbo Books.

Moon, J.M. (2009) Hanok Jikiryoda… Kilburn-Ssi Gajok ui Biguk. [The tragedy of Kilburn family]. *Hankook Ilbo*, 30 October.

Moon, K.H.S. (1997) *Sex Among Allies: Military Prostitution in U.S.–Korea Relations*. New York: Columbia University Press.

Nam, V. (2011) *Goryŏh-in ŭi Yiju wa* Jŏngchesŏng [*The Migration and Identity of Korean-Russians*]. Seoul: Gwanhun Club.

National Geographic Information Institute (2007) *Hankuk Jiriji: Sudogwon Pyun*. [*Korean Geography: Metropolitan Area*]. Seoul: Ministry of Land, Transport, and Maritime Affairs.

National Human Rights Commission of the Republic of Korea (2010) *Yijugwanryon Guknaebop Hyonhwang mit Gukjegijun Yihae* [*Understanding the Status of the*

Immigration-Related Domestic Laws and International Standards]. Seoul: National Human Rights Commission of the Republic of Korea.

Norton, H. K. (1923) *The Far Eastern Republic of Siberia*. London: George Allen & Unwin.

Oliver, P. (2003) *Dwellings*. London: Phaidon.

Ong, A. (1999) *Flexible Citizenship: The Cultural Logics of Transnationality*. Durham, NC: Duke University Press.

Outka, E. (2009) *Consuming Traditions: Modernity, Modernism, and the Commodified Authentic*. Oxford: Oxford University Press.

Park, C.S. (2006) *Apatŭ ŭi Munhwasa*. [*A Cultural History of Apartment Houses*.] Seoul: Salrym.

Park, G.R. (2005) *The DNA of Modern Korean Architecture* [Hanguk Hyondae Gunchuk ui Yujeonja] Seoul: Gonggan.

Park, J.J. (2006) Korean Dream Jjotnun Yibang-indul. [Foreigners following Korean dream]. *Juganhanguk*, 13 January.

Park, S.H. *et al.* (2010) *Reinventing Urban Policy in Response to Ethnic Diversity II: Localizing Immigrant Integration Policy*. Seoul: Korea Research Institute for Human Settlements.

Park, S.M. (2000) Juntong Gwonryuk Gurigo Mat [Tradition, power, and taste: the formation of identity in Insadong through food culture]. *Whedae Sahak*, **13**, pp. 247–282.

Park, S.R. and Kim, D.H. (2008) Gookjejuk Pungmul Sichang: Hanbun Sokju Dobun Soka? [International Pungmul Market: can it be deceived twice?]. *Minjok*, **21**, March.

Park, W.J. (2009) Damunhwa Code-ro bon Itaewon: Damunhwa-song Silhomsil soh Seoul-daum ul Chatda. [Viewing Itaewon with a multicultural code: finding Seoul in a multicultural laboratory] *Jugan Hanguk*, **2296**, pp. 56–59.

Park, W.J. (2010) Ham Gge Hanun DesignSeoul Mandool Uh Yo. [Let's participate in DesignSeoul.] *Weekly Hangook*. 9 June.

Picard, M. (1996) *Bali: Cultural Tourism and Touristic Culture*. Singapore: Archipelago.

Rah, B.T. (2008) Focus Dongdaemun: another multicultural community, 5 October. An interview with IBMK. Available at: http://saladtv.kr/?document_srl=81434.

Robinson, J. (2006) *Ordinary Cities: Between Modernity and Development*. New York: Routledge.

Rudofsky, B. (1964) *Architecture without Architects: An Introduction to Non-Pedigreed Architecture*. Garden City, NY: Doubleday.

Sassen, S. (1991) *The Global City: New York, London, Tokyo*. Princeton, NJ: Princeton University Press.

SDI (Seoul Development Institute) (2001a) *2002 World Cup Gaegi: Bukchon Jangso Maketing Bang-an Yongu* [*For 2002 World Cup: Bukchon Place Marketing Study: The Vitalization of Traditional Districts through the Establishment of the Hanok Lodge System*]. Seoul: Seoul Development Institute.

SDI (2001b) *No Jum-sang GwanLee Bangan Joongjanggi DeaCheck Moseck*. [*Search for the Long-Term Management Plan for Street Vendors*] Seoul: SDI.

SDI (2002a) *A Study on the Improvement of Efficiency of Seoul's Culture Policy: With a Focus on Culture City Strategy*. Seoul: SDI.

SDI (2002b) *A Study on the Spatial Distribution of Cultural Facilities in Seoul*. Seoul: SDI.

SDI (2005) Prospects for Itaewon STZ's change and development measures. *Seoul Research Focus*, **34**, pp. 1–11.

Seoh, Y.Y. (2007) *Uriga Saraon Jip, Uriga Saragal Jip*. [*The House Where We Have Been Living and Will Continue to Live*]. Seoul: Critical Review of History.

Seok, H.H. (2009) Globalization of labor and corporate enterprises in South Korea, in Chang, Y.-S., Seok, H.-H. and Baker, D.L. (eds.) *Korea Confronts Globalization*. London and New York: Routledge.

Seoul Design Foundation (2009) *Dongdaemun Design Plaza and Dongdaemun History & Culture Park: Introduction*. Seoul: Seoul Design Foundation.

Seoul Local City Officials Training Institute (2003) *Problem Solving Working Papers: The Development of Leisure Programs such as Cultural and Tourist Activities According to the Implementation of the Five-Day Work Week*. Seoul: Seoul Local City Officials Training Institute.

Seoul Metropolitan City (2001a) *Bukchon Gakugi Gibon Gyeheok* [*Basic Plan for the North Village*]. Seoul: Seoul Metropolitan City.

Seoul Metropolitan City (2001b) *Hanok Suson Gijun*. [*Standard Guidelines for Repairs of Hanoks*]. Seoul: Seoul Metropolitan Government.

Seoul Metropolitan City (2002) *Hanok Jiwon Jorye*. [*Hanok Aid Ordinance*]. Seoul: Seoul Metropolitan City.

Seoul Metropolitan City (2004) *Seoulsi Dosi Mit Jugohwangyung Jungbi Gibon Goehoek* [*The Basic Plan for the Maintenance of Seoul's Residential Environments*]. Seoul: Seoul Metropolitan City.

Seoul Metropolitan City (2006a) *2020 nyon Seoul Doshigibon Gaehoek* [*The Basic City Plan of Seoul 2020*]. Seoul: Seoul Metropolitan City.

Seoul Metropolitan City (2006b) *Dongdaemun D-dong Sang-ga Cheonggyecheon gwa Hamkke Seropge Danjang* [*The Malls at Dongdaemun D District Newly Designed together with Cheonggyecheon*]. Seoul: Seoul Metropolitan City.

Seoul Metropolitan City (2010) *Where We Meet the Vivid History of Seoul: Dongdaemun History and Culture Park*. Seoul: Seoul Design Foundation.

Seoul Metropolitan City (2011) *Seoul Si Jon Saup Iljari wa Yongye 3man 5 chon-ge Chuga Changchul: Iljari Plus Seoul Project Gadong Uro Olhae 26manyohge Iljari Changchul* [*In Relation to the Former Project to Create 35,000 Additional Jobs: By Operating Iljari Plus Seoul Project 260,000 Jobs are expected to come this year*]. Seoul: Seoul Metropolitan City.

Seoul Tukbyol Sisawiwonhoe (2009) *Simin-ul Wihan Seoul Yuksa 2000 Nyon* [*A 2000-Year History of Seoul for Citizens*] Seoul: Seoul Tukbyol Sisawiwonhoe.

Shin, G.W. (2006) *Ethnic Nationalism in Korea: Genealogy, Politics, and Legacy.* Stanford, CA: Stanford University Press.

Shin, J.J. *et al.* (2004) Chogocheng Gonchukmul ui Gongongsong Jungjinul Wihan Gaehoek Banghyang eh Gwanhan Yongu [A study of the planning strategy for super tall buildings to increase public sharing of urban space]. *Daehangunchukhakhoe Nonmunjip,* **192**, pp. 33–42.

Shin, Y.N. (2005) *Dongdaemun Becksuh 2005 Dongdaemun Sichang ui Byonhwa wa Baljongwajong.* [*Dongdaemun Whitepaper 2005: The Change and Development Process of the Dongdaemun Market*]. Seoul: Dongdaemun Fashiontown Special Tourism District Committee.

Shinyun, D.W. (2007) Itaewon Un Nugu ui Ttang Inga? [Whose land is Itaewon?]. *Hankyoreh 21,* 25 December.

SMBA (Small and Medium Business Administration) (2000) *Venture/Chang Op Gwanryon Juyojiwonjedo 100 Mun 100 Dap. 100* [*Q and As on the Policies to Support Venture Businesses and Chang Op*]. Seoul: SMBA.

Society of Hanok Space (2004) *Cultural Space of Hanok.* Seoul: Kimoonsa.

Solidarity for LGBT Human Rights of Korea and Chingusai (2008) *Gun Gwanryŏn Sŏngsosuja Ingwonjŭngjinŭl Wihan Mujigyebit Yingwon Baram! Gundae ehsŏ Solsol* [*The Comprehensive Sourcebook Regarding the Project to Promote Military-Related Human Rights of Sexual Minorities*]. Seoul: Solidarity for LGBT Human Rights of Korea.

Son, J.M. (2003) *Dosi Gyehoek Iyagi II* [*The Story of Seoul's Urban Planning II*]. Seoul: Hanwul.

Son, J.S. (2010) Magujabi Gukjegyolhon Jongbuga Maknunda. [The government steps in to prevent random marriages]. *Chosun Ilbo,* 12 July.

Song, D.Y. (2004) *Ilryu Hakja Song Doyoung ui Seoul Il-ki* [*An Anthropologist Song Doyoung's Reading of Seoul*]. Seoul: Sohwa.

Song, I.H. (1990) A Study on the Types of Urban Traditional Housing in Seoul from 1930 to 1960. PhD Dissertation, Seoul National University.

Song, I.S. (1995) Hugi Gŭndae Gunchuk ŭi Suyong kwa Kŭ Koer [The acceptance of late modern architecture and the gap (with the concept of architectural amnesia)]. *Gŏnchuk Yŏksa Yŏngu,* **4**(2), pp. 140–145.

Song, J.I. (2000) Insadong ui Jangso Sangpumhwa eh Daeyunghan Jungchesung Undong eh Gwanhan Yongu. [A Study on the Identity Movement in Response to Commodification of Place: A Case Study of Insadong in Seoul]. MS Thesis, Seoul National University.

Song, U.G. (1999) IMF Wa Jungso Gi-op Jongchek [The IMF and policies regarding small and medium businesses]. *Gukhoebo* [*The Newsletter of the National Assembly*], **392**, pp. 24–27.

Suh, C.H. (1987) Woeraegeck ˇul Wihan Sudo-gwˇon Gwan-gwang course gaebal eh Gwan-han Sogo [A study of the metropolitan area tour course development for foreign tourists]. *Hanguk Gwan-gwang Hakhoe Gwan-gwanghak Yongu,* **11**, pp. 77–89.

Tipton, F.B. (1998) *The Rise of Asia: Economics, Society and Politics in Contemporary Asia*. Honolulu: University of Hawaii Press.

Underwood, P. (2010) Multiculturalism in Korea. *Korea Joong Ang Daily*, 26 August.

Veseth, M. (2005) *Globaloney: Unraveling the Myths of Globalization*. Lanham, MD: Rowman & Littlefield.

Vlastos, S. (ed.) (1998) *Mirror of Modernity: Invented Traditions of Modern Japan.* Berkeley, CA: University of California Press.

Woodside, A. (2006) *Lost Modernities: China, Vietnam, Korea, and the Hazards of World History*. Cambridge, MA: Harvard University Press.

Yang, G.Y. (1995) *Dosi Munhwa Jongchek gwa Seoul Si Gohri Chukje* [*Urban Cultural Policies and Seoul's Street Festivals*]. Seoul: Seoul Development Institute.

Yim, S.C. (1995) Sŏyang Gŭndae Gŏnchuk ŭi Suyong kwa Han'guk Hyŭndae Gŏnchuk ŭi Munje [The acceptance of modern Western architecture and the problem of modern Korean architecture]. *Gŏnchuk Yŏksa Yŏngu*, **4**(2), pp. 135–139.

Yongsan Gu Office (2010) *Itaewon-dong Gohju Yoegukin Hyunghwang*. Seoul: Yongsan Gu Office.

Yoon, H.S. (2010) Design Seoul, ga si jok sung gwa e chijoong hat da [Design Seoul has put excessive emphasis on visual accomplishments]. *Eun Pyung Si Min Shinmoon*, 6 September.

Yoon, I.S. (2004) Seoul si Newtown-saup ui munje [The problem of Seoul city's new town projects]. *Doshi wa Bingon* [*City and Poverty*], **69**, pp. 119–138.

Yu, A.R. (1997) *Shikmunhwa ui puri rul chajasuh.*[*Searching for the Root of Food Cultures*]. Seoul: Kyobo.

Yu, G.Y. (1935) The scenery of Kyungsung. *Sahaegongrun*, October.

Yu, H.J. (1993) *Na ŭi Munhwa Yousan Dapsagi* [*My Survey of Cultural Heritage*]. Seoul: Changbi Publishers.

Yu, J.S. (1994) Song gwa sahoe [Sex and society]. *Hanguk Ilbo*, 13 August.

Yu, J.Y. (2002) Seoul Dongdaemun sichang ŭi byunhwa wa jŏngchekjŏk sisajŏm [The change in Dongdaemun Market and some policy suggestions]. *Dosi Munjae* [*The Urban Question*], **399**, pp. 63–71.

Yu, J.Y., Jin, Y. and Kim, H. (2000) *Doshi Munhwa ui Yuksung Bangan* [*Strategies for Culture Industry of City*]. Anyang: Korea Research Institute for Human Settlements.

Yu, S.H. (2011) Leisure Yoesik Tuksu Jonmang … Gajok Danwi Sobi Nuldut [Leisure, eating out industries' boon]. *Hankook Gyongje*, 14 June.

Yu, S.O. (2001) Sarajiryounoon yuksa moonhwa gurirul ouihayuh [For the History and Culture Street about to disappear], in *Moohwa Doshi/Moonhwa Bockji* [*Cultural City/Cultural Welfare*]. Seoul: Hanguk Munhwa Jungchek Gaehalwon.

Yu, Y.W. (2001) Migun-giji hunryonjang 23 got banhwan gwa jonmang [The prospect and return of 23 places of US army training grounds]. *Chosun Ilbo*, 16 November, p. 29.

Yun, B.S. (2005) Soviet gonseol-gi ui goryoh-in sunan gwa gangje yiju [The ordeal of the Soviet-Koreans and the forced relocation]. *JungangSaron*, **21**, pp. 572–594.

Yun, P.H. (2005) Koryoin 3 senun woe jobumo ttang eh-soh jasal het-na? [Why did a third generation Korean-Russian commit suicide in her grandparents' country?]. *Ohmynews*, 14 August.

Index

For Product Safety Concerns and Information please contact our EU representative GPSR@taylorandfrancis.com Taylor & Francis Verlag GmbH, Kaufingerstraße 24, 80331 München, Germany

T - #0202 - 230425 - C0 - 234/156/10 [12] - CB - 9781138777736 - Matt Lamination